Sawday's

Britain's best
dog-friendly
places to stay

D0271262

Contents

SCOTLAND
p256-273

NORTH
EAST
p216-221

NORTH
WEST
p182-199

YORKSHIRE
AND
HUMBER
p202-212

EAST
MIDLANDS
p148-155

WEST
MIDLANDS
p158-179

WALES
p224-253

EAST
OF
ENGLAND
p126-145

SOUTH EAST
p106-123

SOUTH WEST
p28-102

© Maidenhead Cartographic 2019

For the love of dogs

I always feel that it isn't a proper family holiday unless you have your dogs with you. For me, the number one reason for having a staycation rather than a holiday abroad is that it's easier for Lily and Lulu, my border terriers, to come too. If I travel without them I miss them terribly and am always keenly awaiting the daily update. Staying in the UK means relaxing times together, away from the daily routine, which is wonderful for strengthening our bond.

Lily is 16 years old and her grand-daughter Lulu is six. I guess because of the age difference they have never really regarded each other as playmates. Lily retains her characteristic calm wisdom whilst Lulu is full of energy yet incredibly obedient. They definitely go at different paces now – Lulu tends to do the long, hilly walks easily, whereas Lily spends a lot of time in her buggy, observing her surroundings but still joining in and enjoying the scenery.

Exploring a new region of our fair isle with dogs in tow is very satisfying, especially when everyone, including the dogs, is warmly welcomed. There's frankly nothing as wonderful as arriving at a place to stay knowing that they are looking forward to your visit, hounds and all. I love it when we get asked in advance what we might need for the dogs, although there's never much extra we do need, as we always arrive with an enormous armful of beds, treats, food, bowls, poo bags, toys and recently, Lily's doggy stroller. We all love an adventure and exploring new places, and nothing is better than returning after a long day outdoors for a restful evening with the dogs snoozing quietly having been fully exerted.

This makes it so much harder to accept when you're all excited about staying somewhere, call to check if it's ok to bring your furry family and are met with, "sorry, but we do not accept dogs".

My heart sinks and I'm always perplexed. There's nothing worse than being turned away as a pet owner. You look at your beautifully behaved dogs, sigh and walk away feeling rather like a leper. Innkeepers and hotel owners really need not worry about naughty dogs. Owners know perfectly well if their dogs aren't good travellers and are extremely unlikely to take them if they know they won't be perfect guests. I honestly cannot think of a single incident when dogs behaved badly while we've been at lunch, dinner or staying somewhere.

I'm glad to say though that attitudes are changing. More and more places are realising how great four-legged guests are and in all the wonderful places in this book you can count on a warm welcome for your whole family on arrival. Some even serve a doggy menu and I'm delighted to see some favourites here who serve up a range of organic meals, as well as snacks you can buy to take on walks with you.

On behalf of all dog owners, thank you to all the places that appear in this invaluable book. We are incredibly grateful that you are dog friendly and look forward to visiting soon.

Henrietta

FOUNDER OF LILY'S KITCHEN & LILY'S OWNER

6

Henrietta, founder of Lily's Kitchen, and her two dogs

What we look for

We look for special.
We've visited every one of them.
We've written about them honestly.

Our places are not uniform and you'll find everything from a tiny cabin by a river with an outside kitchen to a swish hotel with staff on hand and glorious food. What links them all is that they'll give your dog as happy a welcome as they will you. We look for:

ATMOSPHERE
Relaxed, unstuffy places where staff, guests and other dogs all stop to say hello and ruffle ears. Treats are offered the moment you arrive and nobody minds a bit if dogs go exploring and playing under tables.

CHARACTER
We like our dog-friendly places to be as quirky and individual as they please. We seek dog-friendly differences rather than similarities – and we love surprises!

SPACE
For you and your dog to roam. When you stay at these places you'll find beaches, woods, rivers, fields and all the unconfined space that you and your dog need to get the fresh air and exercise you love.

COMFORTABLE BEDS
Most dogs travel with their own beds but they also like to go to sleep knowing you are right there with them in the room – especially with a cosy blanket provided. So at these lovely places your dog will never be banished to the car, a cold scullery or a lonely kennel outdoors.

GOOD FOOD
You'll find beef bones, dog beer and homemade organic treats for your dog at some of these places – even special things to eat at breakfast (including the odd 'escaped' sausage). Many provide organic biscuits and wet dog food too in case you packed in a hurry.

KIND AND HELPFUL OWNERS
We love it when owners go the extra mile for both you and your dog: birthday cakes for special birthdays, hand-written instructions on the best walks and useful tips on which local cafés and pubs are happy to welcome dogs make your holiday stress-free.

TREATS
Pig's ears, delicious bones and being allowed to eat in the dining room or a special conservatory means your dog won't feel like a second-class citizen in the world of travelling.

WAYS TO KEEP CLEAN AND TIDY
The countryside means mud sometimes, so when you're not at home it's great to find a hosing down spot. Some of these even have warm water! And at many you'll find special dog towels so your dog can go back inside as fragrant as they were pre-walk.

PEACEFUL PLACES TO SNOOZE
After a long walk there's nothing nicer than a long sleep – preferably in front of a real fire. So whether it's lying full length in front of a sizzling log in a pub, hogging the wood-burner in a B&B or edging up to the fire pit, your dog will be happy.

The Meikleour Arms, page 262

The Old Vicarage, page 235

Artist Residence Penzance, page 29

We visit each place so we can make sure your heart won't sink when you step inside. But places to stay (and eat) can be mercurial so let us know if anything less than special has crept in while we weren't looking and we'll be back to visit again.

The Greyhound Inn, page 108

Sawday's top 6

These are our top six picks in categories we think you and your dog will love: the best beaches for that morning stroll, places for amazing walking trails, places to celebrate a special occasion and the best treats. We've also found our favourite pubs with rooms, because the joy of a long country ramble ending by a fireside in winter or in a summery pub garden is one of our enduring loves. Our sister brand, Canopy & Stars, offers something for the wilderness seekers, with glamping spaces that get you deep into the great outdoors.

In each category, we've sought a blend of traditional and trailblazers. Our greatest challenge was to choose only six for each, but these captured our hearts for their passion, imagination and that special something which makes each truly worth a visit.

OUR TOP 6 FOR
Pubs

Pubs were meant to have dogs sleeping in front of fires, searching for dropped treats and lying on your feet as you drink a post-walk beer. These are friendly inns where everyone is welcome to stop for a pint or stay overnight.

1. THE CAT, SUSSEX

The 16th-century building, a fine medieval hall with a Victorian extension, has been comfortably modernised without losing its character. Harvey's Ale and some top-notch pub food attract a crowd of locals, foodies and walkers. Dogs are welcome in the pub but not the dining room. The setting, a pretty, sleepy village opposite a 12th-century church is nothing short of idyllic.

PAGE 118

2. THE HOLFORD ARMS, CLOUCESTERSHIRE

With its own eight-acre garden and orchard, minutes away from wonderful walks in Westonbirt Arboretum, the Holford makes a perfect base for nature lovers. Owners Pete and Tor have a way with food, drink and atmosphere which means the little inn buzzes with happy locals and walkers who've popped in for a pint. All six lovely rooms are dog-friendly.

PAGE 93

The Holford Arms, page 93

3. THE GURNARD'S HEAD, CORNWALL

Outside, the wild west coast weaves up to St Ives; secret beaches appear at low tide, cliffs tumble down to the water and the moorland landscapes are otherworldly. Inside, it's earthy, warm, stylish and friendly, with rustic interiors and fireplaces at both ends of the bar. The food is incredible, with short, fresh, seasonal menus. Rooms are simple and dogs get treats, blankets and more.

PAGE 31

The Inn at Whitewell, page 184

4. THE INN AT WHITEWELL, LANCASHIRE

It is almost impossible to imagine a day when a better inn will grace the English landscape. Everything here is perfect. The inn sits just above the river Hodder, a favourite for dog walkers, and doors from the bar lead onto a terrace where guests can enjoy five-mile views across parkland to rising fells. Except for the main dining room, all areas of the inn are dog-friendly.

PAGE 184

The Felin Fach Griffin, page 245

5. THE FELIN FACH GRIFFIN, POWYS

Quirky and colourful: like you're staying in the home of a fashionable friend. There are maps, guide books and even 'wise old men of the hills' to guide you through the surrounding countryside. They take food and drink seriously too – many ingredients come from a half-acre kitchen veg plot. Four-legged friends are as welcome as their owners and can run around the grassy beer garden.

PAGE 245

The Cat, page 118

6. LORD CREWE ARMS AT BLANCHLAND, NORTHUMBERLAND

Few inns can rival the scale or history of this Grade II listed building. Dogs doze by the inglenook, food is robust modern British and bedrooms are divine. In the wilds of the North Pennine moors, holding court over the honey stone village of Blanchland and crafted by plucky 12th-century monks who headed for the Northumbrian hilltops in search of isolation, it's the perfect hideaway.

PAGE 218

OUR TOP 6 FOR

Beaches

Six places perfectly positioned for days on dog-friendly beaches,
chasing sticks, leaping in the surf and scampering up the coastal paths.

1. THE LIFEBOAT INN, NORFOLK

You're in heaven here, under the big skies of Norfolk's north coast with its sweeping salt marshes, nature reserves and sandy beaches. The Lifeboat, tucked down a lane in pretty Thornham, is smooth and stylish, with glowing fires, scrumptious seafood and the comfiest of rooms. Nearby Holme beach is a true hidden gem and can be almost empty, even in the height of summer.

PAGE 135

2. THE GALLIVANT, SUSSEX

This cool hotel stands across the road from Camber Sands, where five miles of pristine beach backed by tall, grassy dunes are home to kite surfers, beach cricketers and sun worshippers alike. A recent refurbishment has brought The Gallivant a stunning new look to every corner – it's now a chic beach pad with excellent food, a New England feel and stylish bedrooms.

PAGE 121

Aspen Lodge, page 268

3. WATERGATE BAY HOTEL, CORNWALL

Watergate Bay sits directly above the two-mile long beach of the same name, one of the best in the UK. It's all about the views here, through walls of glass in the huge café, or from the 25-metre infinity pool and a terrace strewn with loungers. Walk the spectacular coast path for miles in either direction or set up camp on the beach and watch the sun set directly into the sea.

PAGE 42

4. THE HENLEY HOTEL, DEVON

A small house above Bigbury-on-Sea with fabulous views out to Burgh Island, super bedrooms and some of the loveliest food in Devon. Set within an AONB, the village sits across the South West Coast Path. Warm interiors have wooden floors, the odd potted palm and big windows to frame the view. At high tide surfers ride the waves, at low tide you can walk on the sands.

PAGE 54

The Henley Hotel, page 54

5. SHORT HOUSE CHESIL BEACH, DORSET

A light-and colour filled cottage with gardens and sea views on the UNESCO World Heritage Jurassic Coast. There's plenty of room to roam and no main roads nearby; sheep graze the surrounding National Trust farmland, so keep the lead handy. Only an unspoilt meadow stands between you and the 18 miles of shingle, Chesil Beach, that joins the mainland with the Isle of Portland.

PAGE 78

6. ASPEN LODGE, ARGYLL & BUTE

This cosy lodge is on a little-known Peninsula in the remote and rugged Scottish Highlands, with panoramic views of a sparkling loch and wild moorland. A number of stunning beaches are on the doorstep: Camas Nan Geall, covered in glittering golden sand, Sanna Bay which looks like it should be in the Caribbean, and the Singing Sands which squeaks oddly as you walk across it.

PAGE 268

The Gallivant, page 121

OUR TOP 6 FOR
Treats

Our favourite places to spoil your dog rotten, with beds, bowls, indulgent snacks and entirely dog-friendly menus and the odd free tennis ball.

I. ARTIST RESIDENCE OXFORD, OXFORDSHIRE

This 16th-century boutique hotel is a cool take on all things retro, with quirky art and a little neon thrown in for good measure. Dogs are welcome in four of the bohemian lofts and suites as well as the cosy Mason Arms pub downstairs. Along with lots of fuss, dogs are greeted with a comfy dog bed, bowl and fabulous treats from luxury pet food suppliers Lily's Kitchen.

PAGE 107

2. WIDBROOK GRANGE, WILTSHIRE

A delightful Georgian country house in 11 acres of grounds, where friendly welcomes are always extended to four-legged friends. Not only will your pooch receive a doggy bed and treats in the room, they are also welcome to join you for breakfast and afternoon tea in the conservatory. Expect sausages, 'pawsecco' and 'pupachinos' all round. They'll even get a tennis ball to take home too. **PAGE 91**

Widbrook Grange, page 91

3. THE MASTER BUILDER'S HOUSE HOTEL, HAMPSHIRE

A perfect setting for daydreamers: beautifully groomed lawns, river views and ancient woodland along the water. The hotel greets all its doggy guests with open arms and a little hamper; you'll find a comfortable bed, bowls, treats and toys waiting in the room. There's also a Doggy Room Service Menu available, choose from doggy beef stew, pork sausages and chicken casserole.

PAGE 113

4. ALTON ALBANY FARM, AYRSHIRE

With three of their own, Alasdair and Andrea are extremely fond of visiting dogs at their Bed and Breakfast. Not only is there miles of countryside to run around, but also treats and cocktails sausages, always on hand for a little indulgence. Water bowls, towels, toys, balls and launchers are on offer too, to ensure your dog is thoroughly occupied and happy.

PAGE 258

Artist Residence Oxford, page 107

5. THE SEAFOOD RESTAURANT, CORNWALL

An extension of one of Rick Stein's earliest eateries in Padstow, the Seafood Restaurant is now a place of pilgrimage. When arriving for a stay, all dogs receive a welcome bag filled with goodies; there's a fleece Chalky's blanket, dog toy and personalised dog bowl. You'll also receive some Green and Wild's natural treats, perfect for keeping your pooch busy as you dine on superbly fresh food in the restaurant.

PAGE 45

6. THE CHOLMONDELEY ARMS, CHESHIRE

A light-flooded former schoolhouse with supremely comfortable bedrooms and a brilliant bar downstairs. On the bar, you'll find a jar of homemade biscuits for four-legged friends to enjoy and behind it 'dog bottled beer', a meat-based stock drink that dogs love. Poo bags are free to take whenever necessary, as are dog dinner bowls, so you only have to pack light for your visit.

PAGE 183

The Cholmondeley Arms, page 183

Walks

If there's one thing a dog changes about your life, it's that you're always planning the next walk. These places all have easy access to amazing trails and are welcoming of the muddiest boots and paws.

I. ROSE & CROWN, DURHAM

Everything you'd want of a lovely country inn – relax in front of a fire in the old-school bar, have afternoon tea in the peaceful sitting room or excellent food in the panelled restaurant. Walk the Teesway footpath or drive to Low Force, a series of waterfalls and rapids. From here, follow the river a couple of miles up to High Force, England's tallest waterfall.

PAGE 216

2. BROWNBER HALL, CUMBRIA

This Victorian country house is bright, relaxed and sociable. There's an honesty bar, plenty of space to chill and deeply comfortable beds. The Coast to Coast and the Dales High Way run right past the door, but for something shorter, the route from Smardale Gill Nature Reserve to the viaduct is a real hidden treasure, threading down a secluded valley.

PAGE 189

Brownber Hall, page 189

3. OLD-LANDS, MONMOUTHSHIRE

Immersed in wildlife and rolling hills, this grand gothic house is home to the Bosanquet family, whose love of sustainable farming is inspiring. You'll stay in cosy cottages in the grounds, with the Wye Valley and Black Mountains less than 20 minutes away and the 200-acre estate on your doorstep. Stroll the yew-tree walk and pick up home-grown veg from the honesty shop on the way back. **PAGE 226**

4. OKEL TOR MINE, CORNWALL

It's not often you sleep in a place that's earned both World Heritage and AONB status. Badgers, kingfishers, otters and rare mosses are part of the fairytale landscape surrounding the two cottages that were once part of a Victorian copper and tin mine. Walk the river path to the National Trust's Cotehele House, hike the Bere Peninsula or visit Morwellham Quay port and copper mine. **PAGE 49**

Old-Lands, page 226

5. HIGH HOUSES, CUMBRIA

Tucked away at the quieter end of the Lake District is this beguiling 17th-century hilltop house – all lime-plastered walls, rustic beams, open fires and original flagstones. Beautiful views reach out from every window to 350 acres of wildlife-rich farmland – yours to explore. Walk from the door to Wainwright's Binsey, or venture further to the Lakes and the Solway Plain. **PAGE 199**

6. GREENFIELD COTTAGE, YORKSHIRE

A cosy Victorian cottage in the narrow alleyways that make up Robin Hood Bay's maze of cobbled streets. In creatively-styled rooms, an eclectic art collection competes with the sea views for your attention. Enjoy spectacular walks along the Cleveland Way, amble across the sand to Ravenscar's wild seal colony or bring bikes to pedal the Coast to Coast route, which starts nearby. **PAGE 210**

Rose & Crown, page 216

OUR TOP 6 FOR
Glamping

These are our top six for turning a trip away with your dog into a real outdoor adventure. Explore straight from the door of secluded yurts, boutique bothies and cabins in the woods.

1. MILL VALLEY, CORNWALL

A quirky collection of wooden cabins, yurts, wagons and horseboxes on the edge of a remote valley in north Cornwall. There's no limit to the number of dogs you can bring to Mill Valley, which is no surprise as owners Lisa and Neil have 10 themselves! There are great woodland walks from the door and dogs love the river so much that there's a designated mud room for drying off.

PAGE 46

2. THE YURT SANCTUARY, SOMERSET

This peaceful yurt camp is a private meadow full of little joys – a bench swing, a hot tub and a firepit with tree stump chairs for gathering round the embers at night. Owner Michele offers scent training and grooming – treat your dog to a bath, brush and pamper while you relax in front of the spectacular Mendip views or rest after a day hiking the hills.

PAGE 87

Mill Valley, page 46

3. BOUTIQUE FARM BOTHIES, ABERDEENSHIRE

This gorgeous Scottish estate is made up of two bothies hidden away on a working farm in stunning rural Aberdeenshire and full of innovative upcycling. Dogs are greeted with their very own hamper full of treats and goodies; expect a towel, blanket, bowls, lead and gravy bones. With 45 acres of fields and woodlands surrounding you, there's ample activities to tire your pooch out.

PAGE 273

Boutique Farm Bothies, page 273

4. ACORN FARM, DEVON

A wonderful handmade yurt and spacious shepherd's hut on the edge of peaceful Dartmoor. Owners Chris and Tracey have two of their own dogs, so are always on hand to offer you advice on local walks, dog-friendly beaches and pubs. You'll also be greeted with a hamper; made up of a dog bed, towel, water bowl, ball, brush and food. After a busy day exploring the moors, there's a tap to wash off muddy paws.

PAGE 62

The Chickenshed, page 227

5. COPSE CAMP, DENBIGHSHIRE

Starry skies, cider and quiet seclusion welcome you to your eclectic treehouse in the countryside. Adventurous types will love the variety of activities available here; mountain biking at Llandegla and hiking on the moors are a must. Owners Jenny and Margaret leave complimentary dog beer and natural dog treats that will keep your dog busy while you relax in the hot tub after a busy day.

PAGE 253

6. THE CHICKENSHED, MONMOUTHSHIRE

A striking cabin, beautifully designed with huge windows that frame the views over towards Sugar Loaf in the distance. Dogs will love the surrounding area – there's a large, secure garden for them to run around in and woodland far beyond to explore. With evenings by the crackling fire pit under vivid starry skies you don't have to do much to make time here enchanting and memorable.

PAGE 227

Acorn Farm, page 62

A special occasion

You shouldn't have to leave your dog at home when you're celebrating.
These are our top six places where everyone can share in the treat.

1. NO. 15 GREAT PULTENEY, BATH & N.E. SOMERSET

Style and substance go hand in hand at this art-filled boutique hotel and spa in Bath city. It's made even better by the fact you can bring your dog along for celebrations. Dogs are welcome in almost all of the decadent bedrooms and are greeted with their very own woof-box. Indulge yourselves with afternoon tea and early evening cocktails after being spoilt in the spa.

PAGE 90

2. ANOTHER PLACE – THE LAKE, CUMBRIA

This family-friendly hotel on Ullswater is the perfect place to gather everyone for a celebration. Dogs will love joining you all on long walks around the estate or hopping into the lake to cool off on hotter days. In the evenings, you'll find a brilliant restaurant in The Living Space, a pooch-friendly place to eat, play games and share stories all together.

PAGE 194

Another Place – The Lake, page 194

3. THE SCARLET, CORNWALL

One of the loveliest, most romantic hotels in Britain, with sea views, relaxing rooms and an ayurvedic spa. Eat excellent fresh seafood out on the terrace with your dog at your feet, walk along Mawgan Porth beach (dog-friendly year round) and settle into the wood-fired hot tub high on the cliff top, overlooking the beach below. You will all leave feeling refreshed and revitalised.

PAGE 43

4. THE PEACOCK AT ROWSLEY, DERBYSHIRE

This grand old house dates back to 1652 and is located in the beautiful Peak District National Park. Its four-poster beds (one is from Belvoir Castle), picturesque gardens and impeccable food make it a fabulous place for a romantic celebration. After a long walk in extensive grounds that'll delight both you and your dog, sink into fireside seats or enjoy a G&T out on the terrace.

PAGE 154

The Meikleour Arms, page 262

5. STOW HOUSE, YORKSHIRE

In the heart of the beautiful Yorkshire Dales is this lovingly restored boutique Bed and Breakfast. Each bedroom has been decorated immaculately, boasting restored beams, sash windows, unique artwork and cast iron baths. Dogs are welcome in almost all areas, so enjoy a cocktail in the lounge, a coffee in the snug and dinner in the dining room without them leaving your side.

PAGE 207

6. THE MEIKLEOUR ARMS, PERTH & KINROSS

This historic but brightly renovated country estate in dense, ancient woodland is a wonderful outdoorsy retreat. Go fishing on the Tay, pick vegetables from the garden and walk through the forest. With very few rules, your four-legged friend can accompany you throughout the day. Head to the restaurant and try scallops hand-dived on the west coast and venison from the Meikleour Forest.

PAGE 262

The Scarlet, page 43

South West

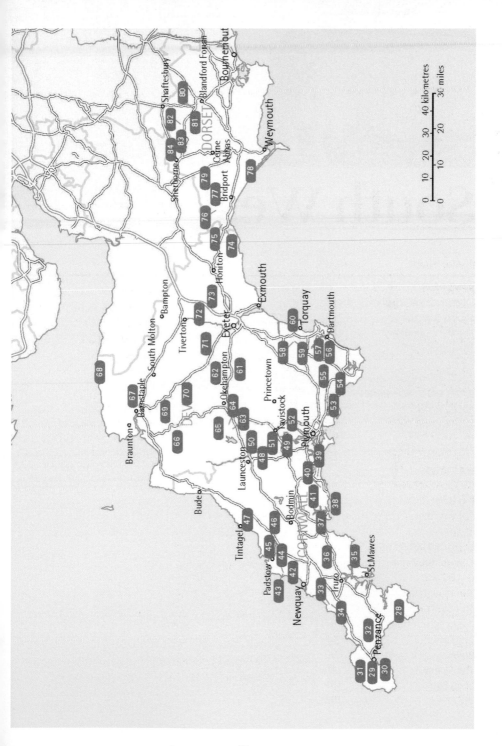

South West

Widbrook Grange, page 91

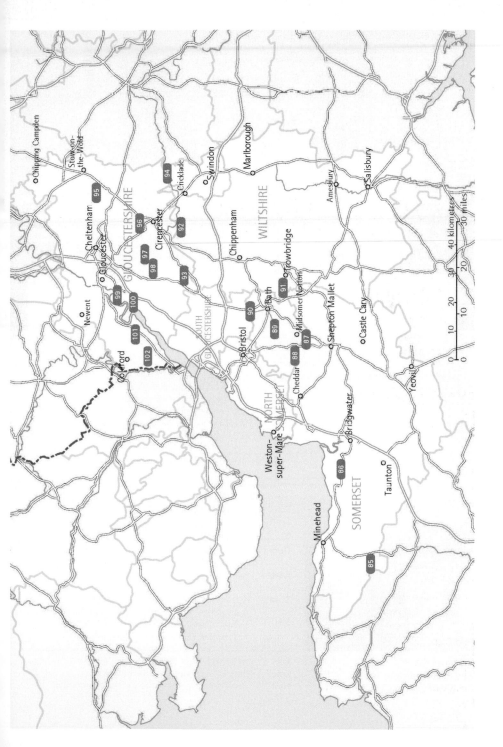

Halzephron Cabin

Up the hill from the village, behind Lucy and Roger's landmark B&B (you won't miss the white crenellations) and across the walled garden, you'll find your snug, seaside hideaway. An unassuming white shack on the outside, the compact interior has been given a full, contemporary makeover. There's a romantic wood-burner for the cooler evenings as well as electric radiators throughout, and a mini kitchen with oak breakfast bar and views of the bay – when it's too dark to admire them you can just turn to the flat screen TV. The bathroom has a beautiful double-ended bath and a nautical porthole window that reminds you of your coastal surroundings, although with the faint sound of the waves lapping below as you drift off, you

probably won't have forgotten. French doors open onto the lawn, and if you go for a little wander you'll find the secret garden overlooking the cove below. From here you can see all the way to St Michael's Mount on a clear day! For more sea and golden sand, Halzephron is a perfect launch pad for miles of secluded beaches and a selection of local fishing villages that offer delicious, fresh seafood. *Secure walled garden. Right on coastal path, by beach; two all year dog-friendly beaches within five minutes*

Rooms	Cabin for 2: from £81 per night Dogs: no charge; max. 1.
Meals	Self-catering.
Closed	Never.
Treats	Advice on walks, river to swim in, coastal path walks, year-round dog-friendly beaches 5-10 min walk, and lovely dog-friendly pub 5-minute walk.

Canopy & Stars
Halzephron Cabin,
Gunwalloe, Helston, TR12 7QD

Tel	+44 (0)117 204 7830
Email	enquiries@canopyandstars.co.uk
Web	www.canopyandstars.co.uk/halzephroncabin

Artist Residence Penzance

Artist Residence's Cornish offering is another cool bolthole from Justin and Charlie Salisbury. The vibe is laid-back: friendly staff stop to chat and you can turn up to dinner in your flip-flops. Choose where to eat – in the restaurant adorned with colourful pop art, in front of the wood-burner in the sitting room-bar or outside in the terrace garden. There's ping pong and table football to play while you wait for dinner from the smokehouse. Breakfast on French toast, local eggs and homemade granola before you whisk yourself off to St Michael's Mount, glimpsed from the hotel, or the Jubilee Pool lido. There's great surfing at Sennen and paddling at Porthcurno, both ten miles, and you can catch the ferry to the Isles of Scilly direct from Penzance. *Minimum stay: 2 nights at weekends in summer. Some bedrooms are dog-friendly. Within walking distance to a dog-friendly pebble beach. Lots of cliff & woodland walks, & other dog-friendly beaches in area.*

Rooms	14 doubles, 3 twin/doubles: £75-£180. 1 suite for 2-3, with sofabed, kitchenette & sitting room: £190-£295. 1 family room for 5: £185-£225. 2 triples: £135-£180. 1 cottage for 6: £270-£385. Singles £65-£120. Dogs £15. Max. 2.
Meals	Lunch & dinner from £6; 3 courses £20-£25.
Closed	Never.
Treats	Bowl, bed & Lily's Kitchen treats.

Tel	+44 (0)1736 365664
Email	penzance@artistresidence.co.uk
Web	www.artistresidence.co.uk/our-hotels/cornwall/

Charlie & Justin Salisbury
Artist Residence Penzance,
20 Chapel Street,
Penzance, TR18 4AW

The Old Coastguard

This seaside hotel stands by the coastal path on the way into Mousehole, one of Cornwall's nicest villages, where kids play on the harbour's sandy beach at low tide. It's a peaceful spot with a clutch of restaurants and galleries, little disturbed since the Spanish raided in 1595. Roguish brothers Edmund and Charles Inkin have form when it comes to creating small hotels of character, and this place bears all their hallmarks, being good value and casual, with relaxed staff and great food. A diverse crowd of guests – couples, families, and ladies lunching – hang out in the rustic-smart bar and dining room. Conversation may stall as you take in the outlook over hydrangeas and palms to intriguing St Clement's Isle and beyond, across the sweep of Mount's Bay to the Lizard. With Newlyn a couple of miles away, locally landed fish features at breakfast. Supper, with a modern British slant, changes with the seasons. Retreat to a lime-washed bedroom hung with Cornish art – all vary in size, character and aspect, and eight have balconies. *Secure garden with sea views. Pebbled beach a stone's throw away & plenty of walks nearby.*

Rooms	8 doubles, 3 twins: £140-£225. 2 suites for 2: £245-£300. 1 family room for 4: £200-£225. Singles £105-£132. Extra bed £30 p.p.p.n.
Meals	Lunch from £12. Dinner, 3 courses, about £30. Sunday lunch from £12.50.
Closed	1 week in early Jan.
Treats	Biscuits, blanket, towels, advice on walks, poo bags & bowls. Very friendly staff too.

Charles & Edmund Inkin
The Old Coastguard,
The Parade, Mousehole,
Penzance, TR19 6PR

Tel	+44 (0)1736 731222
Email	bookings@oldcoastguardhotel.co.uk
Web	www.oldcoastguardhotel.co.uk

The Gurnard's Head

This quirky inn is one of the best – the sort of place a hiker hopes to find. Outside, the wild west coast weaves up to St Ives; secret beaches appear at low tide, cliffs tumble down to the water, wild flowers streak the land pink in summer. Inside, it's earthy, warm, stylish and friendly, with rustic interiors and fires at both ends of the bar. Logs are piled high in an alcove, maps and art hang on the walls, books fill every shelf; if you pick one up and don't finish it, take it home and post it back. Comfortable, cosy bedrooms have views over the Atlantic or the moors. A short, fresh and seasonal menu that changes daily will suit walkers who need a quick fuel stop as well as serious foodies and is served in the bar, dining rooms, or in the garden on sunny days. Choose from three hand-pulled Cornish ales, a choice of good ciders and more than 20 wines by the carafe. *Large back garden. Beautiful coastal path, and a sandy beach if you time the tides right.*

Rooms	3 doubles, 4 twin/doubles: £130-£245. Singles £105-£132. Extra bed/sofabed £25 per person per night.
Meals	Lunch from £15. Dinner, 3 courses from £26.50. Sunday lunch from £21.
Closed	Christmas.
Treats	Biscuits, blanket, towels, advice on walks, poo bags & dog bowls. Very friendly staff too.

Tel	+44 (0)1736 796928
Email	enquiries@gurnardshead.co.uk
Web	www.gurnardshead.co.uk

Charles & Edmund Inkin
The Gurnard's Head,
Zennor, St Ives, TR26 3DE

Deugh An Chy

A truly beautiful home with heaps of interesting books on the shelves, fresh flowers and an eclectic mix of styles – this is a well-loved place, the antithesis of a sterile holiday cottage and families will be very happy here – there's even a piano in the living room if you feel inclined to play. Stand at the bottom of the pretty (enclosed) garden with plenty of lawn, and the 1780s stone cottage appears to be smiling down at you. Inside is bright, light and filled with comfortable seating and lovely big tables for convivial meals. Fling open the wide French doors from the underfloor-heated kitchen; on chillier days there's a big wood-burner, sofas to snuggle in and books to explore. Cooks will be thrilled with the kitchen: find space

for chatterers, loads of cupboards and a state of the art oven. Sleep like logs in peaceful bedrooms with pretty fabrics, smooth white cotton on deep mattresses and views. Walk to the National Trust's Godolphin House; you're close to Porthlevan with its shops and restaurants. Deugh An Chy means 'House of Welcome' and that's certainly how it feels. *Minimum stay: 5 nights. On quiet lane with a secure garden. 100 yards from path through woods & fields to Godolphin Hill.*

Rooms	1 cottage for 7: £525-£1550 per week. Dogs £25 per stay. Max. 1 (or 2 small dogs).
Meals	Pubs/restaurants 0.5 miles.
Closed	Rarely.
Treats	A welcome Bonio, dog gate, towel, garden hose and a downstairs shower for dogs (or children) too enthusiastically covered with mud or sand. Dog rug on request.

Danny & Ann Donovan
Deugh An Chy,
Ruth Dower,
Godolphin Cross, TR13 9QZ

Tel	+44 (0)20 7228 1060
Email	ann@mia.gb.net
Web	www.deughanchy.com

Tree of Life Horsebox

Well-established, beautifully kitted-out and in a corner of dreamy Cornwall, you're welcomed to Tree of Life with produce from the organic smallholding next door – Marie and Sylvia run a veg box business, so know their stuff. You sleep on a double bed above the cab of the lorry, accessed by steps that double as the (very sturdy!) cupboards. Lighting is provided by solar panels, and more romantically by lanterns and tealights. Cook here, in the small kitchen with gas cooker and oven; in the cupboards there are all the pots, pans and utensils you could need. A short distance (15 metres) from the horsebox is a hut with your own compost loo and shower room. The hut also has a large sink to wash up in, a small fridge, and a place to store coats and boots after a walk, or sandy things after a day on the beach at quaint St Agnes. If you have a ploughman's or a good Sunday roast in mind, head to the Miner's Arms in Mithian, a 10-minute walk, and enjoy Cornish real ales while you wait. *Secure garden & an adjoining field to run & play in. Nearby footpath & a small river to paddle in; walking distance to dog-friendly pub*

Rooms	Truck for 2: from £85 per night. Space for 2 adults or children in own tent £10 p.p.p.n. Dogs: £25 per stay; max. 1 dog.
Meals	Self-catering.
Closed	November-April.
Treats	Towels, blankets & a bag of Lily's Organic Training Treats as a welcome treat! Perranporth Beach, sells doggie ice cream.

Tel	+44 (0)117 204 7830
Email	enquiries@canopyandstars.co.uk
Web	www.canopyandstars.co.uk/treeoflife

Canopy & Stars
Tree of Life Horsebox,
Tree of Life Organics, Scala Nij,
Mithian, St Agnes, TR5 0QA

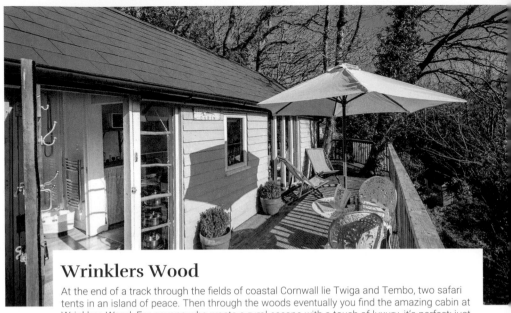

Wrinklers Wood

At the end of a track through the fields of coastal Cornwall lie Twiga and Tembo, two safari tents in an island of peace. Then through the woods eventually you find the amazing cabin at Wrinklers Wood. For anyone who wants a rural escape with a touch of luxury, it's perfect; just leave the low-slung sports car at home. Just in front of the tents a brook winds through thick woodland where deer, badgers and foxes can be heard and even seen if you sit quietly. There's adventure inside the tents too, where pallet wood walls separate the cabin bed and the bunks from the en-suite flushing loo and hot shower rooms and the wood-burner glows at the centre of the comfy living space. There's space for everyone to wander off for naps,

then gather round the table or out on the deck for BBQ meals and board games. Meanwhile, at the Cabin, you'll be strolling out onto the deck for breakfast, or firing up the BBQ and watching the stars come out. It's the sort of place where you ditch your shoes and stroll around barefoot, unwinding with every step. *Babies welcome in cabin; children of all ages welcome in safari tents. Dogs can run freely around the site. Be aware of cattle sometimes in fields surrounding site and keep dogs on a lead when passing fields.*

Rooms	Cabin for 2: from £75. 2 safari tents for 6: from £95. Prices per night. Dogs £25 per dog per stay. Max. 1 small dog
Meals	Self-catering.
Closed	Never.
Treats	Bowls, treats and biodegradable poo bags. Information on great dog-friendly walks & a list of dog-friendly beaches nearby.

Canopy & Stars
Wrinklers Wood,
Mithian Downs, St Agnes, TR5 0PZ

Tel	+44 (0)117 204 7830
Email	enquiries@canopyandstars.co.uk
Web	www.canopyandstars.co.uk/wrinklerswood

Round House East

Standing like sentries guarding the village pub and green below are two whitewashed 1820s roundhouses with thatched roofs and crosses – believed to keep the devil away. Ingenious how everything fits so neatly within the curving walls in this cosy, quirky hideaway that's full of local art and retro touches. Step out from the kitchen extension with a morning espresso, park yourself on a lounger and watch the seagulls swoop in the pretty cottage garden. When night falls, soak in the roll top bath, then retire to an enormous bed under a vaulted ceiling. Bring bicycles, kit for the beach and walking boots for the South West Coast Path; the Roseland Peninsula is awash with secret coves and seaside restaurants. *Local beaches are dog-friendly (on leads 9am-5pm, May-Oct). Coastal path & woodland walks with streams. Local dog friendly pub.*

Rooms	1 cottage for 2: £495-£1015 per week. Dogs £25 per stay. Max. 2 (unless by arrangement).
Meals	Self-catering.
Closed	Never.
Treats	Bowl, towels, poo bags & a dog's cupboard with treats & toys.

Tel	+44 (0)1494 774290
Mobile	+44 (0)7480 198040
Email	ian.rose@telia.com
Web	www.roundhousecornwall.co.uk

Ian Rose
Round House East,
Pendower Road, Veryan,
Truro, TR2 5QL

Benallack Barn

It's easy to reach the best of all things Cornish from this quiet spot sandwiched between the north and south coasts. You're five minutes from the gardens at Trewithen; Eden and Heligan aren't much further. You'll find a good pub, Hawkins Arms, in Probus (3 miles), wild surfing beaches to the north, gentler paddling ones to the south. Vicky and her family live in the main house with their Labrador; you stay in one of the converted farm buildings – bright, fresh spaces made cosy by underfloor heating and wood-burners topped up with unlimited logs. Stick on your favourite tunes and settle in with a good book. Each cottage has lovely views and its own little courtyard. Wander the owners' gorgeous garden; you'll find a lake bustling

with wildfowl and a wooden summerhouse. Have a barbecue here and watch the sun go down on balmy evenings. *Minimum stay: 2 nights; 3 in high season. Completely secure garden and access to four-acre grounds; footpath from door to open countryside; many all-year dog-friendly beaches nearby.*

Rooms	2 cottages for 2: £560-£980 per week. 2-night stay from £200. Dogs £20 per dog. Max. 2.
Meals	Self-catering.
Closed	Rarely.
Treats	All-natural handmade treats, towels, bowls, bags, a throw, gate across stairs and hose right outside. Various crates and beds available on request.

Vicky Goldby
Benallack Barn,
Grampound Road, Truro, TR2 4BY

Tel	+44 (0)1726 884477
Mobile	+44 (0)7740 913818
Email	stay@benallack.net
Web	www.benallack.net

Coriander Cottages

No shortage of natural entertainment here: a gaggle of waddling ducks, a buzzard hovering overhead, a night-time display by bats, a terrace for a ringside view; for a deep-country setting, these converted farm buildings are surprisingly lively! Both cottages combine ultra-green credentials with rustic luxury. Solar panels and geothermal heat ensure energy is renewable, rainwater is harvested, and natural textiles create harmony. Open-plan living spaces are sleek with limestone flooring, wooden beams and stone walls; there are comfortable leather sofas, rugs, plants and toasty wood-burning stove; super kitchens are well-equipped; bedrooms are cosy and inviting; bathrooms are fabulous with TVs, candles and aromatherapy oils. Balconies and terraces have valley views to Fowey, a gentle mile downhill, and charming owner Colin, who lives next door, will drive you if you're not mobile. Beaches, the Coast Path and Saint's Way are close, the Eden Project and Lostwithiel are not much further. Superb. *Pets welcome in White Willow only. Please see website for availability. Due to wildlife dogs to be kept on lead within grounds.*

Rooms	2 cottages for 2: £875-£1015 per week. Max. 2 dogs.
Meals	Self-catering.
Closed	Rarely.
Treats	Coastal, country lane & riverbank walks.

Tel	+44 (0)1726 834998
Email	stay@coriandercottages.co.uk
Web	www.foweyaccommodation.co.uk

Colin King
Coriander Cottages,
Penventinue Lane, Fowey, PL23 1JT

Talland Bay Hotel

The position here is magical. First you plunge down rollercoaster lanes leaving the world behind, then you arrive at this lovely hotel and find a rather good view – a vast carpet of sea that shoots off to the horizon. Pine trees stand guard on one side, an old church crowns a hill on the other, then two acres of lawns roll down to a ha-ha before the land tumbles down to the bay. In summer, loungers and croquet hoops appear on the lawn, and you can nip down to a beach café for lunch by the water. Back at the hotel there's a conservatory brasserie, a sitting room bar and a roaring fire in the half-panelled dining room. You'll find art on the walls, polished flagstones, a terrace for afternoon tea. Follow the coastal path over the hill, then return for a good dinner, perhaps roasted scallops with caramelised orange, loin of venison with chestnut purée, lemongrass panna cotta with peach sorbet. Bedrooms have warm colours, vast beds, beautiful linen, the odd panelled wall. One has a balcony, a couple open onto terraces, all have lovely bathrooms. *Garden, dog-friendly beach & coastal walks. Dogs can dine with owners in the Brasserie; 'canine corner' menu with Alfie & Molly's treats and butchers' sausages.*

Rooms	15 twin/doubles: £160-£290. 4 suites for 2: £260-£350. 3 cottages for 2: £210-£300. Singles £150-£340. Dogs £12.50.
Meals	Lunch from £5.50. Sunday lunch £21.50-£25. Dinner: brasserie from £12.95; restaurant £36-£42.
Closed	Never.
Treats	Pamper pack with luxury blankets, bowls, feeding mats, treats & torches for late night strolls.

Jack Ashby-Wright
Talland Bay Hotel,
Porthallow, Looe, PL13 2JB

Tel	+44 (0)1503 272667
Email	info@tallandbayhotel.com
Web	www.tallandbayhotel.co.uk

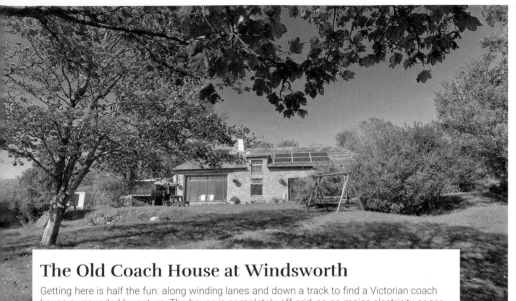

The Old Coach House at Windsworth

Getting here is half the fun: along winding lanes and down a track to find a Victorian coach house surrounded by nature. The house is completely off-grid, so no mains electricity or gas but it's light, comfortable and warm as toast. Fire up the wood-burning stove in the big, handmade kitchen with its large table for convivial meals. The acoustics in here are good and Caroline leaves guitars and African drums so you can rediscover your inner musician. Sea views from upstairs and from the garden are restorative. The outdoors goes on and on – wander the overgrown sub-tropical garden, roam 70 acres of private land, picnic in your own fields and clamber down to a beach below (not for the less than intrepid) for wild swimming. As the stars come out, open the wine or fill up the Kelly kettle for a warming cuppa and revel in your privacy. There's nobody to hear anything – except moles, voles, deer and badger. *Unusual bedroom layout: check before booking. Half-mile of dog-friendly beach; paths through woodland. Free-ranging chickens, as well as sheep, goats, ponies so dogs on lead in some areas.*

Rooms	1 house for 8: £350-£1995 per week. Short breaks from £245. Dogs £20 per stay.
Meals	Pubs/restaurants 1 mile.
Closed	Never.
Treats	Cosy blanket, water bowl & towels.

Tel	+44 (0)1503 262671
Email	stay@windsworth.org.uk
Web	www.windsworth.org.uk/theoldcoachhouse

Caroline Petherick
The Old Coach House at Windsworth,
Windsworth, Looe, PL13 1NZ

Treworgey

A rural idyll within easy reach of coastal treasures. A place to come with the young, the old, with friends or family; children can play, nature lovers ramble, animal lovers get a fix of farming life. Wooden floorboards, rugs, fires, well-equipped kitchens, comfy beds, lovely fabrics and, often, a view of the Looe Valley and, beyond, the sea. Lois is typical of a one-bedroom cottage, cosy and enveloping with a slipper bath and fresh flowers; Trelawney is one of the larger cottages with those views, a grandfather clock, a four poster bed and oak kitchen. The Farmhouse is grander, perfect for a large gathering with its Aga warmed kitchen, sash windows and flagstone floors; Jasmine has a sweet conservatory for meals with views.

All are toasty warm thanks to a Biomass boiler and generous to a fault. You'll find a summer house where you can borrow the computer, a walker's map or a DVD, a games room, a heated pool with spa and sauna, tennis court and an honesty fridge filled with produce. There's a private riding school, too, and home-cooked meals can be delivered. *Each cottage has secure garden. Dog-tie up area with water, shelter & beds (near pool while you swim). Farm & woodland walks; 3 miles to dog-friendly beaches.*

Rooms	1 cottage for 2, 1 cottage for 4, 1 cottage for 6: £412-£2852 1 house for 11: £1263-£3927. Prices per week. Short breaks Nov-April. Dogs £23 per stay. Max. 2.
Meals	Self-catering.
Closed	Never.
Treats	Treats, bowls, towel & a collar tag with local info. Outside hose for washing dogs off.

Holly & Andy Kyte
Treworgey,
Duloe, Looe, PL14 4PP

Tel	+44 (0)1503 262730
Email	stay@treworgeycottages.co.uk
Web	www.treworgeycottages.co.uk

Sangers Showmans Wagon

Roll up, roll up: Sangers Showmans Wagon promises to capture your imagination – and heart – with its charming restoration. Fall asleep under a hand-painted ceiling of swallows and hedgerow flowers, surrounded by vases of blooms, antiques and oriental rugs. In the morning the view from the etched glass windows looks out over the meadow to your neighbours Halcyon and Hobson, the two Exmoor ponies; put the kettle on, throw a log on the cherry red wood burner and park up outside with a cup of tea. A wood shed at the rear contains a flushing loo and hand basin while across the driveway stands a cabin housing the kitchen and shower room. The wagon faces southwest so you're in for some spectacular sunsets: string up a hammock or knock about with the croquet set.
There are blankets to snuggle under while you enjoy the dazzling starlit skies or hop in the hot tub to enjoy the views. The only sounds that will disturb your peace are the mooing of cows and the odd hoot of an owl – often spotted swooping out of the copse in search of supper.
Advice on local woodland, riverside & coastal walks, dog-friendly beaches & pubs. Ponies in field so keep dogs on lead.

Rooms	Wagon for 2: from £95 per night. Jinka's Wagon is available for extra guests in July/August at £25 p.p.p.n; 1 double suitable for a couple or 1 child (14+). Dogs £25 per dog per stay. Max. 2.
Meals	Self-catering.
Closed	Never.
Treats	Two dog bowls, dog biscuits, dog towel, cosy dog blanket.

Tel	+44 (0)117 204 7830
Email	enquiries@canopyandstars.co.uk
Web	www.canopyandstars.co.uk/ sangersshowmanswagon

Canopy & Stars
Sangers Showmans Wagon,
West Lodge, Lanreath, Looe, PL13 2NZ

Watergate Bay Hotel

Grab a surfboard or a kite: this hotel kits you out to ride the waves with the Extreme Academy surf school. But you can still lounge around, and if you have kids, it's a treat; young children can make friends in the popular Kids' Zone while you disappear for a massage or a swim in Swim Club. It's all about the views here, with walls of glass in The Living Space (a huge café/bar), an 25-metre infinity pool that gazes over the ocean, and a terrace strewn with loungers. This large hotel sits directly above one of the best sandy beaches in Britain – two miles long. There's a large ocean room to head home to with an open fire, a sauna and cliff-top hot tub with stunning views, and food that's fresh and delicious. Eat in the bar or Zacry's the grill, it's only 50 paces to the The Beach Hut for a burger and Jamie Oliver's Fifteen Cornwall is right next door. Coastal light floods through the windows of the sea view suites, the family suites have separate bunk rooms for children, The Village apartments have their own kitchens and open-plan lounges. *On year round dog-friendly beach; coast path walks – close to edge in places. Eat at Beach Hut & Living Space with your dog. Certain bedrooms are dog-friendly.*

Rooms	47 twin/doubles: £185-£345. 2 suites for 2, 4 suites for 5, 18 family suites for 4: £285-£450. Singles £120-£268. Dogs £15; £5 for second dog. Max. 2.
Meals	Lunch £10. Dinner, 2 courses, £36.50.
Closed	Never.
Treats	Runs on beach all year round & advice on other dog-friendly beach walks.

Mark Williams
Watergate Bay Hotel,
Watergate Bay, TR8 4AA

Tel	+44 (0)1637 860543
Email	life@watergatebay.co.uk
Web	www.watergatebay.co.uk

The Scarlet

The Scarlet does what few others can – this may be a super-cool design hotel with one of the loveliest spas in the land, but the service here is fantastic: friendly, attentive, ready to help. As for the hotel, it sits above the sea with a vast wall of glass in reception to frame the view. Outside, you'll find a hot tub in the garden from which you can stargaze; inside, there's a stylish restaurant that opens onto a decked terrace, where you scoff delicious Cornish food while gazing out to sea. Elsewhere, an open fire in the sitting room, a pool table in the library, then a cool bar for Cornish wines and ales. Exceptional bedrooms all have sea views, then balconies or terraces, private gardens or viewing pods. Expect organic cotton, oak floors from sustainable forests, perhaps a free-standing bath or a huge walk-In shower. As for the spa, you get tented treatment rooms, chill-out pods that hang from the ceiling, and a couple of swimming pools flanked by sunbeds. Finally, the hotel is green to its core, with a biomass boiler, solar panels and state-of-the-art insulation. *Minimum stay: 2 nights at weekends. Easy access to Coast Path. Mawgan Porth beach, just below, open to dogs year round; a shallow stream runs down one side.*

Rooms	21 doubles, 8 twin/doubles: £210-£405. 8 suites for 2: £210-£460. Dogs £15. Max. depends on breed & size.
Meals	Lunch, 3 courses, £24.95. Dinner, 3 courses, £45.95.
Closed	Rarely.
Treats	Bowls, water, biscuits & an information leaflet about dogs at the hotel.

Tel	+44 (0)1637 861800
Email	stay@scarlethotel.co.uk
Web	www.scarlethotel.co.uk

Meeche Hudd
The Scarlet,
Tredragon Road,
Mawgan Porth, TR8 4DQ

5 & 6 Porth Farm Cottages

The beach is a 10-minute stroll, the cliff path crosses the National Trust coastline, the quiet village has a surf school, shop and fish 'n' chips: all the ingredients for a terrific seaside holiday. The cottages are part of a horseshoe of stone barns with communal gardens, swings and zip wire, all tucked into a hillside with views over the Vale of Lanherne and out to sea. The conversions are impressive, with underfloor heating, elm floorboards and wonderful woodwork. No. 5's staircase spirals up to a gallery landing and comfy bedrooms. Soak in a roll top bath; blast away sand under a huge shower head. Downstairs: cosy up by the fire in an open-plan living room; the kitchen and dining table catch the morning sun. Outside: watch

the sunset over the bay with an evening drink and gaze up at the 'living roof' of flowers. It's a short drive to the Eden Project or St Ives, but mostly you can leave the car behind. The coastal path stretches to Newquay, Watergate Bay and Padstow (good bus service, too) and there's a friendly farm shop down the valley on your way to the ancient village of St Mawgan. *Minimum stay: 3 nights; 7 in high season.*

Rooms	1 cottage for 4, 1 cottage for 6: £430-£1360 per week. 3-night stay £400. Dogs £20 per stay. Max. 2.
Meals	Self-catering.
Closed	Rarely.
Treats	Underfloor heating, advice on walks & poo bags by door.

Carol & Peter Misch
5 & 6 Porth Farm Cottages,
Mawgan Porth, Newquay, TR8 4BP

Mobile	+44 (0)7779 659838
Email	5and6pfc@gmail.com

The Seafood Restaurant

In 1975 a young chef called Rick Stein opened a restaurant in Padstow. These days he has four more as well as a deli, pâtisserie, seafood cookery school and 40 beautiful bedrooms. Despite this success, his homespun philosophy has never wavered: buy the freshest seafood from fisherman on the quay, then cook it simply and eat it with friends. It is a viewpoint half the country seems to share – the Seafood Restaurant is now a place of pilgrimage – so come to discover the Cornish coast, walk on the cliffs, paddle in the estuary, then drop into this lively restaurant for a fabulous meal, perhaps black risotto with Cornish cuttlefish, grilled Padstow lobster with fine herbs, hot chocolate fondant with toasted marshmallow ice cream. Book in for the night and a table in the restaurant is yours, though flawless bedrooms are hard to leave. They are scattered about town, some above the restaurant, others at the bistro or just around the corner at St Petroc's House. All are immaculate. Expect the best fabrics, Vi-Spring mattresses, stunning bathrooms, the odd terrace with estuary views. *Minimum stay: 2 nights at weekends. Walks along Camel Trail by estuary, or across harbour & on to coast paths.*

Rooms	32 doubles, 8 twin/doubles: £165-£315. Dogs £20 for 1st night, £5 thereafter, per dog. Max. as many as can comfortably fit.
Meals	Lunch £38.50. Dinner £58.50.
Closed	25-26 December.
Treats	Fleecy Chalky's pal blanket, guide to dog walks in Cornwall, personal bowls & treats from Green & Wilds with selected breaks.

Tel	+44 (0)1841 532700
Email	reservations@rickstein.com
Web	www.rickstein.com/stay/ the-seafood-restaurant/

Jill & Rick Stein
The Seafood Restaurant,
Riverside, Padstow, PL28 8BY

Mill Valley

Mill Valley is a little idyll: seven places to stay, from wagons on wheels to Hobbit houses all sharing an acre of Lisa and Neil's sustainable smallholding. The simple joy of this sociable site and everything built on it is a perfect reflection of Lisa and Neil's approach to life. It's completely off-grid, encouraging you to escape technology and camp like you used to, exploring nature, getting generally muddy and making new friends. Every space at Mill Valley is a labour of love; Woodland Cabin is handmade entirely from local and upcycled wood, Pixie Yurt is a unique handmade creation too; pop the kettle on the wood-burner for tea and get something sizzling over the campfire for dinner. Settle into the slow life at the Stumpy Hobbit

as you light the wood-burning stove, the BBQ or the pizza oven for dinner and candles for long romantic evenings. The Cornish Hobbit Hut appears to have grown up from the land with its living roof. Finally there are the two horseboxes Nomad and Odyssey, the latest additions to Mill Valley. *Extra children or adults in some spaces with no extra charge. Big secure garden; woodland & riverside walks with heaps of swimming opportunities. Farmland, so beware of livestock. Resident dogs are happy to play.*

Rooms	4 cabins for 2: from £85. Yurt for 4: from £81. 2 horseboxes for 2-4: from £85. Prices per night.
Meals	Self-catering.
Closed	Never.
Treats	Jar of Mera Dog pure goody snacks. The Cabin has a 'mud room' for drying off; Pixie Yurt has space for lots of dog beds. Dog-sitting service.

Canopy & Stars
Mill Valley,
Egloshayle, Wadebridge, PL27 6JQ

Tel	+44 (0)117 204 7830
Email	enquiries@canopyandstars.co.uk
Web	www.canopyandstars.co.uk/millvalley

The Mill House Inn

Coast down the steep winding lane to a 1760s mill house in a woodland setting. Trebarwith's spectacular beach – all surf and sand – is a ten-minute walk away. It's quite a spot. Back at the inn, the bar combines the best of Cornish old and Cornish new: big flagged floor, wooden tables, chapel chairs, two leather sofas by a wood-burning stove. The swanky dining room overlooking the burbling mill stream is light, elegant and very modern. Settle down to some rather good food: firecracker prawns; fillet of sea trout with crushed potatoes, kale, roasted banana shallot, mussel & tarragon cream; coconut panna cotta, torched pineapple, rum sponge. Bar meals are more traditional, they do great barbecues in summer and (be warned) a band often plays at the weekend. In keeping with the seaside setting, bedrooms are simple and uncluttered, with good shower rooms in the smaller standard rooms. If you stay in the little cottage be ready for a steep staircase. Coastal trails lead to Tintagel, official home of the Arthurian legends, there's biking, surfing, crabbing... you couldn't possibly be bored. *Dogs to be kept on a lead please.*

Rooms	6 doubles, 1 twin/double, 1 family room for 4: £75-£130. 1 cottage for 2: £120-£160. Singles £56-£97. Extra bed £20 p.p.p.n. Dogs £7.50.
Meals	Lunch from £7.50. Dinner from £12. Sunday lunch, 3 courses, £17.85.
Closed	Rarely.
Treats	Guidance on local walks. Doc Martin's dog Dodger stays here!

Tel	+44 (0)1840 770200
Email	management@themillhouseinn.co.uk
Web	www.themillhouseinn.co.uk

Mark & Kep Forbes
The Mill House Inn,
Trebarwith, Tintagel, PL34 0HD

Spring Park

The five wagons, tabernacle, cabin and shepherd's hut at Spring Park each have an individual vintage charm and all have their own wood-fired hot tub to soak in. There's Duke, a classic 1940's showman's wagon, with bright vibrant paintwork on the outside and interior furnishings to match. Next, Maiden, a restored railway wagon has been paired up with a large modern cabin, Wisteria Cottage. Then there's Pip, a sturdy 1930's steam roller living van with spacious cabin alongside. Next is The Duchess, bright blue with bathroom in the hut next door. Hercules, a large cedar living van, holds an eclectic mix of antique and vintage finds. St Agnes is a Scandinavian-inspired tabernacle where the nic-nacs take a turn for the

ecclesiastical. The long wagon of Ragnarr is a beautiful, simple space on its own, you can BBQ on the deck and be entertained by the starlit skies. Finally, The Old Potting Shed is a cosy cottage for four, a far cry from a dusty old plant pot shed. Each has its own kitchen and a fifth of an acre of garden, perfect for just lying back and daydreaming in the countryside. *In the Tamar Valley, an AONB with loads of walks & rivers.*

Rooms	5 wagons for 2: from £72. 1 tabernacle for 2: from £76. 1 cabin for 4: from £94. 1 shepherd's hut for 2: from £72. Prices per night. Hot tub £30 per stay. Dogs £20 per dog per stay. Max. 2.
Meals	Self-catering.
Closed	Never.
Treats	Treats, biodegradable poo bags, towels & details of our favourite walks.

Canopy & Stars	**Tel** +44 (0)117 204 7830
Spring Park,	**Email** enquiries@canopyandstars.co.uk
Rezare, Launceston, PL15 9NX	**Web** www.canopyandstars.co.uk/springpark

Okel Tor Mine

It's not often you sleep in a World Heritage Site in an AONB, where flora and fauna – badgers, kingfishers, otters, rare mosses – also mark it as an SSSI. The two cottages – converted buildings of a former Victorian copper and tin mine – sit in a fairytale landscape of ivy-clad chimneys and tree-covered hillsides. Screened from each other, with sweeping views over the river Tamar, their small but thoughtful layouts are perfect for a romantic retreat. Open-plan living areas are cottage cosy with wood-burning stoves, large sofas, rugs on flagstone floors and a table by the window for those views. A simple kitchen and, for wet-weather, books, games and DVDs. Bedrooms, with king-size beds are fresh and unfussy country-pine, with equally neat shower rooms with handmade soaps. Stroll to the village shop and pubs in Calstock, walk along the river to the National Trust's Cotehele House, enjoy walks on the Bere Peninsula or visit Morwellham Quay port and copper mine. Within 30 minutes you could be enjoying Dartmoor, Bodmin Moor or Whitsand Bay. Return to private decking, birdsong, watery views and serenity. *Minimum stay: 2 nights; 7 in high season. River to swim in, woodland & heathland walks from door, far from roads. Short walk to 2 dog-friendly pubs.*

Rooms	2 cottages for 2: £365-£725 per week. Extra bed/sofabed no charge. Dogs £25 per stay. Max. 2 large or 3 small due to cottage size.
Meals	Self-catering.
Closed	Never.
Treats	Throws provided, towels available & wonderful road-free walks.

Mobile	+44 (0)7976 799663
Email	greg1971@mac.com
Web	www.tinmine.com

Greg Smith
Okel Tor Mine,
Calstock, PL18 9SQ

Devon Yurt

This organic farm is as wholesome as they come! Build a fire, wild swim, or pick flowers. Owners Julia and Andrew restored farm house and barns, created veg gardens, dug ponds, planted trees, and stocked the fields with their much-loved rare breed sheep, ponies and good-looking chickens. Great Links is the more remote of the two yurts; it's a whopping 21-foot diameter space with room for kitchen and dining, emperor-size sleigh bed and extra futons for friends and children. Little Links is lovely for couples, and young families may like being closer to the farm. Both are snug with rugs, sheepskins and wood-burner, and each has their own wood-fired hot tub to watch the sun set over the moors and tors and stargaze at night. Great Links has its own outdoor shower and flushing loo, Little Links uses the loo and impressive walk-in shower in the nearby shower barn and has an outdoor bath in a bell tent. There are amazing trails all around and Julia knows the best wild swimming spots. Take a day trip to the Eden Project, walk in the tree tops at Tree Surfers or explore the carved gorge in Lydford. *Dogs over 9 months welcome. Each yurt has own paddock for dog exercise. Please be aware of sheep, chickens & cats on farm. Walks from door; watery fun in Tamar Valley, river Tavy, Dartmoor streams.*

Rooms	1 yurt for 2-6: from £105 per night.
	1 yurt for 2-4: from £99 per night.
	Dogs £25 per dog per stay; £35 for week. Max. 1.
Meals	Self-catering.
Closed	October-March.
Treats	Doggie pack with towel, bowl, treats & more.

Canopy & Stars
Devon Yurt,
Borough Farm, Kelly, PL16 0HJ

Tel	+44 (0)117 204 7830
Email	enquiries@canopyandstars.co.uk
Web	www.canopyandstars.co.uk/devonyurt

The Horn of Plenty

The Horn of Plenty is one of those clever hotels that has survived the test of time by constantly improving itself. The latest addition is six gorgeous new rooms, four of which have terraces or balconies with 40-mile views over the Tamar Valley. Potter about outside and find six acres of gardens, then a path that leads down through bluebell woods to the river. Inside, beautiful simplicity abounds: stripped floors, gilt mirrors, fine art, fresh flowers everywhere. Bedrooms in the main house come in country-house style, those in the garden have a more contemporary feel. All have smart colours, big comfy beds, perhaps a claw-foot bath or a ceiling open to the rafters; ten have a terrace or a balcony. Despite all this, the food remains the big draw, so come to eat well, perhaps beetroot mousse with goat's cheese parfait, grilled duck with chicory and orange, chocolate cannelloni with banana sorbet; views of the Tamar snaking through the hills are included in the price. Afternoon tea is served on the patio in summer. Tavistock, Dartmoor and the Eden Project are close. *The Tamar Valley (2 minutes) provides woodland & river walks. Dartmoor (10-minute drive) offers everything a dog dreams of!*

Rooms	16 twin/doubles: £130-£275. Singles £120-£265. Dinner, B&B £105-£157 p.p. Extra bed/sofabed £25 p.p.p.n. Dogs £10 per night.
Meals	Lunch from £21. Dinner, 3 courses, £52.50. Tasting menu £70. Afternoon tea from £9.50.
Closed	Never.
Treats	Snacks, 5-acre gardens & loads of great local walks.

Tel	+44 (0)1822 832528
Email	enquiries@thehornofplenty.co.uk
Web	www.thehornofplenty.co.uk

Julie Leivers & Damien Pease
The Horn of Plenty,
Gulworthy, Tavistock, PL19 8JD

South Hooe Count House

It's lovely here, so peaceful in your own private cottage perched above the Tamar; the views over the river are glorious and steep steps lead to the shore and a little jetty – borrow a canoe and paddle up stream. Rowers, geese and herons glide by on misty mornings; the woodland garden is full of spring bulbs, vegetables you can pick, free-range hens, chatting guinea fowl and Arabella and Willow the donkeys. Settle on the cushioned window seat in the pretty sitting room with toasty wood-burner, books, art and family photos; copper urns and pewter jugs on a deep slate sill brim with flowers. The cosy kitchen has a lived-in, charming feel with old pine, pretty china, coffee grinder, Belfast sink and cosy Rayburn. Sip coffee on the sheltered terrace

that catches the morning sun. The light-filled bedroom has a comfortable bed, thick curtains and that view to wake to; the double ended rolltop bath is a treat. Delightful Trish can give you routes for good walks, lend you a map and suggest places to visit, boat trips to take. Nearby Tavistock has independent shops, galleries and a lively Saturday market. Live by the tide and emerge refreshed. *Babes in arms welcome. Lovely woodland walks with no sheep. Tamar river below.*

Rooms	1 house for 3: £630 per week. Short breaks of 3+ nights available. Max. 2 dogs.
Meals	Self-catering.
Closed	Rarely.
Treats	Towels, bowls & advice on walks. River to swim in & resident wonder dog Rags to entertain.

Claire Morgan
South Hooe Count House,
South Hooe Mine, Hole's Hole,
Bere Alston, PL20 7BW

Tel	+44 (0)1822 840329
Email	southhooecounthouse@gmail.com
Web	www.southhooecounthouse.com

Carswell Cottages

Deep in the South Hams is a working organic dairy farm with three cottages – ideal for families and outdoorsy couples – and a beach hut for real adventurers. The coastal path is on the doorstep and the sandy beach a short amble. The cottages are nicely spread out so you've got your own space and each is charmingly individual: The Mews (sleeps two) is a stone barn conversion with a funky roll-top bath; charming Crofters (a rustic stone cottage) and The Lodge (timber eco-house) both sleep four and are super dog-friendly. Each cottage has its own garden/outside space, two have wood-fired hot tubs, there's a fabulous kids play area, and you're welcome to come and watch the cows being milked in the dairy. Inside find open-plan kitchen/dining areas, roomy living spaces with wood-burners, comfy beds, cooking basics, and meat from the farm – pop your money in the honesty box. Then there's the stone cabin Beach Hut perched on a private cove – no electricity, compost loo, 15-minute walk from the car but the incredible sea views make it worthwhile. Heaps to do nearby or stay put and watch the sun set, glass of wine in hand. *Minimum stay: 3 nights at weekends & high season; 4 on weekdays. Secure garden. Walks from door; Coast Path 5-minutes. Dog-friendly beaches & pubs.*

Rooms	1 cottage for 2, 1 cottage for 4, 1 cottage for 4: £395-£1475. 1 cottage for 2: £650-£850 for 2 nights. Dogs £3 per dog per night.
Meals	Pub 2 miles.
Closed	Never.
Treats	Biscuits & water bowl.

Tel	+44 (0)1752 830020
Mobile	+44 (0)7771 935732 / 07970 409722 (Geoff)
Email	enquiries@carswellcottages.com
Web	www.carswellcottages.com

Katherine Harding
Carswell Cottages,
Holbeton, Plymouth, PL8 1HH

The Henley Hotel

A small house above the sea with fabulous views, super bedrooms and some of the loveliest food in Devon. Despite these credentials, it's Martyn and Petra who shine most brightly, their kind, generous approach making this a memorable place to stay. Warm interiors have wooden floors, Lloyd Loom furniture, the odd potted palm, then big windows to frame the view. Below, the Avon estuary slips gracefully out to sea. At high tide surfers ride the waves, at low tide you can walk on the sands. There's a pretty garden with a path tumbling down to the beach, binoculars in each room, a wood-burner in the snug and good books everywhere. Bedrooms are a steal (one is huge). Expect warm colours, crisp linen, tongue-and-groove panelling and robes in super little bathrooms. As for Martyn's table d'hôte dinners, expect to eat very well. Fish comes daily from Kingsbridge market, you might find grilled figs with goat's cheese and Parma ham, roast monkfish with a lobster sauce, then hot chocolate soufflé with fresh raspberries. Gorgeous Devon is all around. Better than the Ritz! *German spoken. Minimum stay: 2 nights at weekends. Beach below; only minor restrictions during summer. Coast Path just outside, garden to relax in.*

Martyn Scarterfield & Petra Lampe
The Henley Hotel,
Folly Hill,
Bigbury-on-Sea, TQ7 4AR

Rooms	2 doubles, 2 twin/doubles: £120-£137. 1 suite for 2: £150. Singles from £85. Dinner, B&B £87-£97 p.p. (2 night minimum). Dogs £5. Max. 2 per room.
Meals	Dinner £36.
Closed	November-March.
Treats	Maps & advice on walks, towels on request; entertainment & company from resident Labrador Kasper.

Tel	+44 (0)1548 810240
Email	thehenleyhotel@btconnect.com
Web	www.thehenleyhotel.co.uk

The Batman's Summerhouse

This heritage cabin is beautifully hidden in the woods, but close to fine beaches and great hiking on rugged moorland. Listen to owls as you drift off to sleep, watch buzzards hovering over the valley, spy kingfishers zipping up and down the river and gaze at bright stars in unspoilt skies. The summerhouse is perfect for a couple but roomy enough for a family There's a snuggly double on a mezzanine up generous ladder-style steps and a room for three downstairs (double with single above). It has a wall of glass looking out to the spectacular riverbank setting and a big decked area with fire pit and BBQ. The interior was inspired by family summerhouses in Scandinavia: solid wood floors, airy rooms, original art, natural linen bedding, Marimekko towels and a traditional birch summerhouse broom from Finland!

From the cabin you can walk to the cosy café and boutique shops or enjoy private river frontage with fishing rights. Craft your own bottle of artisan gin at the distillery in Salcombe or go for wood-fired pizzas by the waterside at the Crabshell Inn in Kingsbridge. The local beaches are: Bigbury-on-Sea with the Art Deco Burgh Island hotel, Mediterranean-style Blackpool Sands and Bantham's surf beach. *Miles of riverside walks from cabin, 8 acres of private woodland. Dog-friendly beaches nearby, even in summer.*

Rooms	Cabin for 5: from £130 per night. Dogs £25 per dog per stay. Max. 2.
Meals	Self-catering.
Closed	Never.
Treats	Acres of private woodland for walks in your pyjamas and wellies. Advice on walks and box of maps provided.

Tel	+44 (0)117 204 7830
Email	enquiries@canopyandstars.co.uk
Web	www.canopyandstars.co.uk/batmans

Canopy & Stars
The Batman's Summerhouse,
Riverleigh, Kingsbridge, TQ7 4DR

Big Barn

This versatile barn is tucked away down a private drive and sits by a lake deep in beautiful South Hams farmland. Caroline's restoration has been imaginative: oak beams soar above the vast, vaulted living space and there's a long sociable table with room for everybody. If you want to cook Riverford Organics will deliver, if you don't Caroline can book a chef. Kids can run riot in the open-plan living space when it is wet – in summer spill out to a barbecue terrace where you can sip a sundowner while keeping an eye on the enclosed baby and toddler play area. There's a games room for older children. Bring the dogs for walks along the sands (no fewer than eight dog-friendly beaches nearby). Dartmoor and the coastal rambles of the South Devon peninsula are on the doorstep. *Glorious walks on South Devon coast path and Dartmoor.*

Rooms	1 barn for 10: £1800-£3500 per week. 2-night stay: £1200-£1600; 3-night stay: £1400-£1800. Extra beds available. Dogs £25 per dog per stay. Max. usually 2.
Meals	Self-catering.
Closed	Rarely.
Treats	Blanket, towels & a welcome treat.

Caroline Murray
Big Barn,
East Allington, Totnes, TQ9 7QB

Tel	+44 (0)1548 521670
Email	info@bigbarndevon.co.uk
Web	www.bigbarndevon.co.uk

Fingals Cottage Apartments

Unusual, quirky and fun. Fingals is a magical collection of self-catering cottage apartments and loyal fans return year after year for the old Manor's laid-back charm. In a green valley half a mile from the river Dart, all you need is here: snooker, grass tennis, croquet, pool, gym. Six different spaces have been created, from romantic boltholes to larger escapes for family or friends. The green oak Barn has floor-to-ceiling windows and garden views; The Folly and Barberry Brook overlook the stream; the Wisteria Suite has its own blossom-decked balcony where you can breakfast in the sun; Lower Mill and Upper Mill Houses have private terraces perfect for al fresco dining. Find polished oak floors with faded oriental rugs, well-snuggled-in sofas, rocking horse, piano, minstrel gallery, conservatory, suntrap terraces, books, games and more. Children can knock a ball about, swim, make friends, as you sip your favourite tipple and loll on a steamer chair. Golfers can ask Richard about a discount at the local club, and everyone can head off to the beach, the river, the pub... the area is a treat to discover. *Minimum stay: 3 nights; 7 in high season. Secure garden, woodland & river. Goats, ducks & chickens in walled garden so keep dogs under control in & around hotel gardens.*

Rooms	1 barn for 6: £615-£1475. 2 cottages for 2; 1 apartment for 4: £490-£1050. 1 house for 5; 1 house for 6: £680-£2200. Prices per week. Short breaks £390-£975. Dogs £5. Max. 3.
Meals	Self-catering.
Closed	Never.
Treats	Advice on walks, towels & resident friendly lurchers to play with – & plenty of love & attention!

Tel	+44 (0)1803 722398
Email	info@fingals.co.uk
Web	www.fingalsapart.co.uk/thebarn.html

Richard & Sheila Johnston
Fingals Cottage Apartments,
Old Coombe, Dittisham, TQ6 0JA

Bulleigh Barton Manor

Tea and scones will be waiting. Find long, leafy views to wake up to, a pool for lazy summer days, ponds and a big colourful garden with a summerhouse. Liz and Mark have restored their house with care, uncovering beams and lovely bits of old wood and filling it with original art and books. Bedrooms are inviting: sink-into beds, china pieces on white window sills, a pot of garden flowers, local fudge and homemade cake. They are keen on sourcing the best local produce and their host of hens lay your breakfast eggs. Dartmoor and the south coast are at your feet; return to a friendly hello from Zennor the dog by the fire. *Over 16s welcome. Large garden, alpacas in paddock, sheep in neighbouring fields. Lots of walks nearby. Suite has direct access to garden.*

Rooms	2 doubles: £86-£135. 1 suite for 2: £90-£130. Singles £77-£120. Dogs £7.50 per dog per night. Max. 2 in suite, 1 in Brooking Room.
Meals	Pubs/restaurants 0.5 miles.
Closed	Rarely.
Treats	Devon-made food, handmade liver treats, towels, blanket, shampoo. Info on walks, pubs & beaches; guide to Dartmoor. Tag with local contact details.

Liz & Mark Lamport
Bulleigh Barton Manor,
Ipplepen, Newton Abbot, TQ12 5UA

Tel	+44 (0)1803 873411
Email	liz.lamport@btopenworld.com
Web	www.bulleighbartonmanor.co.ukl

Brownscombe

These luxurious safari tents and cabin in the rolling hills of Devon are perfect for kids or just never-grownups. Bovey and Tamar are the two dog-friendly tents in this two-acre buttercup field that houses all four safari tents at Brownscombe. Or opt for the cabin and soak in the big copper bath with the wall folded back to look out at the valley. Relax in the hot tub or eat out on the deck watching the stars and wake to roe deer grazing in the misty morning fields. By day, adventure in the woods, scramble round the play area at the bottom of the meadow, or join Kate on her farming rounds, feeding the lambs, pigs and chickens with Molly the lab and Margot the pug in tow. Pick teams for rounders, frisbee or football on the lawn, or battle it out over table tennis and foosball in the games room. At night, fire up the hot tub and raid the honesty larder for smores kits and Kate's amazing home-cooked meals, book the BBQ lodge or join in on pizza nights in the barn and get everyone round the table to celebrate. *Both tents have enclosed balcony with gate. Beautiful off lead walks straight from door. Enclosed orchard on site with dog bin for dogs to run off lead. Dogs on lead in glamping area due to livestock.*

Rooms	2 safari tents for 6: from £150 per night. 1 cabin for 4: from £162. Extra £25 per night for hot tub if staying in tent. Dogs £25 per dog per stay. max 1 in cabin; 2 per tent.
Meals	Self-catering.
Closed	November-March.
Treats	Info on local walks, dog friendly beaches & pubs. Basket, towel, bowls & outside tap for muddy paws.

Tel	+44 (0)117 204 7830
Email	enquiries@canopyandstars.co.uk
Web	www.canopyandstars.co.uk/brownscombe

Canopy & Stars
Brownscombe,
Compton Holt, Compton,
Marldon, TQ3 1TA

Cary Arms & Spa

The Cary Arms hovers above Babbacombe Bay with huge views of water and sky that shoot off to Dorset's Jurassic coast. It's a cool little place – half seaside pub, half dreamy hotel – and it makes the most of its position: five beautiful terraces drop downhill towards a small jetty where locals fish. As for the bar, it comes with stone walls, wooden floors, rustic-chic tables and a fire that burns every day, but in good weather you eat on the terraces... start perhaps with seared Brixham scallops, follow with wild mushroom and pistachio roast, finish with elderflower and lime crème brûlée – served on white plates and as pretty as a picture. Then snorkel on mackerel reefs, or hug the coastline in a kayak. *Dogs welcome in main area of inn & garden terraces, but not conservatory. Coast path on doorstep; Babbacombe beach dog-friendly all year round.*

Rooms	7 doubles: £295. 1 suite for 4, 9 suites for 2: £375-£475. 1 family room for 4: £395. Extra bed/sofabed £25 p.p.p.n. Dogs £20 per night. Max. 1-2.
Meals	Lunch from £7.95. Dinner £25-£35.
Closed	Never.
Treats	Biscuits, bed & bowl in room.

David Adams
Cary Arms & Spa,
Beach Road,
Babbacombe, TQ1 3LX

Tel	+44 (0)1803 327110
Email	enquiries@caryarms.co.uk
Web	www.caryarms.co.uk

Mill End

Order a hearty packed lunch the night before, and set off on the Two Moors Way. This is a walkers' hotel run by generous people in a glorious patch of Dartmoor. Tara and Nick give you cream teas, maps of walks straight from the door, high tea for children, and a boot room for your muddy things – including the dog. Outside the river Teign runs alongside the gardens (yes, you can fish; there's even an in-house fly fishing school if you want to learn) and homemade scones with clotted cream and jam are served in the sunshine. Inside are three dapper lounges where fires crackle and burn on chilly days. Order your gin and tonic, play a game of Scrabble then step into the restaurant for fresh fish, locally reared meats and gorgeous West Country cheeses. Bedrooms – some with garden views, others with French windows opening onto the lawns – are all a good size and have comfortable armchairs or sofas if you'd rather stay private. *Minimum stay: 2 nights on weekdays. Amazing walks start directly from hotel onto miles of Dartmoor. Riverside rambles too – usually safe, but in times of spate be cautious.*

Rooms	15 twin/doubles: £105-£200. 6 suites for 2: £190-£260. Singles from £80. Dogs £8 per night.
Meals	Lunch from £6. Dinner, 3 courses, £30-£40. Sunday lunch £22-£26. Afternoon tea £18.95.
Closed	Never.
Treats	Personalised 'Mill End' biscuit bones from Buddy Bakery, welcome pack with chews, spare leads, towels & throwers.

Tel	+44 (0)1647 432282
Email	info@millendhotel.com
Web	www.millendhotel.com

Tara & Nick Culverhouse
Mill End,
Chagford,
Newton Abbot, TQ13 8JN

Acorn Farm

When Chris and Tracey set up home at Acorn Farm they transformed a former chicken shed into their house – they still live there now, but have added a shepherd's hut and a woodland camp to their motley crew of handmade spaces. Here you're tucked away in a peaceful patch of oak and beech woodland – no WiFi, but phone signal if you're desperate – with logs for the wood-burner and hot water bottles to warm you, a chest full of linens and fairy lights twinkling in the gloaming. Both the shepherd's hut and the yurt can be heated, so you'll be cosy year-round. There are lots of spaces around to spread out into, with sports equipment and board games to keep families of all ages entertained. Chris and Tracey really have thought of everything, including treats, toys and blankets for dogs. There's even a treehouse shower halfway up an ancient oak (complete with hot mains water!). *Fencing around hut; 45 acres of fields & woodland; local footpaths. Shower hut dog-friendly. Lots of sheep on farm so take care; local pub dog-friendly. Please bring own dog bed.*

Rooms	Shepherd's hut for 5: from £110. Camp for 5 from £120. Horses £25. Prices per night. Space for 6 adults camping £15 p.p.p.n. Dogs £25 per dog per stay. Max. 2; more by arrangement.
Meals	Self-catering.
Closed	Never.
Treats	Doggy box with towel, blanket, bowls, treats, toys & spare leads.

Canopy & Stars
Acorn Farm,
Spreyton, EX17 5AL

Tel +44 (0)117 204 7830
Email enquiries@canopyandstars.co.uk
Web www.canopyandstars.co.uk/acornfarm

Eversfield Safari Tents

Complete canvas comfort in a quiet wildlife-filled valley. A double room, twin room and a double cabin bed in each means plenty of space for families or groups of friends. There's a sofa, dining table, a blanket box full of games, and a wood-burning stove in the kitchen but, being pitched on a big deck, you can cook outside on the barbecue too and make the most of the lovely views across the lake. Owners Anna and Jon have a farm shop which sells delicious organic stuff. No need to tramp up through the fields either as each tent has its own en suite shower pod and separate loo – just stoke the wood-fired boiler to heat up your water. Eversfield sits on the edge of Dartmoor national park and is a perfect base for walkers who want to discover this famous wilderness. At home there's also plenty on offer – row the boat around the lake or try your hand at fly fishing. If you catch rainbow trout you can cook it for your campfire supper while spotting constellations. If the wind blows in a certain direction you may hear a faint noise from the road but otherwise you'll likely forget all about 'life outside'. *Dartmoor National Park on doorstep, forests & sandy beaches for walks. Organic farm with cattle in fields so dogs must be kept on lead when walking through fields.*

Rooms	2 safari tents for 6: from £116 per night. £250 damage deposit payable before stay. Dogs £20 per dog per stay. Max. 2.
Meals	Self-catering.
Closed	October-February.
Treats	Advice on walks. Dog bowl provided. Good walks nearby over Dartmoor National Park, Roadford Lake and beaches.

Tel	+44 (0)117 204 7830
Email	enquiries@canopyandstars.co.uk
Web	www.canopyandstars.co.uk/eversfield

Canopy & Stars
Eversfield Safari Tents,
Water Meadow, Ellacott Barton,
Bratton Clovelly, EX20 4LB

Great Burrow Cottage

Chickens, children and dogs can roam free here. Mary and Justin will leave out cream teas or cake and some breakfast goodies to get you started – local organic milk and eggs if the hens feel like laying. Watch roe deer wander in the fields, laze in the hammock, snuggle by the wood-burner, sip coffee on the terrace, soak up the views over the Northern Tors of Dartmoor. Kids can play ping-pong, build a campfire and marvel at the stars. The Clovelly Inn for a pie and a pint is a half-hour stroll through the valley and across a stream. Drive to join the Two Castles Trail or West Devon Way at Okehampton – bring back local Curworthy cheese from the market and treats from the deli to cook in the open-plan kitchen, or head to the beaches of North Cornwall for fish, chips and surf. *Minimum stay: 3 nights; 7 in high season. Walks from door, streams to swim in, valleys to run through. On edge of Dartmoor. Free-range chickens so dogs on lead near house.*

Rooms	1 cottage for 6: £450-£950 per week. Dogs £5 per night, £30 per week. Max. 3.
Meals	Self-catering.
Closed	Rarely.
Treats	Basket, towels & treats. Advice on dog-friendly beaches, cafés & great walks.

Justin & Mary Ellery
Great Burrow Cottage,
Bratton Clovelly,
Okehampton, EX20 4JJ

Tel	+44 (0)1837 871623
Mobile	+44 (0)7802 753123
Email	Info@greatburrowcottage.co.uk
Web	www.greatburrowcottage.co.uk

Devon Dens

Jo and Ben have hand-crafted their lovely slice of Devon countryside and the brilliant cabins themselves, to give you a stress-free, tech-free break from hectic modern life. Everything at Devon Dens has been designed to make life flow more naturally. A genuine love of the environment runs through every choice, from the wood-burners, solar power and a dry loo to ladders in the pond for the frogs and newts. You can nip out to the glorious beaches at Bude, just forty-five minutes away, or take the Granite Way cycle path from Okehampton along the old railway lines. You can then enjoy some well earned time out and relax in the wonderful wood-fired sauna. Even if you don't pick up tips on eco-building from your knowledgeable and passionate hosts, you'll come away with a renewed appreciation for the peace and beauty of nature.

Surrounded by livestock, dogs under control on site. Lovely walks around site. Great year-round, dog-friendly beaches within 45-minute drive. Local pub has 1 dog-friendly table.

Rooms	Cabin for 4 from £125. Cabin for 2 from £85. Prices per night. Dogs £20 per dog per stay. Max. 1 per cabin
Meals	Self-catering.
Closed	Never.
Treats	Bowls, eco poo bags, a poo bin & towels.

Tel	+44 (0)117 204 7830
Email	enquiries@canopyandstars.co.uk
Web	www.canopyandstars.co.uk/devondens

Canopy & Stars
Devon Dens,
Germansweek, EX21 5AL

The Woodland Retreat

From the welcome cream tea to the moment you leave, you'll find The Woodland Retreat fits its name perfectly. The cabin is one of our wilder retreats, small and rustic, but with a big double bed and bunks occupying each wall. The wood-burner in the middle does its best to keep out the chill, but don't forget your chunky jumper if you're going in spring or autumn. A few steps away is a converted wood-panelled bus with optional extra sleeping space. The kitchen and shower are outdoor but covered so the terrace with its sofas and table acts as a lounge and dining room. The bell tent is an extra day space, perfect for taking yourself off to read or nap. Owners Lydia and Alex have a long history in the arts and their record label is run

from the on-site recording suite which you can hire if you book their other cabin too, Candyland Studios. They built this 8-person cabin themselves with timber from the woodland, straw bales from the land and a reclaimed tin roof. If you don't feel like making music, head out to the coast at nearby Bude or rack up some miles hiking the stunning surrounding scenery. *Four acres of woodland to explore.*

Rooms	Cabin for 4-6: from £88 per night. Cabin for 8: from £190 per night. The Dodge for 2 adults or children: from £30 p.p.p.n. Max. 2 dogs in Candyland Studios, 4 in Woodland Retreat. Recording studio can be booked £24 per hour.
Meals	Self-catering.
Closed	November-March.
Treats	Blankets & dog biscuits.

Canopy & Stars
The Woodland Retreat,
Stapleton Farm, Langtree,
Torrington, EX38 8NP

Tel	+44 (0)117 204 7830
Email	enquiries@canopyandstars.co.uk
Web	www.canopyandstars.co.uk/woodlandretreat

Coombe Farm

Easy-going, foodie, country-lovers will fit right in here. Lisa and Matt, passionate about real food, cook home-grown dinners; charcuterie a speciality. Their fine old Devon long house sits in a green fold of farmland and you're free to wander the garden, chat to the pigs, plunge in the invigorating pool. Inside find a quirky mix of family and brocante finds, a snug sitting room full of art, colourful comfortable rooms and fab bathrooms. Breakfast is a delicious spread of homemade everything: granola, jams, sourdough bread, sausages and bacon from the rare breed pigs. No 3 cycle route is close by; Exmoor walks and coast are 20 minutes. *Minimum stay: 2 nights at weekends & in high season. Public footpath running through property & into woods. Cattle, sheep, pigs & chickens so dogs must be reliable or on a lead.*

Rooms	1 double, 2 twin/doubles: £75-£90. Max. 2 dogs.
Meals	Dinner from £25. Restaurants 15 minutes walk.
Closed	Rarely.
Treats	Hose to wash muddy paws, stream running through garden to splash in. Towels on request.

Tel	+44 (0)1271 324919
Mobile	+44 (0)7775 941031
Email	info@coombefarmgoodleigh.co.uk
Web	www.coombefarmgoodleigh.co.uk

Matthew Eckford
Coombe Farm,
Goodleigh, Barnstaple, EX32 7NB

Garden Studio, North Walk House

A snug apartment with stunning sea views, close to Exmoor's coastal path as it sweeps dramatically into the Valley of the Rocks. North Walk is a quiet no-through road that crosses – near the top – the funicular linking Lynmouth and Lynton, and the Downings have transformed their house into a calm retreat, with self-catering on the ground floor. Living area, kitchen and comfy brass bed are all in one space – the bed cleverly hidden by a half wall topped with books and walking maps. Wind-blasted wanderers can return to sit on the suntrap terrace with homemade flapjack or cake and watch the boating world go by below, and then get cosy with a DVD. In the morning you may choose to seek out Sarah and Ian's

fabulous local and organic breakfasts in the B&B above – otherwise the kitchen has all the gadgets and the local deli is well-stocked with good things. Your relaxed and charming hosts know the area well and can give you tips for getting the most out of the miles of coast, woods and moorland right on the doorstep – plenty of good pubs and tea rooms along the way too. *Minimum stay: 3 nights. Lovely walks – join the coastal path.*

Rooms	1 apartment for 2: £348-£431 per week. Dogs £5 per night per stay. Max. 2.
Meals	Self-catering.
Closed	Rarely.
Treats	Biscuits, water bowl, towel, throw for furniture & outside tap with hose.

Ian & Sarah Downing
Garden Studio, North Walk House,
North Walk, Lynton, EX35 6HJ

Tel   +44 (0)1598 753372
Email   northwalkhousebb@gmail.com
Web   www.northwalkhouse.co.uk

Welcombe Meadow

Welcombe Meadow is at once disconnected and packed with kit – books and board games, a TV for movie nights snuggled under blankets on the big squashy leather sofa and WiFi too (ask for it to be switched off if you'd prefer to go back to basics). It's slap bang between the moors of Exmoor and Dartmoor and surrounded by wildflower meadows where rabbits and deer roam. The two tents here are named after local rivers – both of which you can walk along – and are angled to enjoy the view, but close enough that you could take over both for a big family bash. Cook together on the wood-burning stove or have the pizza oven wheeled over to your tent and gather at the table for campfire feasts. Pop over to the games room for table tennis and basketball before retreating back to lie in the hammock and stare at the million-tog duvet of stars above you – only the neighbouring sheep and cattle break the silence. *28 acres of farmland for dogs to roam and enjoy smells of farm. Make friends with resident dog Pip. Community wood nearby. Small stream on site to paddle in. Lots of footpaths and walks. Cattle & sheep in fields so dogs on lead in some areas.*

Rooms	2 safari tents for 6: from £124 per night. Up to 2 (own) extra tents per safari tent £25 per night (up to 4-man tent). Dogs £20 per dog per stay. Max 2.
Meals	Self-catering.
Closed	Never.
Treats	Homemade dog biscuits made by the community shop and provided in the tent on arrival. Eco-friendly dog loo.

Tel	+44 (0)117 204 7830
Email	enquiries@canopyandstars.co.uk
Web	www.canopyandstars.co.uk/welcombemeadow

Canopy & Stars
Welcombe Meadow,
Welcombe,
High Bickington, EX37 9BJ

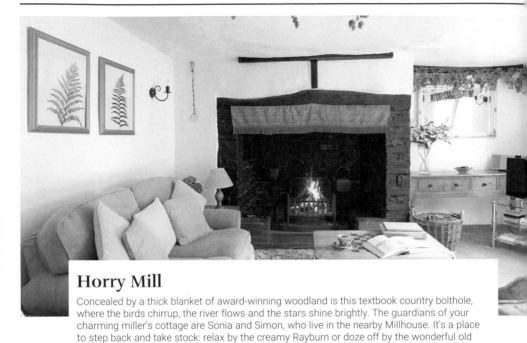

Horry Mill

Concealed by a thick blanket of award-winning woodland is this textbook country bolthole, where the birds chirrup, the river flows and the stars shine brightly. The guardians of your charming miller's cottage are Sonia and Simon, who live in the nearby Millhouse. It's a place to step back and take stock: relax by the creamy Rayburn or doze off by the wonderful old fireplace with limitless logs. A pretty window seat upstairs overlooks the cottage garden – secluded and south-facing, a lovely spot for a summer barbecue. Explore the valley by foot – Simon and Sonia's enthusiasm for the area is infectious and they carefully manage the surrounding area. Bees, birds and bluebells are encouraged, and a small herd of beef cattle, pigs, ducks and hens merrily thrive. *Minimum stay: 7 nights in high season. Woodland walks Chickens & ducks wander into your garden; garden not secure.*

Rooms	1 cottage for 4: £345-£650 per week. Overseas payments to be made in sterling. Max. 2 dogs. Dogs 1+ year allowed.
Meals	Self-catering.
Closed	Never.
Treats	Woodland walks, maps & towels.

Simon & Sonia Hodgson
Horry Mill,
Hollocombe, Chulmleigh, EX18 7QH

Tel	+44 (0)1769 520266
Email	horrymill@aol.com
Web	www.horrymill.com

The Lamb Inn

This 16th-century inn is adored by locals and visitors alike. It's a proper inn in the old tradition with gorgeous rooms and the odd touch of scruffiness to add authenticity to its earthy bones. It stands on a cobbled walkway in a village lost down tiny lanes, and those lucky enough to chance upon it leave reluctantly. Inside there are beams, but they are not sandblasted, red carpets with a little swirl, sofas in front of an open fire. Boarded menus trumpet irresistible food – carrot and orange soup, haunch of venison with a port jus, an excellent rhubarb crumble. You can eat wherever you want: in the bar, in the fancy restaurant, or out in the walled garden in good weather. There's a cobbled terrace, a skittle alley, maps for walkers and well-kept ales. Upstairs, seven rooms have a chic country style. Two have baths in the room, those in the barn have painted stone walls, the suite has a wood-burner and a private terrace. All are lovely with comfy beds, white linen, good power showers and flat-screen TVs. Kind staff chat with ease. Dartmoor waits, but you may well linger. Brilliant. *Secure garden & friendly staff who love dogs; all dogs must be on a lead & well-behaved though, if eating in bar with owners.*

Rooms	5 doubles, 1 twin/double: £95-£140. 1 suite for 3: £145-£180. Extra bed/sofabed £22 p.p.p.n. Dogs £5 per dog p.n.
Meals	Lunch from £6.95. Dinner, 3 courses, £22-£35. Sunday lunch from £10.95- £12.95.
Closed	Rarely.
Treats	Advice on local walks & fresh water bowl.

Tel	+44 (0)1363 773676
Email	thelambinn@gmail.com
Web	www.lambinnsandford.co.uk

Nick Silk
The Lamb Inn,
Sandford, EX17 4LW

Gosling Lodge

The moment Gosling Lodge comes into view as you round the corner of the gravel track, you start to relax. A pocket of trees screen the cabin and its pond from view, leaving you alone with the meadow and the hills beyond crossed only by a distant, quiet road. Handcrafted by a local carpenter, Gosling Lodge is an open space of simple comfort with splashes of blues and green echoing the water outside, where the eponymous birds are often seen in season. Lounging on the veranda or the sofa by the wood-burner, you sink into a dreamlike state of ease. On sunny days, you can splash around in the boat, but even in chillier weather, the covered porch and the cosy cabin itself are lovely spots to curl up and and let the day drift by. Gosling Lodge has a

perfect blend of seclusion and accessibility. Walks across the fields can take you round the corner to meet the inquisitive cows and along a steep track to the local shop at Bradninch, 30 minutes away, or venture further afield to the miles of hillside trails across the Blackdown Hills Area of Outstanding Natural Beauty. *Fifty acres of land to bound across on the doorstep. Lots of local walks and nearby dog-friendly pub. Dogs on a lead at all times during walks due to surrounding wildlife.*

Rooms	Cabin for 2: from £90 per night. Dogs £20 per dog per stay. Max 2.
Meals	Self-catering.
Closed	Never.
Treats	Chewy treat to keep dogs entertained whilst the human guests chill out, dog bowls, outside tap for washing and towel are provided.

Canopy & Stars	**Tel**	+44 (0)117 204 7830
Gosling Lodge,	**Email**	enquiries@canopyandstars.co.uk
Bradninch, EX5 4NP	**Web**	www.canopyandstars.co.uk/goslinglodge

Scorlinch Shepherd's Hut

Your adventure begins with a farm buggy ride through the hay field and straight to your door. The cosy eco-hut is powered by a mini wind/solar-power station and almost everything inside is locally made, from the wool insulation in the walls to the woolly sheep-print curtains. The private decking is all yours, complete with a gazebo to protect you from the elements, a barbecue and a stunning view; you may spot the odd peregrine falcon or stoat. A breakfast basket can be delivered, including homemade butter, jams and bread, local bacon and home-laid eggs. Explore the 20-acre farm – meet the sheep, chickens, turkeys and guinea fowl; you're welcome to collect eggs and feed sheep. There's a footpath that runs all the way to the village with a lunch stop at the Five Bells Pub on the way or you can 'walk the plank' for a shortcut across the river. Dartmoor with its wonderful, wild walks is an easy 40-minute drive, or you might choose not to leave your cosy bolthole and add a touch of luxury by booking the Milking Parlour hot tub, sauna & spa pool before admiring the fantastically clear skies as you wander back to your home for the night. *Fenced (sheep-free) field but dogs can escape under gate. Great dog walks; River Clyst which dogs love to paddle in! Working sheep farm: dogs need up to date worming and to be on lead in fields.*

Rooms	Shepherd's hut for 2: from £88 per night. Use of Milking Parlour: £50 for 2 days; £60 for 3-5 days; £70 for 7+ days; paid on arrival. Dogs £20 per dog per stay. Max. 1.
Meals	Self-catering.
Closed	Never.
Treats	Welcome treat on arrival; towels can be provided.

Tel	+44 (0)117 204 7830
Email	enquiries@canopyandstars.co.uk
Web	www.canopyandstars.co.uk/scorlinch

Canopy & Stars
Scorlinch Shepherd's Hut,
Scorlinch Farm,
Cullompton, EX15 2NJ

The Wellhouse & Wellhayes Barn

Folk with a yen for a country escape close to the coast, and a taste for James Verner's modern rustic design style will love the Wellhouse and next door Wellhayes Barn. Light pours through tall windows into the house's striking open-plan living space, with massive wood-burner, James Verner's furniture and interesting art. The barn is just as bright and lovely, with a wheelchair-friendly downstairs bedroom, an open-plan living area and an upstairs bedroom with long green views and wood-burner. Both kitchens have all you need; catering can be arranged if you come as a group and there are excellent restaurants and markets nearby in Lyme Regis, Bridport and Axminster. Take a boat on, or a plunge into, the lake. Wander the woods with red kites overhead; walk to Lyme Regis in under an hour. *Minimum stay: 3 nights; 7 in high season. House & barn can be booked together to sleep up to 12. A great base for dog walking – explore the footpaths through woods and fields that start and finish at the door.*

Rooms	1 barn for 4: £850-£1550 per week. 1 house for 6: £2500 per week. Extra bed/sofabed no charge in Wellhayes Barn.
Meals	Restaurants 10-minute walk.
Closed	Never.
Treats	Surprise treats in the welcome hamper.

James Verner
The Wellhouse & Wellhayes Barn,
Wellhayes, Harcombe,
Lyme Regis, DT7 3RN

Mobile	+44 (0)7796 991606
Email	stay@wellhayes.com
Web	www.wellhayes.com

The Hut

Through dappled woodland, down a drive swathed with wild flowers in spring to the most romantic, tucked away wooden retreat with stunning views over meadows dotted with Herdwick sheep. You're quite alone and not overlooked so you'll feel free as birds. Inside is warm, unfussy and welcoming with plenty of squishy seats, a sweet kitchen area with a warming Aga (lit in cooler months) and all the stuff even a demanding cook could need. Books, maps and a wood-burner with plenty of logs make rainy days happy too, so hunker down and plan your next outing. Bring bikes and join The Marshwood Vale which passes the top of the drive, explore Charmouth Forest with walking tracks in multiple directions, visit micro-breweries, gin distillers and vineyards, drive to Lyme Regis (12 minutes) for HIX Oyster & Fish House. Beaches (10 minutes) are grand for fossil hunters, Burton Bradstock has the marvellous Hive Beach Cafe. Return to a sundowner on your veranda and watch the stars, and bats, come out *Mobile reception on Vodafone; other networks at top of drive. Secure fenced garden. Walks from door along quiet lanes; Forestry Commission woods & bridleways.*

Rooms	1 cottage for 2: £795-£995 per week. Christmas & New Year £1200 per week. Short breaks from £445. Dogs £20 per dog; £35 per week. Max. 2.
Meals	Self-catering.
Closed	Rarely.
Treats	Rugs, bowls, towel, welcome treats & an Aga & wood-burner to snooze by. List of dog-friendly walks, beaches & places to eat.

Tel	+44 (0)1297 678424
Email	nettlemoor.farm@btinternet.com
Web	www.thedorsethut.co.uk

Susan & Mark Rogers
The Hut,
Fishpond Bottom,
Charmouth, DT6 6NW

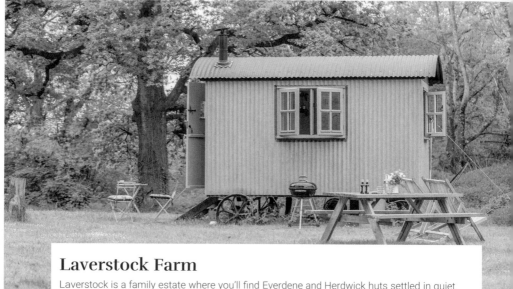

Laverstock Farm

Laverstock is a family estate where you'll find Everdene and Herdwick huts settled in quiet stretches of the Woodland Walk. You are perfectly positioned here for day trips to Lyme Regis, long hikes up Dorset's highest hills, Lewesdon and Pilsdon; climb to the top of the Jurassic Coast's loftiest cliff, then return to your cosy shepherd's hut for a campfire supper in the woodland. Inside each you'll find a comfy double bed, table and chairs and a wood-burner. A camp kitchen is under the awning outside with gas hobs and a big solid sideboard for prepping and cooking. The hot shower and flushing loo are about 100 metres away in the shared purpose-built washroom. There's no electricity in the huts but you'll be given some lanterns which you can recharge in the communal games room, where you'll also find a fridge. There's a welcome pack of Laverstock's own apple juice, freshly baked cake and eggs, if the chickens have been on form, and you can order a farmhouse breakfast. From then on, you can simply relax into the gentle Dorset countryside, or head out seeking adventure. *Woodland & grounds with stream to cool off in, info pack, lots of dog-friendly walks, pubs & restaurants nearby.*

Rooms	2 shepherd's huts for 2: from £75 per night. Extra space to pitch two tents £20 per night per tent. Dogs £20 per dog per stay. Max. 2.
Meals	Self-catering.
Closed	Never.
Treats	Basket, towel, bowl & biscuits. Hose available for muddy dogs!

Canopy & Stars
Laverstock Farm,
Laverstock, Bridport, DT6 5PE

Tel	+44 (0)117 204 7830
Email	enquiries@canopyandstars.co.uk
Web	www.canopyandstars.co.uk/laverstock

Camping Coach

The quirky train carriage gleams inside and out. Turn the chunky brass handle on the door of this ancient London Brighton & South Coast Railway carriage and enter another era. Find original fittings (luggage racks, rounded windows, leather straps and brasswork), but the tradition gives way slightly in the presence of a fully equipped kitchen and adjoining loo and shower at one end. In the main saloon there is a long bench seat that converts into a double bed and at the other end there is a wonderful antique French stove to keep you warm. Of course, you could spend your days in the living van a few steps from the coach, which is gaily decorated and equally comfortable. The van's seating can also convert into two single beds (ideal for children), so you can sleep four people in the whole camp altogether. There are pubs and restaurants, markets and teashops where you can explore the area's varied produce. You're a fossil's throw from the Jurassic Coast for some lovely beach walks and surrounded by endless fields and hills. *Children over 5 welcome. Fabulous walking area.*

Rooms	Train carriage for 4: from £98 per night. Space for 2 extra adults from £10 per adult per night; children over 5 £5 per night. Dogs £10 per dog per stay. Max. 1 well-behaved dog. (Two by arrangement).
Meals	Self-catering.
Closed	Never.
Treats	Towels & advice on walks.

Tel	+44 (0)117 204 7830
Email	enquiries@canopyandstars.co.uk
Web	www.canopyandstars.co.uk/campingcoach

Canopy & Stars
Camping Coach,
High Cross Cottage, Whitecross,
Netherbury, DT6 5NH

Short House Chesil Beach

Drive through swaying pampas grass and umbrella pines to this newly-restored Purbeck stone and pink rendered cottage: the deep blue sea shimmers in the distance and a solemn terracotta warrior stands guard. Sheep graze the surrounding National Trust farmland and you've only an unspoilt meadow between you and Chesil Beach. Charming owners Andrew and Julie, live in the 18th-century house next door and stock up the cottage with wine and local Dorset delights from the farm shop. Find a large, sociable, open plan kitchen dining and sitting room with high ceilings, bright kilims, oak floors and purple doors. Julie's bold canvasses hang on the walls, there's comfortable furniture, piles of books and DVDs, even an

excellent Bose sound system. The bedrooms have finely dressed beds in feather and down, glorious watery views and smart bathrooms with roll tops and travertine stone walls and open onto a west-facing terrace overlooking the garden and sea. You can play tennis, hop on a horse from the riding stables, visit Abbotsbury Gardens or ancient Swannery by foot, or tackle wonderful coastal walks from the door. *Minimum stay: 3 nights; 7 in high season. Secluded location, no main roads nearby. 400-metre walk to beach across field.*

Rooms	1 house for 5: £750-£1500 per week. Extra beds/sofabeds no charge.
Meals	Pubs/restaurants 1 mile.
Closed	Never.
Treats	Beach runs & towels for drying after splashing in sea.

Andrew Wadsworth
Short House Chesil Beach,
Labour-in-Vain Lane,
West Bexington, DT2 9DE

Tel	+44 (0)1305 871600
Mobile	+44 (0)7836 262222
Email	aww11@mac.com
Web	www.short-house.co.uk

The Acorn Inn

Perfect Evershot and rolling countryside lie at the door of this 400-year-old gem in Thomas Hardy country. Natalie and Richard took the reins to revive its fortunes, with head chef Robert Ndungu cooking hearty food. It's very much a traditional inn; locals sup pints of Otter Ale in the long flagstoned bar and guests sample good food sourced within 25 miles. In the dining room, the atmosphere changes to rural country house with smartly laid tables, terracotta tiles, soft lighting and elegant fireplaces. Good gastropub fare is taken seriously, be it an Acorn Inn homemade burger, or open lasagne of confit rabbit followed by twice cooked pork belly, and a warm sticky toffee pudding. Little ones have their own menu, and stacks of colouring books and crayons to keep them busy while they wait. Service is helpful and friendly. Bedrooms creak with age and style; there are antiques and fabric wall-coverings, super little bathrooms, perhaps a wonky floor or a lovely four-poster. It's worth splashing out on a larger room if you want space. *Footpath through 900-acre parkland in village; countless other paths in all directions. Coastal path 20-minute drive.*

Rooms	4 doubles, 2 twin/doubles, 3 four-posters: £105-£180. 1 suite for 3: £170-£230. Singles £89-£205. Dinner, B&B £80-£133 p.p. Extra bed/sofabed £20 p.p.p.n. Dogs £12.
Meals	Lunch & dinner £5.25-£22.95. Bar meals from £4.95.
Closed	Rarely.
Treats	Dog-friendly guide, water bowl, towel & treats. Walking map & treats in bar.

Tel	+44 (0)1935 83228
Email	nread@rchmail.com
Web	www.acorn-inn.co.uk

Natalie & Richard Legg
The Acorn Inn,
Evershot, Dorchester, DT2 0JW

53 Durweston

Rural chic at its best! A thatched 18th-century cottage bursting with character and clutter-free style. Dreamy window seats, an inglenook fireplace, oak floorboards and latch doors, exposed beams, cob walls, wood-burners, a rustic antique dining table, a vintage leather armchair... fresh flowers, soft furnishings, candles and contemporary artwork complete the picture. Picasso line drawings dot the kitchen – a long, narrow Victorian addition with stone flooring, a painted dresser and all you'll need. Up the cottagey stairs to the two oh-so-pretty bedrooms, light and luxuriously carpeted with views of church, water meadows and woods beyond. Both have king-size, French style, cream iron beds, crisp white cotton and chests of drawers; the larger gets a buttonback chair, the smaller, a cast-iron fireplace, and the spacious bathroom between them has sumptuous towels and toiletries. All this, and a herb and flower-planted garden, in the quietest part of a beautiful Dorset village. Fantastic for cycling and chalk ridge walks, and a ten-minute drive from Georgian Blandford. It'll be hard to leave. *Secure garden & miles of beautiful country walks right on doorstep.*

Rooms	1 cottage for 4: £750-£1450 per week. Dogs £10 per dog per stay. Max. 2. Short breaks available.
Meals	Self-catering.
Closed	Never.
Treats	Water bowl, food bowl & a treat.

Emma Perry
53 Durweston,
Blandford Forum, DT11 0QA

Mobile	+44 (0)7966 490836
Email	emmaperry_uk@yahoo.co.uk
Web	www.53durweston.com

Loose Reins

Follow the strums of country guitar ballads and the smell of smoked chilli beans and it will lead you to the old-time wild west of Loose Reins. Choose between three wooden-crafted cabins or three canvas lodges, nestled along the edge of a shallow valley in the foothills of Shillingstone Hill (and all kept nice and private by trees and shrubs!). Sleeping up to six, the three canvas lodges are a perfect fit for families, with comfy beds, fully-equipped kitchens with gas hobs, proper loos, and electricity. Meanwhile, the inspired cabins have everything you need to go trailing on four legs or two, knowing you'll come back to a hot shower, cold drinks in the fridge and a rocking chair on the porch to watch the sun go down over the ranch and the Blackmore Vale. *Lots of nearby woodland to explore, or scaling Hambledon Hill might just tire out even the most energetic puppy.*

Rooms	3 cabins for 2: from £99. 3 safari tents for 6: from £120. Prices per night. Dogs £25 per dog per stay. Max. 2.
Meals	Self-catering.
Closed	November-March.
Treats	Bowls, beds, towels & treats. Welcome pack with dog-friendly places to eat & visit in area

Tel	+44 (0)117 204 7830
Email	enquiries@canopyandstars.co.uk
Web	www.canopyandstars.co.uk/loosereins

Canopy & Stars
Loose Reins,
Ridgeway Farm, Lanchards Lane,
Shillingstone, DT11 0TF

Colber Farm

The Happy Hare and The Pleasant Pheasant shepherd's huts on this peaceful Dorset farm are surrounded by miles of country footpaths. Arrive to a cream tea or cake and settle in to a slice of cosy, quiet rural heaven. Each hut has a comfy bed, ample storage, a cunning en suite bathroom and wonderful green views of the open countryside. Sit in bed and watch the sunrise. Essentials are provided along with marshmallows, fresh herbs are planted around the huts and breakfast hampers are available on request: bread, sausages, bacon, mushrooms, eggs, butter, homemade jam. Whip up coffee and cook on your gas hob; or there's the hot plate on the wood-burner and a tripod for the fire bowl, if you love the smell of wood smoke and fancy being outside. Rambles start from your hut door, the river Stour runs through the farm and you can see swans and herons. You'll hear the cows go back and forth, meet the resident pheasants and if you're lucky spot the eponymous hares. It's a 20-minute walk to the pubs and local shops of Sturminster Newton – have a long, starry soak in your own hot tub when you get back. *Miles of walks; maps with marked walks; river Stour nearby; dog-friendly pubs & cafes within walking distance. Working farm so dogs to be kept under control/on tether.*

Rooms	2 shepherd's huts for 2: from £75 per night. Wood-fired hot tub £30 per stay. Dogs £10 per dog per stay. Max. 1 medium/large or 2 small dogs.
Meals	Self-catering.
Closed	Never.
Treats	Treats or pig's ears, wash-down kit with towels & shampoo, poo bags. Long tether so owners can use hot tub without dog running off!

Canopy & Stars
Colber Farm,
Stalbridge Lane,
Sturminster Newton, DT10 2JQ

Tel	+44 (0)117 204 7830
Email	enquiries@canopyandstars.co.uk
Web	www.canopyandstars.co.uk/colberfarm

Stock Gaylard

Down a farm track, just above the small stream and just around the corner from the deer park you'll find heaps to choose from: yurts, a woodsman's wagon and shepherd's hut or a double decker bus and cabin. Each camp has its own spot within Stock Gaylard, and the whole site faces west so whether you're lying in bed or toasting marshmallows over the fire, you'll get the best of the sun setting below the Dorset horizon. Owners Andy and Josie had the yurts built (using the estate's very own ash) by a local joiner, who also made all the bespoke furniture. You'll find cosy rugs and notoriously comfy beds, with compost loo and outdoor shower just on the edge of the deck, and a wood fire-heated bath under the stars (flushing toilet and electric shower up at the farm buildings too). Cosy Sawpit Wagon and hut have uninterrupted views; Parsons Camp bus has an alfresco dining top deck. Fry up some venison sausages from the estate on the campfire or walk to the local pub for supper. There are 1,800 acres of land to explore, with beautiful mixed woodland. Head out for fishing, archery, llama trekking and paintballing. *Lots of woodland walks on the estate and surrounding area. Animals in nearby fields so keep dogs on leads when out walking.*

Rooms	1 camp for 14 : from £130. 1 camp for 12: from £100. 1 camp for 11: from £118. 1 wagon for 2-4: from £80. Prices per night. Extra space for 2 children in Sawpit Wagon: £20 per child per night. Max. 1 dog.
Meals	Self-catering.
Closed	October-March.
Treats	Advice on walks.

Tel	+44 (0)117 204 7830
Email	enquiries@canopyandstars.co.uk
Web	www.canopyandstars.co.uk/stockgaylard

Canopy & Stars
Stock Gaylard,
Sturminster Newton, DT10 2BG

The Eastbury Hotel

Delightful staff make you welcome with their smiley efficiency and local lad Matt Street, MasterChef contestant and finalist in the prestigious Roux Scholarship, heads up the kitchen. The food is great and as much thought goes into the children's menu as it does to the seven-course taster menu. You eat in the restaurant overlooking the walled garden. Elegant Sherborne is there to delve into and you can walk everywhere. The Abbey is stunning and the castle gardens (landscaped by Capability Brown) are inspiring. While away an afternoon browsing independent shops; stop in a café for tea and cake. There's a comfortable lounge, sunny morning room with magazines and games and a library for loafing which you can also hire for special dinners. The walled garden is set in an acre of mature trees and plants, and plans are afoot for five garden rooms and a mini spa. *Minimum stay. 2 nights. Dogs welcome throughout hotel & upper deck of restaurant. Walled garden. Purlieu Meadow 5-minute walk away (river to splash in); nearby Sherborne Castle grounds for longer walks.*

Rooms	17 doubles: £195-£205. 3 suites for 2: £315-£350. Singles £110. Dogs £20 per dog per night. Max. 2 per room. Dogs welcome in 4 bedrooms.
Meals	Small plates from £2.50. Dinner, 3 courses from £30.
Closed	Never.
Treats	Dog biscuits are free. Chicken and rice £5 per dog bowl. Dog grooming can be booked.

Ian Crighton
The Eastbury Hotel,
Long Street, Sherborne, DT9 3BY

Tel	+44 (0)1935 813131
Email	relax@theeastburyhotel.co.uk
Web	www.theeastburyhotel.co.uk

Streamcombe Farm Shepherd's Hut

A peaceful spot in the woods just south of Exmoor: a break from city life. The area is a dark sky reserve completely unspoilt by light pollution and the woods near the hut shelter a herd of wild deer among other forest creatures. You can see them all on the two-mile hike over the hills to Dulverton, where you'll find some lovely pubs and shops. The Shepherd's Hut itself was built in the late 19th century and retains its original oak panelling and floors. It has been redecorated in the simple plain colours of Shaker style and positioned near the house but shielded by the barn, set up to catch the morning sun on the front door. The hut is off grid, lit with candles and heated by the big wood-burner. The shower, sink and organic chemical loo are all housed in the barn a few yards away. Karen and Ian have started a cookery school here where you can learn game or fish cookery, so of course the food available is superb. You can book BYO evening meals or have breakfast and lunch hampers delivered to the hut and eat surrounded by the sounds of the country. Free-range chickens and sheep everywhere: leads at all times please. Exmoor is a dog-walker's paradise.

Rooms	Shepherd's hut for 2: £80 per night. Max. 2 dogs.
Meals	Self-catering.
Closed	October-March.
Treats	Maps & advice on local walks.

Tel	+44 (0)117 204 7830
Email	enquiries@canopyandstars.co.uk
Web	www.canopyandstars.co.uk/streamcombe

Canopy & Stars
Streamcombe Farm Shepherd's Hut,
Streamcombe Lane,
Dulverton, TA22 9SA

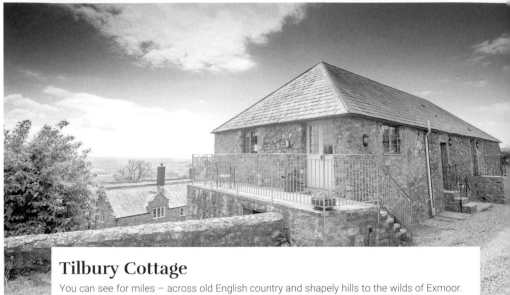

Tilbury Cottage

You can see for miles – across old English country and shapely hills to the wilds of Exmoor. Walks from the door pass through valleys and woods via great pubs dishing up good food. Return to an upside-down cottage muddy and ruddy after bike rides; bring your own or hire from the shop down the road – Matt and Jenny can point you in the right direction. There's space for two in the sociable kitchen where you can cook and chat together, eating outside on the balcony which is perfectly angled for the sun and the view. All the basics are waiting for you and there's a generous hamper of milk, best bacon and bread for easy breakfasts. Spend evenings gazing up at a million-tog duvet of stars. You'll share the outside space with other

cottages and shepherds' huts at the farm, but it's a short trip down the winding lanes to National Trust properties, villages and the moors. *Minimum stay: 2 nights; 3 in high season. Small nursery field that dogs can run around in off the lead. Dogs on lead around animals on farm & ponies. All breeds welcome except Bulldogs.*

Rooms	1 cottage for 2: £490-£630 per week. Dogs £10 per night. Max. 1.
Meals	Pub 10-minute walk. Free breakfast hamper available.
Closed	Never.
Treats	Pig's ears, blankets & towels.

Matt & Jenny Ambler
Tilbury Cottage,
Tilbury Farm,
West Bagborough, TA4 3DY

Tel	+44 (0)1823 299222
Email	matt.ambler@gmail.com
Web	www.tilburyfarm.co.uk/cottages/

The Yurt Sanctuary

This pretty yurt camp sits behind a wicker fence under the trees, through your own private meadow at Orchard House. It has stunning views of the Mendips and owners Michele and Dan have thought of everything: big, iron-framed double bed, chunky wooden furniture, quirky trinkets, colourful rugs. There are cosy pubs for hearty food, but you could rustle up something in the kitchen hut and crack open the welcoming supply of local cider. After dinner, lounge by the wood-burner, watch the sunset from the bench swing, fire up the hot tub for soaking and stargazing. There are camp beds for children – they'll love to join the early morning feeding of chickens and pygmy goats. Michele offers grooming or training for your four-legged friends and you could take advantage of Dan's sports therapy work with the slightly larger beasts of Bath Rugby team by booking a massage. A peaceful place (occasional road sound at busier times) with warm, caring hosts who make you feel instantly at home. *Canine sensory enrichment garden for dogs to explore. Wonderful walks nearby including Cheddar Gorge; 3 dog-friendly local pubs.*

Rooms	Yurt for 2 (+2 children on camp beds): from £100 per night. Children £15 per child per night. Dogs £20 per stay. Max. 6.
Meals	Self-catering.
Closed	October-March.
Treats	Doggy treat tin. Book your dog in for bath, brush & pamper, with a blueberry & vanilla facial! Scent work & tracking sessions can be booked in advance

Tel	+44 (0)117 204 7830
Email	enquiries@canopyandstars.co.uk
Web	www.canopyandstars.co.uk/yurtsanctuary

Canopy & Stars
The Yurt Sanctuary,
Orchard House, Emborough,
Radstock, BA3 4SA

The Litton

You're perfectly placed for Bath and Bristol here, tucked into the Mendips in a pretty village that's fallen in love with its new inn – and it's easy to see why. The Litton is a gem, where owner Sally and her team work hard and happily to make you feel at home. As soon as you duck inside, you're wrapped in comfort, from reindeer skins on the sofas to mulled cider warming on the bar. Tuck yourself into a corner and order up a Welsh rarebit, or grab a Moroccan blanket and an armful of cushions and head for the riverside terrace where fire pits blaze, and kids can perch on colourfully upcycled beer barrels. The whisky bar is a temptation all of its own, as are the splendid Sunday roasts. Bedrooms, some above the bar, some in the adjoining mill, are individually and stylishly decorated. Beds are big and comfy, baths and showers sparkle. Clever cottage-style suites on the ground floor let you bring the family without feeling cramped; one is considerately designed for the less able. It's not often an owner has thought of everything but Sally is a star, and the Litton shines out as special. *Open garden areas. Beside river with walks around Mendips & Litton lakes. Some walks need dogs on leads because of livestock.*

Rooms	10 doubles: £120-£180. 2 suites for 4: £160-£320. Singles £100-£320. Extra sofa bed available. Dogs £25 per stay. Max. 3.
Meals	Starters from £6. Mains from £12. Sunday lunch from £12.95.
Closed	Never.
Treats	Beds, food, water bowls, towels & treats.

Sally Billington
The Litton,
Litton, Near Wells, BA3 4PW

Tel	+44 (0)1761 241554
Email	contact@thelitton.co.uk
Web	www.thelitton.co.uk

Abbey Hotel

A super central hotel with views to the medieval Abbey and gentle Somerset hills. Originally three Georgian townhouses, now its rooms are bright, art-filled spaces – although not huge – best to choose one at the back if you want somewhere quieter. The feel is relaxed: chatty, professional staff look after you smoothly. Breakfast on croissants, bread from Bath's best baker, or cooked treats in the restaurant. Enjoy cocktails or a G&T – the gin list is impressive – in the cool ArtBar after a full day getting acquainted with lovely Georgian architecture or walking in the surrounding Cotswolds. Bath Abbey – fan-vaulted, imposing tower, stained-glass windows – is just across the square, the Roman Baths not much further; escape the crowds and walk over Pulteney Bridge for a gentle ramble beside the river Avon. *Small doubles not dog-friendly. Parks a few minutes' walk away. Dogs welcome in bar & lounge area; full dinner menu available throughout.*

Rooms	46 doubles, 10 twin/doubles: £130-£500. 6 family rooms for 4: £200-£600. Dogs £15 per dog per stay. Max. 2.
Meals	Breakfast £10.50. Lunch from £7.50. Dinner, 3 courses, £35-£45; pre-theatre menu £21.50-£27.50 (5.30pm-7pm). Sunday lunch £24-£28.
Closed	Never.
Treats	Bed, bowl & advice on walks.

Tel	+44 (0)1225 461603
Email	reception@abbeyhotelbath.co.uk
Web	www.abbeyhotelbath.co.uk

Reservations
Abbey Hotel,
North Parade, Bath, BA1 1LF

No. 15 Great Pulteney

You're on the grandest street in Bath, once home to Jane Austen; the Holburne Museum of Art stands at one end, Robert Adam's famous Pulteney Bridge at the other. As for No.15, it's a super-chic boutique hotel that doubles as a contemporary art gallery. You'll find collections of curios all over the place – art books, hand-blown lights, chandeliers by the score; there's a golden bar for drinks before dinner, a small spa with treatment rooms, a sauna and a hot tub in the original stone vaults. Bedrooms are sumptuous regardless of size, each with an original piece of art on the walls. You get Hypnos mattresses, cashmere throws, and stunning bathrooms, perhaps a copper basin, a walk-in shower or a claw-foot bath. Vast suites flood with light courtesy of high windows, while a help-yourself larder waits on the landing for popcorn, soft drinks and ice cream. Back downstairs, Café 15 offers delicious food all day: prosecco 'on the house' at breakfast, perhaps a feisty fish pie at lunch, then chicken with lemon and thyme at dinner. There's a small garden and a car park for guests, too. Hard to beat. *Advice on walks & park very close by.*

Rooms	25 doubles: £140-£500. 15 suites for 2: £250-£1200. Dogs £15 per night. Max. 2.
Meals	Lunch from £6.50. Sunday brunch from £25. Dinner, 3 courses, £30-£40. Afternoon tea £28.
Closed	Never.
Treats	'Woof Box' with treats, bowl, Lily's Kitchen dog food, tennis ball & poo bags. Blanket provided overnight too.

Ian & Christa Taylor
No. 15 Great Pulteney,
15 Great Pulteney Street,
Bath, BA2 4BS

Tel	+44 (0)1225 805879
Email	enquiries@no15greatpulteney.co.uk
Web	www.no15greatpulteney.co.uk

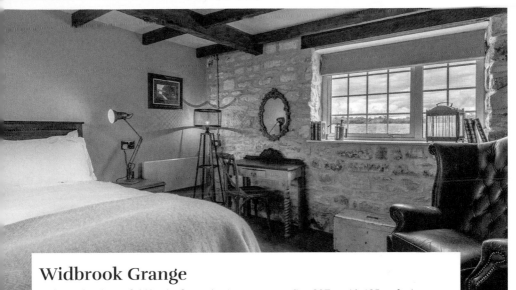

Widbrook Grange

Sink into the chesterfield by the fire and enjoy an outstanding G&T – with 125 craft gins on the menu and 14 tonics this is G&T Central. Not only that, the food is largely locally sourced with herbs from the garden and a sophisticated menu, and you can have your wedding party or special gathering here. We love this Georgian country-house hotel in 11 acres of grounds at the end of a track, close to Bath and Bradford-on-Avon. Choose from bedrooms in the house or those over in the ground-floor stables. You'll find the staff a delight and their welcome extends to families and dogs: note the dog baskets and the rabbit-rich grounds. Stroll down to the canal and walk along the tow path, or hire a narrow boat for the day. Stay put and use the gym and indoor heated pool, book a massage and treatment, have afternoon tea. *Kennet and Avon Canal minutes away, 11 acres of grounds & fields to roam. Guests with dogs welcome to eat in conservatory.*

Rooms	6 doubles, 8 twin/doubles: £105-£220. 1 suite for 2; 4 family rooms for 3: £145-£220. Dogs £15.
Meals	Lunch from £13. Dinner, 3 courses, £35. Sunday lunch £24.95. Afternoon tea from £8.95.
Closed	Never.
Treats	Welcome box with ball, poo bags, Lily's Kitchen wet dog food & organic biscuits. Bowls, bed, puppachino & pawsecco too.

Tel	+44 (0)1225 864750
Email	stay@widbrookgrange.co.uk
Web	www.widbrookgrange.co.uk

Hakan Tiryaki
Widbrook Grange,
Bradford on Avon, BA15 1UH

Big Box

Down a sleepy country lane on the edge of the Cotswolds in Wiltshire might be the last place you'd expect to find a stunning piece of modern design, but Big Box, the newest addition to a small clutch of renovated farm buildings, is exactly that. The huge glass front lets the light flood in and the doors all open wide to let you bring nature right inside. The fully fitted bathroom shared by the two bedrooms is decorated in soft grey and blue tiles, while the bedrooms and the living area are a beautiful blend of stripped wood, Indian murals and the owner's unique style. With examples of owner Peter Lavery's world-renowned photography and Kimberly's flair as an ex-costume designer, it feels like a funky New York loft has retired to the country. On Peter and Kimberly's 35 acres of land you'll find peaceful woodland, wildflower meadows and quiet spots to picnic. A little lake with rowing boat is a short walk from the cabin, where you'll also find a BBQ and outdoor bar for catching the last of the day's sun with a chilled beverage and cooking under an open sky. Right next door to the cabin there's a tennis court and Cotswold Water Park is just 5 minutes up the road. *Fenced garden. Walks without leads from Box; 4 mile round trips. Swimming in small lake. Bring own bedding*

Rooms	Cabin for 2: from £185 per night; double sofa bed: £25 p.p.p.n. Dogs £25. Max 1.
Meals	Self-catering.
Closed	Never.
Treats	Towels for drying, water and food bowls.

Canopy & Stars
Big Box,
Brandiers, Crossing Lane,
Upper Minety, SN16 9PZ

Tel	+44 (0)117 204 7830
Email	enquiries@canopyandstars.co.uk
Web	www.canopyandstars.co.uk/bigbox

The Holford Arms

At the side of the long road that takes you into Tetbury sits this unassuming country inn with its whitewashed exterior hiding more secrets than you can shake a stick at. Owners Pete and Tor have worked a special magic here. Whether it's building more stylish 'shacks' in the big field at the back, or pressing their own apples, they have a way with food, drink and atmosphere which would be the envy of many a new pub entrepreneur. Their hands-on approach means the little inn buzzes with happy locals and nature lovers who've popped in for a pint or a Sunday roast after exploring nearby Westonbirt Arboretum. Inside, all is snug and homely. The bar winks with bottles, or try one of the local ales. Young chefs serve up tasty classics and treats; on Wednesdays you can tuck into a three-course Thai feast for a bargain price. Upstairs, six pretty bedrooms with crisp white linens and splashes of colour. Take the big twin/double under the eaves with a day bed that doubles as a window seat. Very special. *Seven-acre garden & minutes away from wonderful walks in Westonbirt Arboretum.*

Rooms	4 doubles, 2 twin/doubles: £74-£170. Singles £74-£124. Extra bed/sofabed £30 p.p.p.n.
Meals	Starters from £5. Mains from £15.
Closed	Christmas.
Treats	Treats & water bowl.

Tel	+44 (0)1454 238669
Email	info@theholfordarms.co.uk
Web	www.theholfordarms.co.uk

Pete Heathcock
The Holford Arms,
Knockdown, Tetbury, GL8 8QY

Great Farm

Wind your way along the leafy path through the trees and cross the narrow footbridge over the river – young-at-heart adventurers will love it here. Otter Camp, Nightingale Camp and Barn Owl Camp are close together but secluded with a private clearing. Cross the water again and you'll have The Island at Great Farm all to yourself. Otter and Nightingale are intimate and off-grid, though the swish bathrooms are a step above camping. The river Coln forms a boundary to the front, there's woodland at the rear, and sheep and cattle nearby – keep dogs on leads! Each spot has its own private hot-tub, campfire, kitchen with gas hob (some outdoors), flushing loo and shower – and many thoughtful touches. Leonie can provide a

hamper of local ingredients for breakfast and picnics; dinner can be delivered too. If the river is too chilly, Otter, Nightingale and The Island have their own hot tubs. You're on a family-run working farm in the rural heart of the Cotswolds, with pretty villages and pubs galore and great walks. Go down river to Lechlade, or the Cotswold Water Park – Leonie will give you a map. If you're lucky, you'll spot an otter... *Children welcome in Shepherd's Hut, Camp and Train Carriage. Great walks, river to play in. Dogs need to be on a lead near livestock.*

Rooms	2 cabins for 2; 1 train carriage for 2 (space for own cot); 1 shepherd's hut for 2: from £95. Camp of 2 gypsy wagons for 4-6 (extra space for 10/own tents): from £105. Prices per night. Dogs £20 per dog per stay. Max. 2.
Meals	Self-catering.
Closed	October-March.
Treats	Advice on walks.

Canopy & Stars	**Tel** +44 (0)117 204 7830
Great Farm,	**Email** enquiries@canopyandstars.co.uk
Whelford, Fairford, GL7 4EA	**Web** www.canopyandstars.co.uk/greatfarm

The Plough Inn

Take a pint to the terrace on a summer's day and watch village life tick by. This spruced-up 17th-century inn is as inviting as can be, thanks to new owner Tom and his team. The food is locally sourced and delicious, the gins zing, and ales come straight from the cask. What's more, for the Cotswolds, the wines are very well priced. Tourists flock to Bourton on the Water with its five little bridges (two miles). The famous Daylesford Farm Shop is a 20-minute drive... pop by for an organic lunch, or a picnic for the Windrush Way. Westwards is leafy Cheltenham (15 miles), with Regency streets, a theatre, posh shops, and a racecourse in the lee of the hills. Return to sweet, cosy bedrooms upstairs. With two dog-friendly bedrooms, and dog meals on request, you're not the only one who is made welcome here. *Quiet village with lots of walks on doorstep.*

Rooms	1 double, 2 twin/doubles: £99-£150. Dogs £10 per stay. Max. 2 medium or 1 large per room.
Meals	Starters from £6.95. Lunch from £7.50. Mains from £13.50.
Closed	Never.
Treats	Homemade dog biscuits in room & a doggy dinner if guests would like one rustled up.

Tel	+44 (0)1451 822 602
Email	thughes@coldastonplough.com
Web	www.coldastonplough.com

Thomas Hughes
The Plough Inn,
Chapel Lane, Cold Aston, GL54 3BN

The Guest House

Your own timber-framed house with masses of light and space, a sunny terrace, and spectacular valley and woodland views... A peaceful secluded place, it's full of books and mementoes of Sue's treks across the world; the large living room has wooden floors, lovely old oak furniture and French windows onto the rose-filled garden. Sue brims with enthusiasm and is a flexible host: breakfast can be over in her kitchen with delicious farm shop sausages and bacon, or continental in yours at a time to suit you. There's a wet room downstairs, and you hop up the stairs to your charming up-in-the-eaves bedroom with oriental rugs and a big comfy bed. Wonderful! *Minimum stay: 2 nights at weekends Easter-October. 2.5-acre fenced garden in glorious rural Cotswolds with walks straight from the door. Dogs must be completely sheep-proof as surrounded by breeding ewes.*

Rooms	1 double, with sitting room & kitchenette: £150-£170.
Meals	Dinner, 2 courses, from £17.50; 3 courses, from £22.50; 4 courses, from £28. Pub 1 mile.
Closed	Christmas.
Treats	Dog-sitting, towels & advice on walks – or walks with Manor Cottage dogs.

Sue Bathurst
The Guest House,
Manor Cottage, Bagendon, GL7 7DU

Tel	+44 (0)1285 831417
Email	sue.bathurst@icloud.com
Web	www.cotswoldguesthouse.co.uk

Cockshutt Cottage

Tumble down the track to Westley Farm and break free. Families with children will love Dan and Ali's 70 acres which you are encouraged to enjoy. Two friendly dogs, free-range chickens and ponies to ride add to the fun. There are woods to explore (and make dens in), meadows to picnic in and wildlife to spot. Your one-storey retreat is open plan and well-equipped with logs for the fire, books, games and a telly if the weather turns foul. You'll find a homemade cake, and a private view-filled walled garden – a serene spot for a sundowner. A ten-minute walk will take you to Chalford and the Lavender Bake House for tea and cakes or hop in the car to explore Stroud and stock up at the farmers' market every Saturday and The Brewery. You can also walk there along footpaths then get a taxi back. On some evenings you can gather round the communal pizza oven while the children make new friends, or amble across fields to The Crown. *Minimum stay: 3 nights. Walk to Nature Reserve; towpath to dog-friendly pub. Farmland criss-crossed with woodland paths; dogs on leads with animals. Farm borders Bathurst Estate: 9 miles of off-lead walking.*

Rooms	1 cottage for 4: £700-£950 per week. Dogs £25 per dog per stay. Max. 2-3.
Meals	Self-catering.
Closed	Never.
Treats	Towels for muddy paws & handwritten maps of walks nearby.

Tel	+44 (0)1285 760262
Email	info@westleyfarm.co.uk
Web	www.westleyfarm.co.uk

Dan & Ali
Cockshutt Cottage,
Westley Farm, Chalford, GL6 8HP

The Close

Up a hill of pretty Cotswold-stone houses, this large Queen Anne house with handsome sash windows delivers what it promises. Step into a stone-flagged hall with grandfather clock and Georgian oak staircase; take welcoming tea with Karen in the drawing room – all gracious sofas and charming chandelier; then upstairs to three light and airy bedrooms softly furnished with antiques. Window seats, shutters and views over garden or pretty street add to the restful atmosphere. Karen, as gracious and relaxed as her house, serves excellent breakfasts in the polished dining room. An elegantly hospitable base for exploring the Cotswolds. *Minimum stay: 2 nights at weekends. Garden, lots of footpaths & walks on Minchinhampton Common. Many dog-friendly pubs/cafés.*

Rooms	2 doubles, 1 twin: £95-£105. Singles £75-£85. Dogs £10 per stay.
Meals	Pubs/restaurants 1-minute walk.
Closed	January – February.
Treats	Advice on walks & large dog-friendly garden.

Karen Champney
The Close,
Well Hill, Minchinhampton,
Stroud, GL6 9JE

Tel	+44 (0)1453 883338
Email	theclosebnb@gmail.com
Web	www.theclosebnb.co.uk

Belle

The Glamping Orchard is a sleepy little spot, usually scented with campfire smoke. Belle is hidden in one corner of the apple orchard, with the majestic Warwick Knight in the other – although the glorious views are the only thing you'll share! A comfy double bed is made up with blankets and hot water bottles and the woodburner chucks out plenty of heat. There's room for five so you can add a couple of futons or just enjoy all the extra space. Home comforts are plentiful but the charm and wonder of the great outdoors is never lost here. Meet the resident chickens, take a rustic woodfired shower in the hut on wheels or adventure through the leafy fringes of the Cotswolds on foot or by horse-drawn carriage – both are equally magical. Cooking over a glowing firepit is highly encouraged by the owners (and simple living enthusiasts) Ali and Rich, but it's sometimes just as nice to take shelter in the kitchen hut, as rain taps down on its roof. *Great walks on doorstep. Walk Cotswold Way to local pub. Dog sitting service available.*

Rooms	Bell tent for 4: from £90 per night. Dogs £25 per dog per stay; £35 for 2. Max. 2 dogs.
Meals	Self-catering.
Closed	November-April.
Treats	Dog beds and bowls provided and the area around Belle is totally secure to allow four-legged friends to roam around freely.

Tel	+44 (0)117 204 7830
Email	enquiries@canopyandstars.co.uk
Web	www.canopyandstars.co.uk/belle

Canopy & Stars
Belle,
Peglass Cottage, Bow Lane,
Longney, GL2 3SW

The Grange

The largest green in England and this house is at a leafy corner. Rosanne has that happy knack of making you feel at home. Gibraltarian and keen cook too, her breakfasts come with a continental edge – eggs with chorizo, homemade baked beans; her Spanish soup suppers are hearty. The house has stories – ask about Miss Kickler... Family photos, art, quirky monkeys add warmth, the guest sitting room has original wood panelling with the Clifford Crest, inviting bedrooms are all different; there's an indoor pool, gym, playroom, places to read – dogs Spud and Otto keep you company. Walk to Slimbridge, have fun at Frampton's festivals. *Garden enclosed – Houdini the Labrador has tested it! Walks from gate away from roads; sheep in some fields. Lakes for swims; beautiful wooded areas.*

Rooms	1 twin/double; 2 doubles, each with separate bathroom: £95-£125. 1 child's room sharing bath with nearby double: £80-£140. Dogs £10 per stay.
Meals	Soup with bread, £10. Restaurant & 2 pubs 3 miles.
Closed	Rarely.
Treats	Bowls, high quality food, beds, hose & local ID tag.

Rosanne Gaggero-Brodermann
The Grange,
The Green,
Frampton on Severn, GL2 7DX

Tel	+44 (0)1452 740654
Email	rockape@mac.com
Web	www.atthegrange.com

Legg Barn

Ted and Paddy's barn is a surprise. Tucked off the High Street, it has four acres of garden with space for pigs, chickens, veg, sunny seats, trees – and for collie Bill to chase squirrels. The long hall has a quirky line of antique high chairs, and there's a soaring living space beyond with a big wood-burner and comfy sofas; the white theme throughout contrasts with honey-coloured wood and odd splashes of colour. Bedrooms – one up spiral stairs on the sitting room mezzanine – have lovely linen and piles of pillows. Paddy is a good cook – her generous breakfasts often include their own sausages. Walk from the door into the Forest of Dean. *Forest walks nearby; four-acre meadow to romp in which is surrounded by a brook – perfect for muddy dogs to get clean in.*

Rooms	1 double; 2 doubles sharing bathroom: £80-£90. Max. 2 dogs.
Meals	Restaurant 2-minute walk; pub 10-minute walk.
Closed	Christmas & occasionally.
Treats	Dog bowls & beds.

Tel	+44 (0)1594 510408
Email	paddy@leggbarn.co.uk
Web	www.leggbarn.co.uk

Paddy Curtis
Legg Barn,
Church Square,
Blakeney, GL15 4DP

Up^

Your spirits lift arriving at Up^ and climbing the 20 steps to the broad, raised deck among the trees... hence the name. Light streams through the glass front and into every room and the views of the Wye Valley are amazing. Watch the sunset from the comfort of your double bed, before picking some herbs from the indoor herb wall and cooking up a fragrant feast on the barbecue. When night sets in, a clear sky can be enjoyed with the powerful telescope or the naked eye, and naked everything else, from the outdoor bathtub on the deck, private despite the nearby minor road. During the day, the cabin has plenty to keep you busy. Brush up your piano skills on the baby grand, put some LPs on the record player if you remember how, lounge on the suntrap deck, or use the complimentary yeast and flour to try out owner Jill's open-fire bread recipe. It'd be a shame not to head out and hike, bike or canoe your way around the Area of Outstanding Natural Beauty on your doorstep, but when you're somewhere this relaxing, it can just be too hard getting Up^ in the morning... *Enclosed garden, but not dog proof. Exciting walks from the door; walk to local dog-friendly pub; list of more dog-welcoming pubs that can be combined with a walk. No dogs on furniture but dog bed provided. Must have up to date flea control.*

Rooms	Cabin for 2: from £100 per night. Dogs £15 per dog per stay. Max. 2; more by arrangement.
Meals	Self-catering.
Closed	Never.
Treats	Biscuits, a chew, sometimes a piece of ham. Outside bath for dogs who love to roll in muddy puddles (candles optional). Deck to sit on – doggy heaven sharing a BBQ with their owners!

Canopy & Stars
Up^,
Coldharbour Road,
Brockweir, NP16 7PH

Tel	+44 (0)117 204 7830
Email	enquiries@canopyandstars.co.uk
Web	www.canopyandstars.co.uk/up

The Slate Shed at Graig Wen, page 248

South East

The Cat, page 118

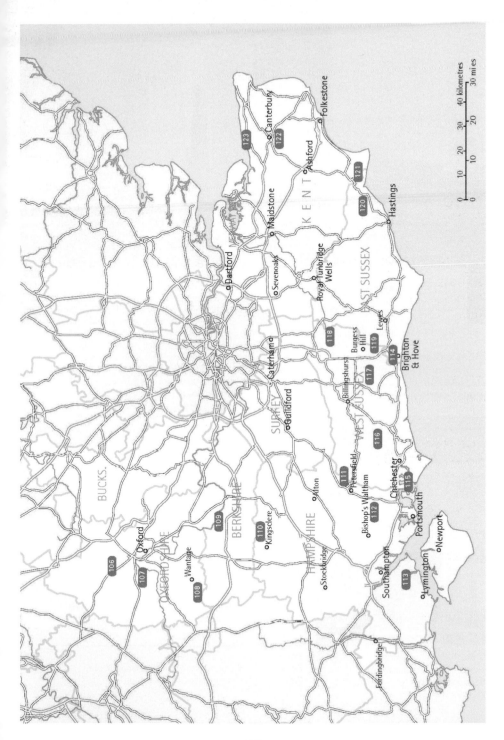

The Killingworth Castle

The family behind The Ebrington Arms has renovated this 17th-century inn, around the corner from Blenheim Palace, to its former glory with beautifully restored bedrooms too. Wood floors sweep from side bar to main bar to dining room, burners in brick fireplaces belt out heat and the set menu is a steal. Smiling staff ferry own-brewed Yubby Bitter, Goldie and Yawnie to locals, dog walkers and drinkers; the rest are here for the food: roast venison and faggot croquette with beetroot dauphinoise, kale and juniper; blackberry and frangipane tart. And possibly the best chips in Oxfordshire! The pub won three stars from the Soil Association for its commitment to organic food but you'll also find organic wine. There's a nifty selection of malt whiskies, or try a pint of their home-brewed in the garden. Bedrooms are upstairs and down all have original art, handmade sturdy beds and the softest linen. Muted tartan blankets keep you warm and there are organic toiletries and roll top baths. *Seven-mile walk Wychwood forest; eight-mile Wootton Circular walk; short rambles too. Two dog-friendly rooms.*

Rooms	10 doubles: £99-£180.
	Dogs £10 per dog per night.
Meals	Starters £6-£8. Mains £13-£21.
	Midweek set menu 2 courses £11.95.
Closed	Rarely.
Treats	A box of dog treats, water bowls and a beer garden to snooze in.

Grace Ford
The Killingworth Castle,
Glympton Road,
Wootton, OX20 1EJ

Tel	+44 (0)1993 811401
Email	reservations@thekillingworthcastle.com
Web	www.thekillingworthcastle.com

Artist Residence Oxford

Justin and Charlie's ability to create beautiful small hotels at the speed of light is unprecedented. Their fourth – lost in the country a few miles west of Oxford – is a reinvention of the country pub, though not as you might think. This isn't a stripped-back monument to contemporary design, rather a cool take on all things retro with quirky art and a little neon mixed in for good measure. You'll find vintage wallpapers, vivid colours, glass cabinets filled with curios, then a pink, upcycled sofa in the cocktail bar. Country rugs cover flagstone floors, a fire burns on both sides in the bar, an original pine bench comes with plumped-up cushions. You eat in the restaurant amid ferns and flock wallpaper, perhaps Dorset crab with sorrel sauce, local venison with rainbow chard, gin and tonic panna cotta, there's a pie and a pint at the bar, too, and a dining terrace that overlooks the kitchen garden. Stunning bedrooms set the standard for others to follow: fat beds, exposed timbers, robes in flawless bathrooms, old tea chests for bedside tables. We've hardly scratched the surface. Exceptional. *Minimum stay: 2 nights at weekends. Six dog-friendly rooms, 3 with private terraces. In countryside with plenty of woodland walks, streams & fields.*

Rooms	5 doubles, 1 twin: £140-£290. 3 suites for 2: £180-£350. Extra beds £40 p.p.p.n. Under 12s £30. Dogs £15 per dog p.n. Max. 2.
Meals	Lunch from £6.50. Dinner, 3 courses, about £40. 5-course tasting menu, £60. Sunday lunch from £15.95.
Closed	Never.
Treats	Bowl, bed & Lily's Kitchen treats.

Tel	+44 (0)1993 656220
Email	oxford@artistresidence.co.uk
Web	www.artistresidence.co.uk/our-hotels/oxford/

Charlie & Justin Salisbury
Artist Residence Oxford,
Station Road, South Leigh,
Witney, OX29 6XN

The Greyhound Inn

Close to the white chalk horse at Uffington – the walking is grand round here – is a beautiful red-brick pub on the quiet road that winds through Letcombe Regis. The new owners have kept the fine old windows and the irresistible fireplaces and have added a garden at the back, a bright, cheerful décor, and a diamond of a chef in Phil Currie. Menus change with the seasons, and whether you go for cider braised lamb shoulder, or beer battered haddock and chips with mushy peas, this is cooking of a high order. Our two-course 'Midweek Fix' was a steal: a cheddar and leek tart followed by new season lamb steak, both delicious. If the pub is Georgian on the outside, it's country-trendy within. Racing scenes adorn the walls, dog biscuits beautify the bar, and you can pop in for a latte, a well-kept pint or a hedonistic meal. It's the sort of pub we all love. *Secure garden; country walks; maps. Close to Ridgeway path; woods, streams & fields too; horses & sheep so some signs for dogs on leads. 2 dog-friendly rooms.*

Rooms	4 doubles, 2 twin/doubles: £95-£125. 1 suite for 4, 1 suite for 5: £145-£205. Singles £80-£130. Extra bed/sofabed £20-£40 p.p.p.n. Dog £15 per dog per night.
Meals	Lunch from £7. Dinner from £11.
Closed	Christmas, 5-17 January.
Treats	Selection box of tasty treats, comfy bed, water bowl, towel to dry muddy paws & poo bags.

Catriona Galbraith
The Greyhound Inn,
Main Street,
Letcombe Regis, OX12 9JL

Tel	+44 (0)1235 771969
Email	info@thegreyhoundletcombe.co.uk
Web	www.thegreyhoundletcombe.co.uk

The Elephant at Pangbourne

In the centre of well-heeled Pangbourne, The Elephant is a stroll to chi-chi gift shops, an award-winning cheese shop – Cheese Etc – and the Thames. Amble along it; hire a boat or kayak if you fancy a splash about. This is also a handy base for the Henley Regatta. Inside, smiley staff buzz around and colonial era glamour reigns: wooden floors, club chairs to recline in, old tea chests – and quite a lot of elephants! Book in for afternoon tea or settle down for sandwiches, sharing plates or a salad in the Baba bar. The Herd Restaurant is open in the evenings – treat yourself to a steak, they are sublime. There are no fewer than 56 gins on the menu – fun to sit in the bar at a table made from an old aeroplane wing to sample a couple of them. Upstairs, grand bedrooms continue the old school sophistication.
The garden annexe rooms have the best views across the gorgeous gardens to the church next door. *Hotel gardens; banks of the river Thames nearby with great walk through Pangbourne Meadow. Dogs welcome in all areas of hotel except restaurant; dine with your dog in the bar area.*

Rooms	20 doubles: £85-£150. 2 singles: £65-£110. Extra bed £20 p.p.p.n. Dogs £20. Max. 2.
Meals	Bar meals from £6.50. Dinner from £11.50.
Closed	Never.
Treats	A warm welcome & a woof box with a ball to take home, choice of Lily's Kitchen wet food, organic biscuits & poo bags. A comfy bed & special treats.

Tel	+44 (0)118 984 2244
Email	reception@elephanthotel.co.uk
Web	www.elephanthotel.co.uk

Nick Dent
The Elephant at Pangbourne,
Church Road,
Pangbourne, RG8 7AR

The Wellington Arms

Lost down a web of lanes, the 'Welly' draws foodies from miles around. Cosy, relaxed and decorated in style – old dining tables, crystal decanters, terracotta floor – the newly extended bar-dining room fills quickly, so make sure you book to sample Jason's inventive modern cooking. Boards are chalked up daily and the produce mainly home-grown or organic. Kick off with home-grown courgette flowers stuffed with ricotta, parmesan and lemon zest, follow with rack of home-reared lamb with root vegetable mash and crab apple jelly, finish with elderflower jelly, strawberry and raspberry sorbet. Migrate to the huge garden for summer meals and views of the pub's smallholding: little pigs, woolly sheep, a few bees and almost 100 assorted hens; buy the eggs at the bar. Stay over and get cosy in any one of the four rooms, housed in the former wine store and pig shed. Expect exposed brick and beams, vast Benchmark beds topped with goose down duvets, fresh flowers, coffee machines, mini-fridges, and slate tiled bathrooms with underfloor heating and walk-in rain showers. Breakfast too is a treat.
Open fields and woodland walks; footpath from pub.

Rooms	4 doubles: £125-£220. Dogs £10.
Meals	Lunch, 2-3 courses £17.50-£19. Dinner £11-£21.
Closed	Rarely.
Treats	Lily's Kitchen Bedtime Biscuits, bones, sheepskin rug, water bowl, towels, maps & advice on walks.

Jason King & Simon Page
The Wellington Arms,
Baughurst Road,
Baughurst, RG26 5LP

Tel	+44 (0)118 982 0110
Email	hello@thewellingtonarms.com
Web	www.thewellingtonarms.com

Adhurst

The Yurts at Adhurst are set in the ancient woodland of the South Downs National Park just an hour and a half from London, the perfect place for getting back to nature. Owners Guy and Alison are passionate about sustainable living and invite you to set the fire, tramp through the woods and immerse yourself in a slower, more basic, way of life. The site is completely off-grid and the four yurts share a camp kitchen but each has its own gas-powered hot shower and compost loo. You can choose between an idyllic, relaxing stay wandering in the woods and sipping hot chocolate, or a wilderness adventure tackling trails and picking up skills - or a combination of the two! Go from raiding the blanket box and bedding down in the comfort of the yurt, to trying your hand at bread baking, slow cooking or fly fishing, with the choice of a gillie or a crash course in ponassing (a hand-filleting technique) when you reel one in. The local hikes come in all sizes too, from the one-hour Adhurst circular, to the 21 miles of Hangers Way or strolling straight onto a section of the Serpent Trail or the South Downs Way. *Yurts are away from road & each has own space for dogs. River & woods. Be aware of deer & sheep. Three dog-friendly pubs in walking distance.*

Rooms	4 yurts for 2: from £169 per night. Space for 2 children on camp beds. Dogs £25 per dog per stay. Max. 2 – please call before booking.
Meals	Self-catering.
Closed	November-March.
Treats	Advice on walks and river swims.

Tel	+44 (0)117 204 7830
Email	enquiries@canopyandstars.co.uk
Web	www.canopyandstars.co.uk/adhurst

Canopy & Stars
Adhurst,
Steep, GU31 5AD

Wriggly Tin

Wriggly Tin shepherd's huts were born out of a family holiday where Alex Evans and his two daughters got out into the countryside and never looked back. That defining stay was in tipis but Alex's love of all things mechanical has lead him to hand build these lovely off-grid huts in a wooded corner of Hampshire. Butser, named after the highest point in the area, sleeps two and has a hot tub and there are four others, varying in size; Boundary is the biggest and can sleep five but all have enough space for a dog to sleep in comfort. Showers and loos are shared and housed in, unsurprisingly, a cunningly converted shepherd's hut. You're far enough apart to feel on your own, with your own fire pit, tripod, cast iron griddle and plenty

of wood and kindling for adventurous campfire cooking. The 100-year-old Old Winchester also has its own wood-fired hot tub to soak in. Wriggly Tin gives you a chance to relax in to the slow lane. Keep a pan of water on the wood-burner for tea and stroll through the surrounding bluebell woods with your canine companion. *Dogs to be kept on lead on site. Think twice before bringing a wolfhound, as space is limited! Butser, Barrow & Old Winchester have most space for a dog bed.*

Rooms	4 shepherd's huts for 2; 1 shepherd's hut for 2-3; 1 shepherd's hut for 2-5: from £93 per night. Extra guests £9 p.p.p.n. Bedding £18 p.p. Dogs £6 per dog per stay. Max. 2.
Meals	Self-catering.
Closed	Never.
Treats	Map showing walks and advice on days out.

Canopy & Stars
Wriggly Tin,
15 Beckless Cottages,
Brook Lane, Hambledon, PO7 4TF

Tel	+44 (0)117 204 7830
Email	enquiries@canopyandstars.co.uk
Web	www.canopyandstars.co.uk/wrigglytin

The Master Builder's House Hotel

The position here is hard to beat: lawns run down to the river, yacht masts flutter in the breeze, ancient woodland runs along the water, soundproofing this beautiful landscape. As for the house, it dates to 1729 and was home to the shipwrights who built Nelson's fleet; several ships built here saw action at Trafalgar. These days peace reigns. A chic sitting room opens onto a smart garden, where gravel paths weave past colourful beds to tables for lunch in the sun. There's a lovely old bar and an airy restaurant – both have terraces that drink in the view, and both serve tasty local fare, too, perhaps a pizza or posh fish and chips in the bar; smoked rabbit chorizo, pot au feu with local veg, salted butterscotch crème brûlée in the restaurant. Bedrooms in the main house have big views, Indian furniture, then colour and character in spades. Those in the annexe, recently refurbished (a few await their turn), come in crisp blues and whites, with a wall of wood, Bose sound systems and excellent walk-in showers. As for the New Forest, walk, cycle or kayak though it. A great forest base. *Reasonably secure garden (not for smaller dogs). Dogs need to be on lead in village but can go off lead on two-mile river walk to Beaulieu, and can jump into the river!*

Rooms	17 doubles, 9 twin/doubles: £95-£320. 2 cottages for 4: £500-£1400. Dogs £20. Max. 2.
Meals	Lunch from £5. Dinner in bar from £12; in restaurant, 3 courses, £30-£35. Afternoon tea from £15. Sunday lunch £19.95-£23.95.
Closed	Never.
Treats	Bed, fleece & biscuit, plus a delicious Doggy Room Service menu.

Tel	+44 (0)1590 616253
Email	enquiries@themasterbuilders.co.uk
Web	www.themasterbuilders.co.uk

Reservations Team
The Master Builder's House Hotel,
Bucklers Hard,
Beaulieu, SO42 7XB

Artist Residence Brighton

At the top of a square, looking down to the sea, a cute hotel with an arty vibe. You're bang in the middle of Brighton with all the stuff you'd want on your doorstep: galleries, bars, the Pier and the Royal Pavilion. As for the hotel, good food, great staff, relaxed informality and a playful style are the hallmarks here. You get stripped boards, exposed brick walls and an old garage door that slides back to reveal The Set Restaurant with an open kitchen. In typical AR style, it's now one of the best places to eat in Brighton with seasonal, modern British food as well as a 10-course tasting menu on The Chef's Table. You'll find cool art, the odd wall clad in corrugated iron, even an ornamental drainpipe! Bedrooms come in different

styles. Some have Pop Art murals, others come in Regency colours, a new batch are super-cool with baths in the room. Most have small, stylish shower rooms, one has a decked terrace. There's the quirky cocktail bar, The Fix, overlooking the West Pier, a ping pong table that doubles as a boardroom, then lunch in the restaurant with views through big windows down to the sea. The beach waits below. *Minimum stay: 2 nights at weekends. On seafront & in walking distance to dog-friendly beaches towards Hove.*

Rooms	17 doubles, 5 twins: £95-£250. 1 suite for 6: £280-£380. 1 quadruple: £145-£190. Singles £95-£165. Extra beds available in twin rooms. Dogs £15 per dog per night. Max. 2.
Meals	Breakfast £2.50-£8. Lunch from £7. Dinner, 4 courses, about £30. Restaurants within 500m.
Closed	Never.
Treats	Bowl, bed & Lily's Kitchen treats.

Charlie & Justin Salisbury Artist Residence Brighton, 34 Regency Square, Brighton, BN1 2FJ	**Tel** +44 (0)1273 324302 **Email** brighton@artistresidence.co.uk **Web** www.artistresidence.co.uk/our-hotels/brighton/

8 Coastguard Cottages

Step through a white gate, down the garden path and into the porch of your cottage; one in a neat row of whitewashed 19th-century dwellings. Downstairs there's a fresh nautical feel with white, grey and blue tones and seascapes on the walls. The cosy living room, dining area and well-stocked kitchen are all open plan; and the spick and span family bathroom is downstairs too. Take your morning Nespresso outside to the terrace while you plan your day – perhaps a yomp through miles of rolling Sussex landscape, a jaunt to boaty Chichester or a wander down to wonderful West Wittering beach, a ten-minute walk, for some twitching: swifts and swallows in spring, oyster catchers and geese in autumn. You're left a generous pile of logs for the open fire, a TV and plenty of books and board games – there's also a shed in the garden bursting with outdoorsy things: bikes, body boards, buckets, spades and crabbing nets. Upstairs to three restful bedrooms that continue the seafaring theme, the double has a distant view of the sea and one of the twin rooms is best suited to little ones. *No dogs in July & August. Secure garden; coastal walks, dog-friendly sandy beach nearby. Don't leave dogs alone if they bark or cry, and don't allow on furniture.*

Rooms	1 cottage for 6: £865-£1350 per week. Short breaks occasionally available. Dogs £10 per stay. Max. 3 (depending on size and age).
Meals	Pubs/restaurants 5-minute walk.
Closed	Never.
Treats	Bowls & towels.

Tel	+44 (0)20 7351 6009
Mobile	+44 (0)7984 808575
Email	admin@snowhillproperties.com
Web	www.snowhillproperties.com

Pilar Lafuente
8 Coastguard Cottages,
Coastguard Lane,
West Wittering, PO20 8AT

Rubens Barn

Pheasant strut, shy deer bounce by – sure signs that you're immersed in the Goodwood Estate. This little flint barn is tucked into one of the most unspoilt woody corners of Sussex. Rush hour here, on a leafy lane, consists of the occasional tractor, car or combine. Renovated and decorated to the highest order – in duck-egg blue with hints of gold – this is one stylish retreat. Downstairs, a luxurious bedroom with a huge bed, silk throws, velvet cushions and a shower room with slate tiles, heated rails and fluffy bathrobes. In the living room, cream sofas, fresh flowers, a Shaker kitchen. Upstairs, a big twin bedroom, a roll top bath, soft lights and white towels. A welcome pack of fruit, ham, cheese, coffee and croissants is provided by

the lovely owners who live in the main house – as are binoculars so you can spy on the wildlife! Sit out on the neat little patio through the French windows, enjoy a game of tennis, borrow the barbecue. Or set off for East Dean – it has two wonderful pubs. Sussex at its best, hidden well away yet never far from civilisation: historic Chichester is close by. *Minimum stay: 2 nights. Secure garden; surrounded by walks through forests & farmland. AONB in South Downs National Park.*

Rooms	1 barn for 4: £750-£1200 per week.
	Dogs £30 per dog per stay. Max. 2.
Meals	Self-catering.
Closed	Rarely.
Treats	Advice on walks & dog-friendly pubs nearby.

Rob & Rachel Hill	**Tel** +44 (0)1243 818187
Rubens Barn,	**Email** info@rubensbarn.co.uk
Droke Lane, East Dean, PO18 0JJ	**Web** www.rubensbarn.co.uk

Merrion Farm

Local and sustainable are the two principles at the heart of Merrion Farm. Withyfield Cottage is half rustic log cabin, half comfortable cottage, this incredible straw bale structure was designed by Ben Law, builder and permaculture expert whose project was voted the most popular ever to feature on Channel 4's Grand Designs. Throughout, modern comfort blends seamlessly with rustic design. It's a graceful work of art: exposed timber beams sweep down from the high, arched ceiling and sink into the worktops and floor, framing the open plan kitchen and living room. One of the bedrooms has its own bathroom, two are on the ground floor; all are simply decorated, letting the breathtaking quality of the workmanship shine through. From the veranda, you can see the very

woodlands where the timber to clad the exterior was cut and then replenished. A ten-minute walk away (sharing the woods with badgers, woodpeckers and barn owls) you'll find Withywood Shepherd's Hut, a private hideaway for up to four. Further afield is the Sussex landscape, criss-crossed with walking trails taking in places of history and beauty. *Heaps of lovely walks, private garden & lots of good smells for dogs!*

Rooms	Cottage for 6: from £131. Shepherd's hut for 4 (space for 2 extra children): £100. Prices per night. Hut: £15 per dog per stay; max. 1. Cottage: £20 per dog per stay; max. 2, extras by arrangement.
Meals	Self-catering.
Closed	Never.
Treats	Towels, advice on walks from door. Dog sitting available.

Tel	+44 (0)117 204 7830
Email	enquiries@canopyandstars.co.uk
Web	www.canopyandstars.co.uk/merrionfarm

Canopy & Stars
Merrion Farm,
Partridge Green, Horsham, RH13 8EH

The Cat

Owner Andrew swapped grand Gravetye Manor for the buzzy, pubby atmosphere of The Cat in 2009; he hasn't looked back. The 16th-century building, a fine medieval hall house with a Victorian extension, has been comfortably modernised without losing its character. Inside are beamed ceilings and panelling, planked floors, splendid inglenooks, and an airy room that leads to a garden at the back, furnished with teak and posh parasols. Harvey's Ale and some top-notch pub food, passionately put together from fresh local ingredients by chef Alex Jacquemin, attract a solid, old-fashioned crowd: retired locals, foodies and walkers. Tuck into rare roast beef and horseradish sandwiches, Rye Bay sea bass with brown shrimp and caper butter, South Downs lamb chops with dauphinoise (and leave room for treacle tart!). The setting is idyllic, in a pretty village opposite a 12th-century church – best viewed from two of four bright and comfortable bedrooms. Crisp linen on big beds, rich fabrics, fawn carpets, fresh bathrooms and antique touches illustrate the style. A special retreat in a charming village backwater. *Lots of walks in the area.*

Rooms	4 doubles: £130-£165. Singles £95-£110. Dogs £10 per stay. Max. 2.
Meals	Lunch & dinner from £12. Bar meals from £6. Sunday lunch, 3 courses, £26.
Closed	Rarely.
Treats	Poo bags, biscuits & towels for drying.

Andrew Russell
The Cat,
Queen's Square,
West Hoathly, RH19 4PP

Tel	+44 (0)1342 810369
Email	thecatinn@googlemail.com
Web	www.catinn.co.uk

Ditchling Cabin

Ditchling Cabin is the embodiment of the words, 'idyllic lakeside retreat'. Just you and whoever you brought along, alone by a private lake and free to canoe on it, fish in it, jump into it and swim in it. There's a BBQ and seating on the deck that encourage you to live outdoors as much as possible, but inside, the kitchen and the lounge have lake views through the folding glass frontage and the roll top bath upstairs looks down the length of the water. Whether you're lying on the sofa with the woodburner crackling, you've bust out the board games or you're just making breakfast, the sights and sound of the lake are always with you. It'll be hard to leave the sanctuary of the cabin, but day trips down to the beach at Brighton or the vineyards of Ditchling might tempt you out and the South Down National Park offers some great walking and cycling. Local shops and farms (try Mac's for great organic eggs) or there are lovely country pubs such as the Bull in Ditchling if you feel like eating out. *Secure area & lots of amazing walks in South Downs National Park.*

Rooms	Cabin for 4: from £320 per night. No charge for dogs; max. 1.
Meals	Self-catering.
Closed	Never.
Treats	A private lake for doggy paddles

Tel	+44 (0)117 204 7830
Email	enquiries@canopyandstars.co.uk
Web	www.canopyandstars.co.uk/ditchlingcabin

Canopy & Stars
Ditchling Cabin,
Whiteland's Cottage, Underhill Lane,
Hassocks, BN6 9PL

Strand House

As you follow the Royal Military Canal down to miles of sandy beach, bear in mind that 600 years ago, you'd have been swimming in the sea. This is reclaimed land and Strand House, built in 1425, originally stood on Winchelsea Harbour. Outside, you find wandering wisteria, colourful flowerbeds and a woodland walk that leads up to the village. Inside, medieval interiors have low ceilings, timber frames and mind-your-head beams. There are reds and yellows, sofas galore, a wood-burner in the sitting room, an honesty bar from which to help yourself. It's a home-spun affair: Hugh cooks breakfast, Mary looks after guests in style. Quirky bedrooms sweep you back in time. One has an ancient four-poster, some have wonky

floors, three open onto a terrace, all have good beds and robes for tiny shower rooms. As for the cottage, airy rooms have more space, and the suite, with its balcony and views across fields, is a treat. The house, once a work house, was painted by Turner and Millais. Local restaurants wait: Webbe's at the Fish Café, The Kings Head in Rye, top notch food at the Curlew in Bodiam. *Minimum stay: 2 nights at weekends & in high season. Towpath in front of hotel. Lots of local walks & places to eat.*

Rooms	5 doubles, 1 twin/double; 1 double with separate bath: £80-£150. 1 suite for 4: £180. 5 triples: £80-£150. Singles from £60. Extra beds £25 p.p. Dogs £7.50; 3 dog-friendly rooms.
Meals	Dinner for groups by arrangement (minimum 8 people).
Closed	Rarely.
Treats	Homemade biscuits, towels & drying room.

Mary Sullivan & Hugh Davie
Strand House,
Tanyards Lane,
Winchelsea, TN36 4JT

Tel	+44 (0)1797 226276
Email	info@thestrandhouse.co.uk
Web	www.thestrandhouse.co.uk

The Gallivant

This cool little hotel stands across the road from Camber Sands, where five miles of pristine beach are home to kite surfers, cricketers and sun worshipers alike. As for the Gallivant, a recent refurbishment has brought a stunning new look to every corner. Bedrooms, small and large, and now things of great beauty. Snug cabin rooms are clad in wood with brass lamps hanging from the ceiling; baby Hamptons have daybeds and marble bathrooms; deck rooms at the back come in cool whites with doors onto private terraces. Then come the garden rooms – heaven for hedonists – with double-ended baths in the room (and doors that slide for privacy), then small decks in the garden, where you'll also find a massage hut and deckchairs in summer. All have great storage, flawless bathrooms and crisp linen for Hypnos beds. As for the food, most is sourced within 10 miles and you eat in an airy restaurant that opens onto a terrace, perhaps cod with lime and cucumber, salt marsh lamb with root veg, chocolate torte with Frangelico jelly. There's tea and cake 'on the house' every afternoon, too. *Minimum stay: 2 nights at weekends. Secure coastal garden, but not for unsupervised dogs. Sandy beach a 5-minute walk. Dogs welcome when you dine, please mention when booking.*

Rooms	20 doubles: £135-£245. Singles £85-£240. Dogs £15 per dog per night. Max. 2.
Meals	Lunch from £16. Dinner, 3 courses, from £35.
Closed	Rarely.
Treats	Rug, biscuits & water bowl. Priced snack basket in room & jar of treats in reception.

Tel	+44 (0)1797 225057
Email	enquiries@thegallivant.co.uk
Web	www.thegallivant.co.uk

Elise Roberts
The Gallivant,
New Lydd Road,
Camber, TN31 7RB

Stable West

Who would imagine, at the end of the humble track, fields of blackcurrants, a newly planted vineyard and a beautifully converted Edwardian stable block? The friendly owners live at one end of the stables, you live at the other, and all you hear are the birds and the sheep. There are free logs for the wood-burner, wine and flowers for the table, and heaps of country-house space. So: enter a hall with white paintwork and chequer tiles, a lofty sitting room in duck-egg blue, a big fresh kitchen/dining room with all you need, and an airy sun room, perfect for the papers. The en suite bedroom is downstairs and the rest are up: a twin/double; a single; a bathroom under the eaves. Colours are muted, carpets soft, beds comfortable and everything

shines. Outside? Rolling views of Kentish countryside from a well-tended pretty garden, a pool enclosed by a rose-tumbled wall, a wild meadow sprinkled with flowers. Swimming and tennis can be arranged, historic Canterbury is up the road, and if you fancy a well-pulled pint – or a top-notch Sunday roast – you simply stride across the fields. *Minimum stay: 3 nights; 7 in high season. Secure garden & beautiful walking countryside from door.*

Rooms	1 house for 5: £800-£1400 per week. 3-night stay from £525. Max. usually 2 dogs.
Meals	Pub 15-minute walk.
Closed	Rarely.
Treats	Biscuit treats, rugs for furniture & towels.

Charlie Markes
Stable West,
Heppington,
Street End, CT4 7AN

Mobile	+44 (0)7779 350305
Email	stablewest@btinternet.com

Heron House

Welcome to Heron House – spruce and perfectly placed, between the high street and the sea. Its restoration, from 'sorry state' to much-loved home (neat-as-a-pin but not precious) is down to Julie, who has thought in much detail about your stay. Her passion for the place, and her love of Whitstable and all it offers, will rub off on you the moment you meet her. Downstairs are two sitting rooms, one smaller (with a wood-burner), one large, and a kitchen-diner in the extension, in beautiful, bright, Victorian-modern style. Find a table topped with candles and a basket of nice things, and doors to a pretty courtyard with a garden room for dreaming on a day bed. Bedrooms on the upper floors are a mix of vintage pine pieces and Farrow & Ball colours, new rugs on stripped floors, bathrooms with thick towels and shining sash windows – only the best. For a group of friends or two families it's perfect. Wander through trendy Whitstable, it has it all: shops, galleries, restaurants, pubs, oysters, chips, beach huts by the sea, and a proper coffee shop in Tankerton called Jo Jo's. *Minimum stay: 3 nights; 7 in high season. Secure small garden, beach & woodland walks, dog-friendly restaurants & pubs.*

Rooms	1 house for 8: £1225-£1890 per week. Max. 3 dogs.
Meals	Pubs/restaurants 2-minute walk.
Closed	Never.
Treats	Towels, blankets, biscuits & water bowls.

Mobile +44 (0)7734 663589
Email   info@heronhousewhitstable.co.uk
Web   www.heronhousewhitstable.co.uk

Julie FitzGerald Vitelli
Heron House,
Nelson Road,
Whitstable, CT5 1DP

East of England

Hare Field Cabin, page 131

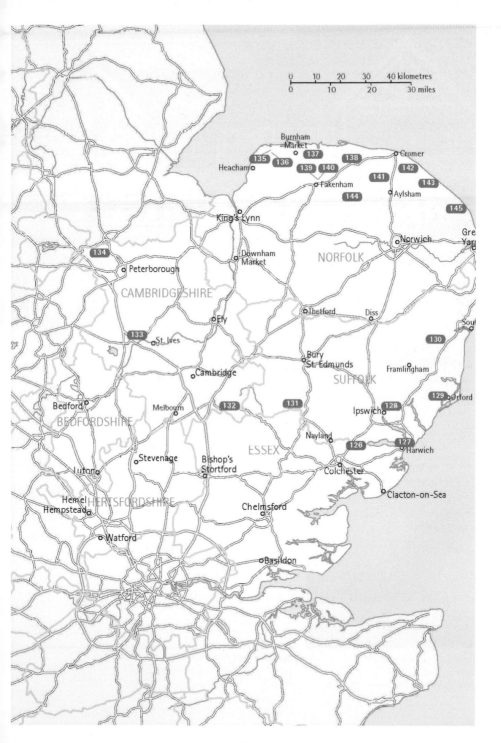

Maison Talbooth

The outdoor swimming pool is heated to 29°C every day, a chauffeur is on hand to whisk you down to the hotel's riverside restaurant, a grand piano waits in the sitting room, where guests gather for a legendary afternoon tea. They don't do things by halves at Maison Talbooth, a small-scale pleasure dome with long views across Constable country. The house, an old rectory, stands in three acres of manicured grounds; the pool house is a big draw with its open fire, honesty bar, beautiful art and treatment rooms. Interiors are equally impressive. There are no bedrooms, only suites, each divine; all pamper you rotten with flawless bathrooms, fabulous beds, cool colours and hi-tech excess. At dinner you're chauffeured to

the family's restaurants (both within half a mile): Milsoms for bistro food served informally; Le Talbooth on the river Stour for more serious fare, perhaps poached lobster with orange and fennel, saddle of venison with plums and bitter chocolate, pineapple and coconut soufflé with piña colada ice cream. A great escape. *Lots of walks through woods & by river. Livestock around part of the year on some walks.*

Rooms	12 suites for 4: £210-£420. Singles from £170.
Meals	Dinner at Milsoms £25; at Le Talbooth £35-£50.
Closed	Never.
Treats	Biscuits, blankets & towels.

Paul & Geraldine Milsom
Maison Talbooth,
Stratford Road, Dedham, CO7 6HN

Tel	+44 (0)1206 322367
Email	maison@milsomhotels.com
Web	www.milsomhotels.com/maison-talbooth/

The Pier at Harwich

They don't do things by halves at the Pier – a cool £1.5 million has recently been spent on a 21st-century makeover for this iconic coastal hotel. It sits on the harbourside with views of town and water, its front terrace a big draw in good weather. Inside, a cool new look captivates. A chic warehouse feel waits in the bar – stripped walls, hanging lamps, leather bar stools, big windows to frame the view. You get craft beers and cask ales, a gin library and prosecco cocktails, then small plates of Nordic design if you fancy a light bite. Hungry souls fly upstairs to the famous first-floor brasserie, where mirrored booths and leather banquettes now come as standard, and doors open onto a balcony, where you can tuck into your lobster Thermidor while gazing out onto the estuary. Bedrooms – some above, others next door in a former inn – have fancy bedheads, seaside colours, crisp white linen and super bathrooms; the suite, with its vast window, has a telescope with which to scan the high seas. Coastal walks and blue flag beaches wait, as does the Electric Palace, the second oldest cinema in Britain. *Beach & promenade to walk on, sea to swim in.*

Rooms	10 doubles, 3 twins: £120-£170.
	1 suite for 2: £200-£230. Singles from £95.
	Dinner, B&B from £100 p.p.
Meals	Lunch from £6.50. Sunday lunch from £19.50.
	Dinner à la carte £25-£40.
Closed	Never.
Treats	Blankets, towels, advice on walks, doggy
	dinners, bowls & treat.

Tel	+44 (0)1255 241212
Email	pier@milsomhotels.com
Web	www.milsomhotels.com/the-pier/

Paul & Geraldine Milsom
The Pier at Harwich,
The Quay, Harwich, CO12 3HH

Kesgrave Hall

This Georgian mansion sits in 38 acres of woodland and gardens, sound-proofing it from the outside world. It was home to US airmen during WWII, but the locals have reclaimed it as their own now and they come for the easy style, the excellent service, the delicious food and the informal vibe. The emphasis here is firmly on the food, so it's almost a restaurant with rooms, albeit quite a grand one. Inside, you find wellington boots in the entrance hall, high ceilings in the big sitting room, stripped boards in the humming bistro and doors that open onto a terrace in summer. Colourful bedrooms have lots of style. One is huge and comes with a free-standing bath and a faux leopard-skin sofa. The others might not be quite as wild, but they're

lovely nonetheless, some cosy in the eaves, others in beautifully refurbished outbuildings. Expect warm colours, crisp linen, good lighting and fancy bathrooms. Back downstairs, tasty food flies from the kitchen, perhaps smoked haddock fishcakes, a char-grilled steak, a delicious coffee cheesecake with Tia Maria ice cream. Suffolk's magical coast waits. *Woods to roam in & lawns to run on. Beach & rivers about 20 minutes away.*

Rooms	10 doubles, 7 twin/doubles: £130-£230. 6 suites for 2: £275-£300. Dogs £10.
Meals	Breakfast £10-£16. Lunch & dinner, 3 courses, £25-£30.
Closed	Never.
Treats	Blankets, towels, walks, bowls & doggy dinners.

Oliver Richards
Kesgrave Hall,
Hall Road, Kesgrave, IP5 2PU

Tel	+44 (0)1473 333741
Email	reception@kesgravehall.com
Web	www.milsomhotels.com/kesgrave-hall/

The Crown & Castle

A great place to wash up for a few lazy days. Orford is hard to beat, a sleepy Suffolk village blissfully marooned at the end of the road. River, beach and forest wait, as does the Crown & Castle, a welcoming English hostelry where the art of hospitality is practised with unstinting flair. The inn stands in the shadow of Orford's 12th-century castle. Uncluttered interiors have a warm, airy feel with stripped floorboards, open fires, wonderful art and flickering candles at night. Chic bedrooms have Vi-Spring beds, fancy bathrooms, lovely fabrics, the odd armchair. Four in the main house have watery views, the suite is huge, the garden rooms big and light, the courtyard rooms a real delight. All have crisp white linen, TVs, DVDs and digital radios. Wellington boots wait at the back door, so pull on a pair and explore Rendlesham Forest or hop on a boat and chug over to Orfordness. Ambrosial food awaits your return, perhaps potted brown shrimps, a faultless steak and kidney pie, crushed pistachio meringue with a chocolate ice-cream sundae. Sutton Hoo is close. *Minimum stay: 2 nights at weekends. Children over 8 welcome. Lots of walking by river & in forest.*

Rooms	18 doubles, 2 twins: £90-£250. 1 suite for 2: £150-£163. Dinner, B&B from £100 p.p. Dogs £10 per room per night. Max. 2.
Meals	Lunch from £8.50. À la carte dinner around £35.
Closed	Rarely.
Treats	Homemade treats, towels, walks, & a bookable "doggie table" in restaurant.

Tel	+44 (0)1394 450205
Email	john.morrell@crownandcastle.co.uk
Web	www.crownandcastle.co.uk

John Morrell
The Crown & Castle,
Orford, IP12 2LJ

Oak Tree Farm

A magnificent ancient oak tree stands guard over this 300-year old Georgian-fronted farmhouse. John and Julian love all things Art Nouveau/Art Deco and their home is filled with pieces from those periods, including china with masses of different patterns; fine books galore too, and peaceful bedrooms with smart white linen. Breakfast is a moveable feast: in the conservatory in summer, or by the fire in the dining room in winter; the bird feeders get moved too so you're kept entertained while you tuck in! You can wander the five-acre garden and meadows, pretty Yoxford village has antique shops to browse, and Snape Maltings is a hop. *Minimum stay: 2 nights at weekends. Plenty of space to exercise dogs & throw balls. Dogs don't usually need to be on leads (check in case chickens are free-ranging). Many lovely walks around area.*

Rooms	3 twin/doubles: £90. Singles £70.
Meals	Pubs/restaurants 5-minute walk.
Closed	Christmas, 1 November-28 February.
Treats	Doggy towels & poo bags.

Julian Lock & John McMinn
Oak Tree Farm,
Little Street,
Yoxford, IP17 3JN

Tel	+44 (0)1728 668651
Mobile	+44 (0)7969 459261
Email	oaktreefarmyoxford@gmail.com
Web	www.oaktreefarmyoxford.co.uk

Hare Field Cabin

Hare Field Cabin is an effortless escape for the work-weary city dweller. Just a hop out of London takes you to a quiet spot in the heart of Suffolk countryside, but the cabin's modern elegance keeps the best of urban comfort close to hand. Laze in the king-size bed to the sound of birdsong, pad across the heated floor to the monsoon shower, then throw open the doors to the terrace while you cook breakfast in the fabulous kitchen. Owners Richard and Rachel have considered the environment in everything from the reclaimed wood of the veranda and the air-source heat pump, to the careful positioning that blends the cabin into its surroundings and even hides it from their house just over the drive. Follow the miles of footpaths and bike trails that criss-cross the sleepy landscape to medieval towns and villages, or make a day trip to the coast. Come home via the local farm shop to pick up something for the barbecue or marshmallows for the firepit, then lie back on the loungers and watch the stars. There's even a spa nearby, although with the cabin itself working its mellowing magic on you, you'll hardly need it. *Public footpath opposite cabin; large field that dogs can roam; advice on other nearby walks, including a riverside one for a quick dip. Lots of dog-friendly pubs in Long Melford.*

Rooms	Cabin for 2: £104 per night. Dogs £30 per dog per stay. Max. 1 small/medium dog.
Meals	Self-catering.
Closed	Never.
Treats	Treats, bowl & towel; other items can also be supplied: leads, spare bed, food.

Tel	+44 (0)117 204 7830
Email	enquiries@canopyandstars.co.uk
Web	www.canopyandstars.co.uk/harefieldcabin

Canopy & Stars
Hare Field Cabin,
Mill Road, Foxearth,
Sudbury, CO10 7JF

The Three Hills

Originally opened as an alehouse in 1847 this rural inn has been bought and refurbished with aplomb. It's the only pub in this tiny village of just over a hundred souls and doubles up as the village hall, the library and all-round buzzing hub. Food is taken seriously: classic British with a twist and sourced locally as much as possible – touchingly there is also a discount for the villagers. There's a warm buzz inside with muddy-booted walkers, lycra-clad cyclists and families with children who spill outside to the pretty garden on warm days – a pizza oven and barbecues are planned. Find a cosy spot by the roaring fire and choose a book from the library, eat in the light and airy Orangery overlooking the terrace, retreat to bedrooms (two upstairs) with soft wool throws and fresh flowers. It's great walking and cycling country so you can set off straight from the village but you're a short hop in the car from Cambridge, Ely and Newmarket for culture, cathedral and shopping. *Dogs welcome in the bar & garden. River & lovely open countryside to explore. The four guesthouse rooms are dog-friendly, not the two in the pub.*

Rooms	5 doubles, 1 twin: £130-£150. Dogs £10 per night. Max. 2.
Meals	Breakfast from £6. Lunch, 2 courses, £17. Starters from £6. Mains from £15.
Closed	Rarely.
Treats	Blankets, towels, beds & bowls.

Michelle Wood
The Three Hills,
Dean Road,
Bartlow, CB21 4PW

Tel	+44 (0)1223 890500
Email	michelle.wood@thethreehills.co.uk
Web	www.thethreehills.co.uk/

The Old Bridge Hotel

The Old Bridge is one of those places that mixes old-fashioned hospitality with contemporary flair, a template of excellence for others to follow. It's a big hit with the locals, who come for delicious food and exceptional wines, and it inspired the founders of Hotel du Vin, who were amazed how busy it was. Ladies lunch, businessmen converse, kind staff weave through the throng. You can eat wherever you like: in the beautifully refurbished restaurant; on a sofa in the lounge; or sitting in a winged armchair in front of the fire in the bar. You feast on anything from homemade soup to rack of lamb (starters are available all day), while breakfast is served in a panelled morning room with Buddha in the fireplace. It's all the work of owners John and Julia Hoskins. Julia's interiors are dreamy, with style and comfort going hand in hand. Beautiful bedrooms have fresh colours, chic fabrics, crisp linen, padded bedheads. All have posh TVs and robes in excellent bathrooms, some of which overlook the river Ouse. John, a Master of Wine, has a wine shop in reception; you can taste before you buy (and you will). *In town but there are easy walks from the door.*

Rooms	18 doubles, 1 twin, 3 four-posters: £145-£230. 2 singles: £95-£125. Dinner, B&B £104-£150 p.p.
Meals	Lunch & dinner £5-£35.
Closed	Never.
Treats	Water bowls, towels & biscuits in room.

Tel	+44 (0)1480 424300
Email	oldbridge@huntsbridge.co.uk
Web	www.huntsbridge.com

John & Julia Hoskins
The Old Bridge Hotel,
1 High Street,
Huntingdon, PE29 3TQ

The White Hart

Wash up at the White Hart and mix with the locals drawn by the lovely lived-in farmhouse feel and the big, beamy bar. The ales are good too: Oakham Jeffrey Hudson, Tim Taylors, Grainstore's Red Kite. Farmers gather on Fridays, the cricket team drops by on Sundays; in summer life spills onto the terrace. Flags, floorboards and a crackling fire continue the rustic feel; railway signs, wooden pitch forks and hanging station lamps add colour. You can eat simply or more grandly, anything from a ploughman's to a three-course feast, with memorably good Sunday roasts full of flavour. Walk through rooms with lovely scrubbed tables to the orangery, a glass-gabled restaurant furnished with Lloyd Loom chairs. Bedrooms (some above the bar; the rest across the way) are simple and spotless, with crisp white linen and feather pillows, free WiFi and an honest price. One is airy and lovely, with period lounge chairs and views across the fields to the church; another has a four-poster bed. This forgotten slip of England – Stamford is five miles – is prettier than people imagine. *Secure garden; pub is surrounded by lots of good lead-free walks if dogs reliable (no main roads nearby). Sheep in neighbouring field.*

Rooms	10 doubles, 2 twins: £80-£130.
	Extra bed £15 p.p.p.n. Dogs £15 per night.
Meals	Lunch, 2 courses, £14.95. Dinner from £10.50.
	Sunday lunch, 2 courses, £19.90.
Closed	Rarely.
Treats	Water bowl & hose for washing off muddy paws.

Lisa Olver
The White Hart,
Main Street, Ufford, PE9 3BH

Tel	+44 (0)1780 740250
Email	info@whitehartufford.co.uk
Web	www.whitehartufford.co.uk

The Lifeboat Inn

You're in heaven here, under the big skies of Norfolk's north coast with its sweeping salt marshes, nature reserves and sandy beaches. The Lifeboat sails a smooth and stylish path with glowing fires, scrumptious seafood and the comfiest of rooms. Tucked down a hidden lane in pretty Thornham, the inn's darkly-beamed bar conjures a smugglers retreat, while the conservatory and restaurant are light, bright and contemporary. Settle by a crackling fire with a pint of Woodforde's Wherry and plan a day's bird- or seal-spotting. In summer, the sun-trap courtyard beckons, or book one of two cedar wood pavilions for private dining. Wherever you settle, the menu will tempt you with seasonal specials, cream teas, hearty sandwiches and children's treats. Our Brancaster mussels were the juiciest and tastiest we've eaten, and where else could you find roast beef in a Yorkshire pudding with horseradish sauce and a jug of gravy as a (bargain-priced) bar snack? Bedrooms (most are upstairs, one is on the ground floor) are wonderfully comfy with colour schemes that reflect the long landscape views. Bathrooms sparkle, and breakfasts are a treat. *Minimum stay: 2 nights at weekends. Walks on marshes, nearby beaches & Thornham Harbour.*

Rooms	13 doubles: £145-£225. Extra bed £25 p.p.p.n. Dogs £10 per dog per night. Max. 2.
Meals	Lunch from £6.50. Dinner from £9.95.
Closed	Never.
Treats	Blanket & bowl with treats in room on arrival. Treats behind bar & a sausage for breakfast.

Tel	+44 (0)1485 512229
Email	info@chequersinnthornham.com
Web	www.lifeboatinnthornham.com

Ewen Thomson
The Lifeboat Inn,
Ship Lane, Thornham, PE36 6LT

The Chequers Inn

Cheerful Chequers, beloved by locals and visitors alike, is thriving under the new care of Agellus. General Manager Ewen takes the helm and all is smooth sailing – with some of the best seafood you'll find in this lovely part of the world. Thornham is a pretty little village nestled along the coast, close to spectacular scenery and nature reserves, where Chequers gleams with its whitewashed walls and red pantiles. Inside, the fireplace glows and crackles, fresh flowers sit on scrubbed tables and the menu beckons. Our tempura of Brancaster mussels with tartar espuma and chilli vinegar (part of their Norfolk tapas range) was bursting with delicate flavours, but you might try slow-cooked crispy belly of pork with cider potato fondant, black cabbage, black pudding bonbon and grain mustard velouté. Pizzas are a treat too (crispy duck caught our eye) and there's private dining in the all-weather Pavilions outside. Both Sandringham and Holkham Hall are close. *Minimum stay: 2 nights at weekends. Maps with local walks available.*

Rooms	11 doubles: £120-£195. Extra bed/sofabed £25 p.p.p.n. Dogs £10 per dog per night. Max. 2.
Meals	Breakfast from £15. Tapas from £3.95. Lunch from £8.95. Dinner from £13.95.
Closed	Rarely.
Treats	A dog blanket in room & a tasty sausage for breakfast.

Ewen Thomson
The Chequers Inn,
High Street,
Thornham, PE36 6LY

Tel	+44 (0)1485 512229
Email	info@chequersinnthornham.com
Web	www.chequersinnthornham.com

The Globe Inn at Wells-next-the-Sea

It's as English as England can be – a beautiful inn on a Georgian green, where Nelson used to catch the coach to London. Potter down to the water and find a sandy beach for family fun, then a small harbour, where day boats land their catch on the quay. As for the Globe, it's an inn for all seasons. Outside, there's a sun-trapping terrace at the front, a flower-filled courtyard where you can eat in summer, then a colourful roof terrace for guests. Inside, wood-burners sit at both ends of the bar, there are sofas and armchairs, games for rainy days, then local ales and excellent wines with which to wash down delicious local food. You eat in an airy restaurant with local art of the walls, perhaps clam linguini with chilli and garlic, dressed Wells crab or a rib-eye steak, then chocolate mousse with pistachio ice cream. Rooms above have the comfiest beds in the land. Those at the front have views of the green, all have crisp linen, padded heads and vintage tiles in sparkling bathrooms. Rooms connect for families, boat trips can be arranged. Sandringham is up the road. *Minimum stay: 2 nights at weekends. Huge dog-friendly beach. Woods & miles of Coast Path to explore. Return on coasthopper bus when you & the pooch have had enough!*

Rooms	10 doubles, 5 twin/doubles: £110-£190. 3 suites for 2: £190-£250. 1 single: £60-£100. Extra bed £30 p.p.p.n. Dogs £15 per night. Max. 2 small or 1 large per room. 3 dog-friendly rooms.
Meals	Lunch from £6. Dinner, 3 courses, £25-£30.
Closed	Rarely.
Treats	Homemade biscuits, blankets & soft bed, bowls, feeding mat, poo bags. Towels & drying room.

Tel	+44 (0)1328 710206
Email	hello@theglobeatwells.co.uk
Web	www.theglobeatwells.co.uk

Antonia & Stephen Bournes
The Globe Inn at Wells-next-the-Sea,
The Buttlands,
Wells-next-the-Sea, NR23 1EU

Hill Cottage

Tucked behind a short row of houses in a peaceful cul de sac, with common land to one side and woodland to the other, is an 1800s drover's cottage. Step in to discover fresh flowers and a basket of logs, rose-strewn curtains and a duck egg-blue sofa, a hand-crafted kitchen and a colourful kilim: all you need to keep you cosy on the wintery-est night. Everything has been stripped back to its original style, and great comfort added. The steep winding stair is soft-carpeted and rope-bannister'd, the bedroom's beams are perfectly limewashed, the fireplace has a wood-burner that belts out the heat. For summer? Two levels of lawn separated by a flower bed, a furnished patio for meals, a bench facing south. The area is famous for its

houses – Holkham, Blickling, Felbrigg, Houghton Hall – there's golf at Sherringham, and the 'Poppy Line' – full steam ahead – is down the road; best of all, the delights of the Georgian market town of Holt are a five-minute stroll from your door. Then it's home to a deep soak in a free-standing tub and sweet dreams; the simple bedroom is a gorgeous treat. *Please see website for availability. Garden enclosed with flint walls & panel fencing. Front gate leads onto Common; many walks around Holt.*

Rooms	1 cottage for 2: £620-£730 per week. Dogs £15 per stay. Max. 1.
Meals	Restaurant 5-minute walk.
Closed	Never.
Treats	Biscuits & poo bags.

Amanda Agnew
Hill Cottage,
57 New Street,
Holt, NR25 6JQ

Mobile	+44 (0)7920 776635
Email	holiday@hillcottageholt.co.uk
Web	www.hillcottageholt.co.uk/availability.html

Banes Cottage

A Tudor manor house complete with a moat and a brick and flint cottage which once belonged to Banes, the gardener. You're free to roam the gardens on open days in spring and summer; guided tours of the house take place occasionally during the year. It's cosy inside with a real coal fire, plenty of games, books and DVDs; store your boots, bikes and muddy dog towels in the scullery to the side. You're welcome to use the tennis court, and the lovely garden space with far-reaching views is the best place for a barbecue. You can walk bridle paths or drive to the coast for wonderful beaches and salt marshes. The Georgian town of Holt and the market town of Fakenham are both seven miles equidistant; Binham Priory is two miles away and Walsingham Abbey five miles.

Wells-next-the-Sea is a pretty harbour town with a nature reserve and a stunning beach. *Minimum stay: 3 nights; 7 in high season. Unfenced lawns; easy walking from door & adjacent to a bridle path. Nearest beach, Morston, is dog-friendly; various local pubs too.*

Rooms	1 cottage for 4: £550-£1050 per week. Dogs £20 per stay. Max. 1.
Meals	Self-catering.
Closed	Never.
Treats	Towels & metal food bowls.

Tel	+44 (0)1328 878226
Email	info@hindringhamhall.org
Web	www.hindringhamhall.org/holiday-cottages/

Lynda Tucker
Banes Cottage,
Hindringham Hall,
Hindringham, NR21 0QA

Dockings Cottage

This tranquil cottage is next to open fields and Hindringham Hall's gorgeous gardens, 12th-century moat and medieval pond. The barn was converted after the war for the head herdsman, Mr Docking, who lived here with his bride. Inside, amuse yourself with games, books and cards next to the cosy wood-burner. Outside, light the barbecue and admire the roses in the enclosed garden while you cook supper, or there's a tennis court you're welcome to use by prior arrangement. Gardeners will love visiting the Hall grounds, which are open on Wednesday mornings and Sunday afternoons between April and the end of September. A bridle path for walks leaves from the door, and the North Norfolk coast is only ten minutes' drive – take the dogs to wide sands of Holkham and Wells-next-the-Sea, and the enticing aromas of Stiffley Marshes. Don't miss the six pretty villages called the Burnhams near Brancaster, the best-known being Burnham Market. There are also five stately homes nearby: Blickling Hall, Felbrigg Hall, Sandringham House, Houghton Hall, Oxburgh Hall. *Fenced rear garden. Beside bridle path. Space for dog baskets. Advice on walks & dog-friendly beaches.*

Rooms	1 cottage for 4: £530-£980 per week. Short breaks available.
Meals	Self-catering.
Closed	Never.
Treats	Towels for drying.

Lynda Tucker
Dockings Cottage,
Hindringham Hall,
Hindringham, NR21 0QA

Tel	+44 (0)1328 878226
Email	info@hindringhamhall.org
Web	www.hindringhamhallfarm.uk/ dockings-cottage/

Saracens Head

Lost in the lanes of deepest Norfolk, an inn that's hard to match. Outside, Georgian red-brick walls stand to attention at the front, but nip round the back and find them at ease in a beautiful courtyard where you can knock back a pint of Wherry in the evening sun before slipping inside to eat. Tim and Janie upped sticks from the Alps, unable to resist the allure of this lovely old inn. A sympathetic refurbishment has worked its magic, but the spirit remains the same: this is a country-house pub with lovely staff who go the extra mile. Downstairs the bar hums with happy locals who come for Norfolk ales and good French wines, while the food in the restaurant is as good as ever: Norfolk pheasant and rabbit terrine, wild duck or Cromer crab, treacle tart and caramel ice-cream. Upstairs, there's a sitting room on the landing, then six pretty bedrooms. All have smart carpets, wooden furniture, comfy beds and sparkling bathrooms. There's masses to do: ancient Norwich, the coast at Cromer, golf on the cliffs at Sheringham, Blickling Hall, a Jacobean pile. Don't miss Sunday lunch. *Many local walks for dogs & owners; beaches nearby too. Dogs on leads please as sheep & cattle very near.*

Rooms	5 twin/doubles: £110-£130. 1 family room for 4: £110-£160. Singles £75. Extra bed £25 p.p.p.n. Dogs £5 per night. Max. 2.
Meals	Lunch from £6.50. Dinner, 3 courses, £25-£35.
Closed	Rarely.
Treats	Dog bed, & towels for drying off wet, nicely tired out dogs.

Tel	+44 (0)1263 768909
Email	info@saracenshead-norfolk.co.uk
Web	www.saracenshead-norfolk.co.uk

Tim & Janie Elwes
Saracens Head,
Wolterton, NR11 7LZ

The Willows Cottage

Two cottages – two staircases – neatly woven into one, and a tiny sun room tucked onto the end. This is a sweet Norfolk brick and flint house, 180 years old, quintessentially English and idyllically positioned on a small-village road close to the coast. Over the garden gate is a huge wildlife-rich nature reserve of reed beds and woodland bisected by pushchair-friendly boardwalks – a privileged spot. Step through the door and into the dining room to low ceilings, a wooden floor and a lovely feeling of homeliness. Then the kitchen: low-beamed, well-equipped – the bathroom too is off here – and the sitting room, cosy with books, sculptures, squishy sofas and a wood-burner with logs on the house. Then up the steep narrow stairs to inviting bedrooms with sloping ceilings, low windows and doors to duck; the twin is nautically themed, the double a dream, with a carved mahogany bed and a glass chandelier. Feather toppers, scented candles, gorgeous linen... you are shamelessly spoiled. Brilliant for families, walkers, romantic couples – and dogs, enticed with biscuit snacks, holiday tags and a list of all the best walkies. *Dogs free to roam in secure garden, walks from door, splashy river & dog-friendly beach nearby.*

Rooms	1 cottage for 4: £470-£695 per week. 3-night stay £315-£455. Dogs £15 per stay.
Meals	Self-catering.
Closed	Rarely.
Treats	Tasty biscuits, bowls for feeding, blankets for snuggling, throws for furniture.

David Sewell
The Willows Cottage,
Lower Street, Southrepps, NR11 8UL

Tel +44 (0)1608 686351
Email norfolkholidaycottage@gmail.com
Web www.thewillowsnorfolk.co.uk

The Old Rectory

Conservation farmland all around; acres of wild heathland busy with woodpeckers and owls; the coast two miles away. Relax in the big drawing room of this 17th-century rectory and friendly family home, set in mature gardens full of trees. Fiona loves to cook and bakes her bread daily; food is delicious, seasonal and locally sourced, jams are homemade. Comfortable bedrooms have *objets* from diplomatic postings and the suite comes with mahogany furniture and armchairs so you can settle in with a book. Super views, friendly dogs, tennis in the garden and masses of space. If you fancy self-catering then opt for an independent break in the Garden Room. *Wonderful walks & dog-friendly beaches nearby; garden is not enclosed. Dogs welcome downstairs only.*

Rooms	1 double, 1 suite for 2: £80-£100. Singles £50. Garden Room for 2-4: £250-£400 per week.
Meals	Dinner from £25. Pubs 2 miles.
Closed	Rarely.
Treats	Locally made biscuits & occasional dog sitting if owners have to leave dogs for the day.

Tel	+44 (0)1692 650247	**Peter & Fiona Black**
Mobile	+44 (0)7774 599911	The Old Rectory,
Email	ridlingtonoldrectory@gmail.com	Ridlington, NR28 9NZ
Web	www.oldrectorynorthnorfolk.co.uk	

Stables & Coach House B&B

You stay in converted outbuildings in the back garden of this Georgian house in the centre of the village. Both have a separate entrance and look out on to the vegetable patch and gardens. Karena has thought of everything. You have your own kitchenette and dining/sitting area, a large comfortable bedroom and drench shower above and use of the garden. A continental breakfast is left for you: homemade bread, fruit, yogurt and muesli. Take your morning coffee outside to a suntrap bench and plan your days – Karena has heaps of information about the area. Join the Marriott's Way, take a trip to the coast, hunt for antiques in Holt. Return to your cosy bolthole for tea and biscuits and walk to The Queen's Head for supper. *Minimum stay: 2 nights. Large garden; walks from door; wood & nature reserve nearby.*

Rooms	1 double, 1 twin/double: £78-£120. Dog £20 per dog per stay. Max 2.
Meals	Pub 2-minute walk.
Closed	Rarely.
Treats	A basket with a blanket for sofa, poo bags, biscuits & towel.

Karena Taylor
Stables & Coach House B&B,
1 Hindolveston Road,
Foulsham, NR20 5RX

Tel	+44 (0)1362 683241
Email	stablesandcoachouse@gmail.com
Web	www.norfolkbandb.co.uk

Mill Farm Eco Barns

In the grounds of Mill Farm where the owners live (he's an ecologist, she's an organic food specialist), is a big beautiful barn with space to spread out. Views reach over farmland and Shetland ponies, while brick and flint walls and willow screens create privacy from next door; the big patio is a safe place for children. Enter an open-plan living room with vaulted ceilings and a bright airy feel; the central oak staircase winds you to the mezzanine and bedrooms above (two are up, two are down). Fossil-stone slabs line the floor, sleek leather sofas are deliciously comfy and children will love the hanging chair. Delightful Emma gives you a fabulous hamper (veg from the allotment, home-baked cake and more), logs for the woodburner, and has a wonderful eye for colour and design

Bedrooms are spacious and calming, one with a balcony for sundowners; bathrooms are the bee's knees. Hay Barn is close by – snug for two (and space for a little one) with a wood-burner and enclosed patch of garden. There are books, games, TV, bikes to borrow and toddlers' seats, and you can walk to pub, fish shop, small store and beach. *Secure garden, all-year dog-friendly beach, countryside walks & local walking guide. Chickens on site, so sadly no puppies.*

Rooms	1 barn for 2, 1 barn for 8: £320-£1950 per week. Short breaks off-season: Hay Barn £220-£440; Mill Farm Eco Barn £625-£1560. Dogs £15 per dog per stay. Max. 2 in each barn.
Meals	Self-catering.
Closed	Never.
Treats	Treats on arrival & bowls provided.

Mobile	+44 (0)7900 376462
Email	millfarmecobarn@gmail.com
Web	www.millfarm-ecobarn.co.uk

Emma Punchard
Mill Farm Eco Barns,
Mill Farm, Hemsby Road,
Winterton-on-Sea, NR29 4AE

East Midlands

Fern Cottage, page 152

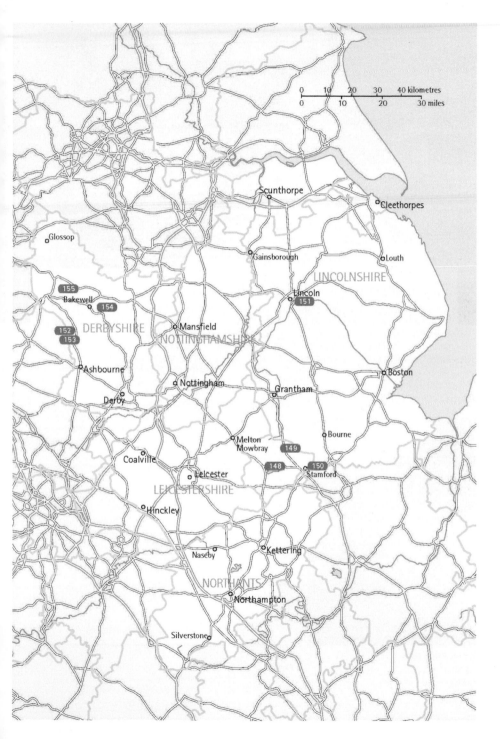

Hambleton Hall Hotel & Restaurant

Hambleton is matchless, one of the seven wonders of English country-house hotels. It sits on a tiny peninsular that juts into Rutland Water. You can sail on it, cycle round it, or watch terns and osprey commute across it. Back at the house the undisputed wonders of Hambleton wait: sofas by the fire in the panelled hall, a pillared bar in red for cocktails, a Michelin star in the elegant dining room. French windows in the sitting room – beautiful art, fresh flowers, the daily papers – open onto fine gardens. Expect clipped lawns and gravel paths, a formal parterre garden that bursts with summer colour and a walled swimming pool with views over parkland to the water. Bedrooms are flawless: hand-stitched Italian linen, mirrored armoires,

Roberts radios and marble bathrooms. Stefa's eye for fabrics, some of which coat the walls, is impeccable; the Pavilion, a two-bedroom suite, has its own terrace. Polish the day off with ambrosial food, perhaps beetroot terrine with horseradish sorbet, fallow venison with Asian pear, passion fruit soufflé with banana sorbet. Barnsdale Gardens are close. *Minimum stay: 2 nights at weekends. Great walks around Hambleton; maps provided. Livestock in fields so please keep dogs on leads.*

Rooms	15 twin/doubles: £290-£725. 1 suite for 4: £510-£725. Singles £200-£220. Dinner, B&B £210 p.p. Extra bed £35 p.p.p.n. Dogs £10. Max. 2.
Meals	Lunch from £29. Sunday lunch £58. Dinner, 3 courses, £73. Tasting menu £92.
Closed	Never.
Treats	Leads, bedding, poo bags, bowls, food & biscuits. Crates, toys, waterproof coats & towels.

Tim & Stefa Hart
Hambleton Hall Hotel & Restaurant,
Ketton Road, Hambleton,
Oakham, LE15 8TH

Tel	+44 (0)1572 756991
Email	hotel@hambletonhall.com
Web	www.hambletonhall.com

The Olive Branch

Start the evening with a local, seasonal, hedgerow cocktail – try a crab-apple bellini. Move onto dinner: the menu changes each day. All the produce is lovingly sourced – eggs from the hens, veg from the garden, local meat and fish – then cooked with passion by Sean and his team. Set off for Stamford (ten miles), a town rich in history, notable for its medieval Sheep Market, All Saints Church (climb the bell-tower), and numerous side streets to get lost down. The town's prosperity is linked still to Burghley House, the finest Elizabethan house in England. Take a pub picnic to its lawns. As for the pub, it's 400 years old and an absolute gem. It stands at the end of a tree-lined avenue, next to a beautiful stone barn (the pub's dining room). Bedrooms lie in Beech House across the lane, three with private terraces. Everyone's welcome, from children to dogs. *Lots of countryside walks nearby.*

Rooms	5 doubles: £120-£210. 1 family room for 4: £250-£270. Singles from £97.50. Extra beds £30. Dogs £10.
Meals	Lunch from £8.50. Dinner, 3 courses, £28.50-£40. Sunday lunch from £24.50.
Closed	Rarely.
Treats	Advice on walks.

Tel	+44 (0)1780 410355
Email	info@theolivebranchpub.com
Web	www.theolivebranchpub.com

Ben Jones & Sean Hope
The Olive Branch,
Main Street, Clipsham,
Oakham, LE15 7SH

The William Cecil

This attractive townhouse hotel stands yards from the gates of the Burghley estate. Inside, interiors offer a pleasing mix of English quirkiness and splendour. Downstairs, informality reigns. There are armchairs in front of the fire in the bar, smart wicker tables in the conservatory, doors onto a lovely terrace in summer, then hanging lamps and half-panelling in the colourful restaurant. The food is fresh and local with seasonal delights that include game from the estate. You might find lobster mousse with avocado ice-cream, slow-cooked Burghley venison casserole, lemon curd pie with lime sorbet. You can walk it all off through historic Stamford or spin over to Burghley for one of the finest Elizabethan houses in the realm. Come back to country-house bedrooms that mix eclectic Rajasthan furniture with a little English decorum. You'll find beautiful art, a wall of paper, perhaps a day bed or a ceiling rose. Some have views onto the estate, all have good bathrooms, the best with roll top tubs and vast walk-in showers. Dogs don't fare badly either with Union Jack beds. *Access to Burghley Park for walks: dogs have to be on leads. Short walk to Stamford Meadows with long walks along river.*

Rooms	20 doubles, 7 twin/doubles: £100-£180. Dogs £20 per stay. Max. 2 per room.
Meals	Lunch from £6.50. Dinner from £12. Sunday lunch, 3 courses, £24.50.
Closed	Never.
Treats	Beds, bowls & dog room service menu including sausage, chicken & steak.

Reservations Team
The William Cecil,
St Martins,
Stamford, PE9 2LJ

Tel	+44 (0)1780 750070
Email	enquiries@thewilliamcecil.co.uk
Web	www.thewilliamcecil.co.uk

Washingborough Hall

In its day Lincoln was one of the most important cities in England. Its castle holds one of the four original copies of the Magna Carta and was built by William the Conqueror in 1068; its cathedral dates to 1090 and remains one of the finest in Europe. All of which makes it a great city to visit, and if you want to beat a peaceful retreat into the country at the end of the day, this is the place to stay. It sits two miles east of Lincoln in a small village on the river Witham – footpaths by the water lead back into town. As for this Georgian rectory, you'll find smart lawns to the front, then a big welcome within – Edward and Lucy go out of their way to make your stay special. There's a wood-burner in the hall, a breakfast room with garden views, a sitting-room bar for afternoon tea, then a light-filled orangery restaurant. Stylish bedrooms offer unstinting comforts. Rooms at the front are bigger and have the view, all have good beds, bold wallpapers, excellent bathrooms, a sofa if there's room. As for the food, there's posh fish and chips in the bar or sea bass with spring greens in the orangery. *Small woodland within grounds & open countryside within half a mile.*

Rooms	12 doubles, 3 twin/doubles, 2 four-posters: £85-£175. 1 suite for 2: £175-£195. 2 singles: £65-£85. Dogs £10. Max. 2.
Meals	Lunch from £5.50. Dinner, 3 courses, £25-£35. Sunday lunch from £18.50.
Closed	Never.
Treats	Bowls, biscuits & advice on walks.

Tel	+44 (0)1522 790340
Email	enquiries@washingboroughhall.com
Web	www.washingboroughhall.com

Lucy & Edward Herring
Washingborough Hall,
Church Hill,
Washingborough, LN4 1BE

Fern Cottage

Up a steep, bumpy road, with no sign of habitation... a mystery tour? Then a sturdy, limestone cottage, with deep-set windows and handsome proportions appears. Turn around, and you'll be staggered at the views over the hills; there's even a wall seat from which to enjoy them. Originally the mine manager's house for nearby copper workings, and then the owners' family home, it's been thoughtfully updated without losing authentic charm. Window seats, alcove cupboards and original fireplaces mix with pale colours, cottagey furnishings and a sprinkling of well-chosen antiques to create a calm, tranquil atmosphere. Pale-painted floorboards lend an airy feel to the small, well-kitted kitchen. A window seat plump with cushions and a wood-burning stove make the sitting room cosy while a sunny conservatory extension cleverly doubles as a dining space. Large, light-filled bedrooms and bathroom are comfortably pretty yet unfussy, with wake-you-up views. Go walking and cycling; explore Chatsworth and local industrial heritage. The biggest joy is the secret corners in the terraced gardens, perfect for reading and dreaming. *Minimum stay: 3 nights at weekends & high season; 4 on weekdays. Enclosed garden; walks from door.*

Rooms	1 cottage for 4: £650-£790 per week. Dogs £15 per dog. Max. 3.
Meals	Restaurants 3 miles.
Closed	Rarely.
Treats	Treats, water, food bowls & poo bags.

Robert & Jo Wood
Fern Cottage,
Ecton,
Ashbourne, DE6 2AH

Tel	+44 (0)1335 310393
Email	stay@alstonefieldmanor.com
Web	www.alstonefieldholidaycottages.com/ fern-cottage/

Wisteria Cottage

Heavenly walks start from the door – then it's back to a cosy wood-burner, and bathrooms made for lingering. High in the hills above Dovedale is a handsome 19th-century cottage swathed in wisteria, a former blacksmith's workshop. There's a walled garden at the back (lawns, shrubs, trees, French tables and chairs), a stylish New England feel within. The space has been beautifully designed, with open-plan living downstairs, a bathroom and a twin, and a dreamy bedroom with a big shower up the runner'd stair. From the porch you enter the boot room (handy!), then the dove-grey kitchen, a chef's delight, and the sitting room, charming and immaculate, with a leather sofa and tartan wool cushions, a renovated stone fireplace and logs on the house. Bedrooms are fresh and sophisticated, with a quirky dash of vintage. Best of all? The George lies across the road, a timeless village inn where the chefs get creative with seasonal produce. Charming. *Minimum stay: 3 nights at weekends & high season; 4 on weekdays. Enclosed garden, walks from door & a boot room.*

Rooms	1 cottage for 4: £750-£910 per week. Dogs £15 per dog. Max. 2.
Meals	Self-catering.
Closed	Never.
Treats	Treats, water, food bowls & poo bags.

Tel	+44 (0)1335 310393
Email	stay@alstonefieldmanor.com
Web	www.alstonefieldholidaycottages.com/ wisteria-cottage/

Robert & Jo Wood
Wisteria Cottage,
Alstonefield,
Ashbourne, DE6 2FX

The Peacock at Rowsley

The Peacock sits between two fine houses, Haddon Hall and Chatsworth House. You can follow rivers up to each – the Derwent to Chatsworth, the Wye to the hall – both a stroll through beautiful parkland. As for the hotel, it was built in 1652 and was home to the steward of Haddon. Inside, old and new mix gracefully: mullioned windows, hessian rugs, aristocratic art, then striking colours that give a contemporary feel. You'll find Mouseman tables and chairs in the restaurant, where French windows open onto the terrace. Elsewhere, a fire smoulders in the bar every day, the daily papers wait in the sitting room, the garden lawn runs down to the river. Stylish bedrooms have crisp linen, good beds, Farrow & Ball colours, the odd antique; one has a bed from Belvoir Castle. Good food waits in the restaurant, with meat and game from the estate, perhaps venison terrine, roast partridge, Bakewell Tart with buttermilk ice cream. There's afternoon tea in the garden in summer and you can fish both rivers, with day tickets available from reception. Guests also receive a discount on entry to Haddon Hall. *Minimum stay: 2 nights at weekends. Lots of walking in woodland & fields. Peak Park area – follow countryside code. Derwent & Wye rivers.*

Rooms	10 doubles, 2 four-posters: £165-£310. 1 suite for 2: £250-£310. 2 singles: £130-£145. Dinner, B&B £142-£195 p.p. Dogs £10. Max. 2.
Meals	Lunch from £4.50. Dinner £60. Sunday lunch £22.50-£29.50.
Closed	Rarely.
Treats	Biscuits at turndown, towels & lots of walking information.

Laura Ball
The Peacock at Rowsley,
Bakewell Road, Rowsley,
Matlock, DE4 2EB

Tel	+44 (0)1629 733518
Email	reception@thepeacockatrowsley.com
Web	www.thepeacockatrowsley.com

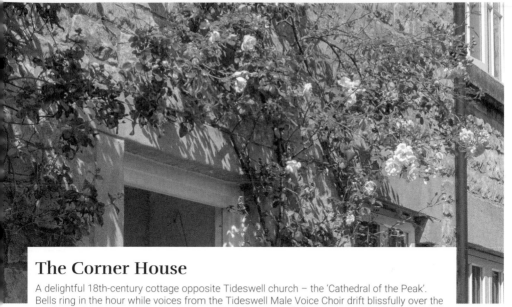

The Corner House

A delightful 18th-century cottage opposite Tideswell church – the 'Cathedral of the Peak'. Bells ring in the hour while voices from the Tideswell Male Voice Choir drift blissfully over the garden. Oak beams and flagstone floors recall the cottage's fascinating past, while John and Nikki have introduced modern comforts from an Aga to White Company towels, Laura Ashley bed linen and country antique furniture. A generous welcome hamper including tea, coffee, local handmade sausages, bread and a Tidza pud awaits in the kitchen, which has a sociable table for six. Plump sofas surround a wood-burner stocked with logs in the cosy sitting room. Head up the wide, carpeted staircase to sleep in peaceful bedrooms; doubles have comfy king-size or super king-size beds, while the twin overlooks the church. There's a spacious bathroom on the first floor and a small shower room up the next flight of stairs. In sunny weather, you can breakfast al fresco in the pretty garden alongside the churchyard. Stroll to pubs and cafés from the front door, or put on your walking boots to explore the Peak District. *Minimum stay: 3 nights; 7 in high season. Separate walled & gated garden. Please keep dogs on leads as lane has occasional passing cars.*

Rooms	1 cottage for 6: £560-£1125 per week. Max. 2 dogs.
Meals	Pubs/restaurants 5-minute walk.
Closed	Rarely.
Treats	Bed, bowls & treats, towels & poo bags. Advice on local dog-friendly cafés, pubs & walks.

Mobile	+44 (0)7876 763730
Email	info@thecornerhousetideswell.co.uk
Web	www.thecornerhousetideswell.co.uk

Nikki Turton
The Corner House,
1 Pursglove Road,
Tideswell, SK17 8LG

West Midlands

Lakeside Retreat, page 171

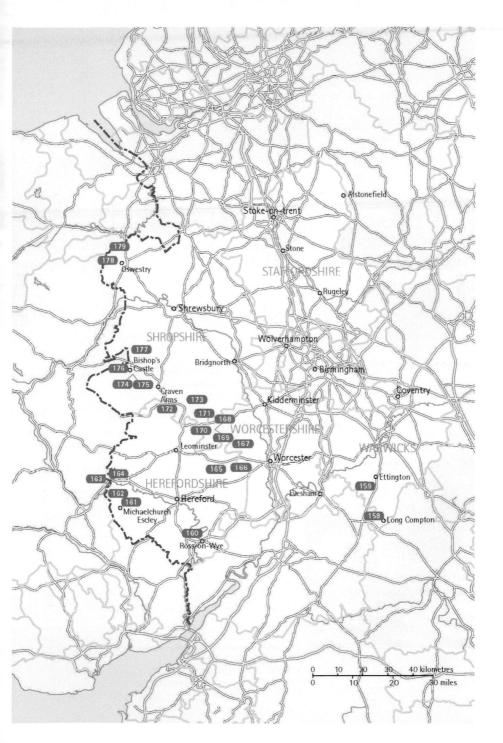

The Red Lion

Dogs are welcome in this ancient warren of a pub where canine sketches adorn the walls; 'the Landlady' – the pub's own chocolate lab – is often around. Enter to a mouthwatering aroma of imaginative dishes from chef/co-patron Sarah Keightley. Crispy-battered cod and chips with caper berries and mushy peas are served on The Red Lion Times, and pork tenderloin comes wrapped in pancetta with apple purée and black pudding. A meltingly warm pear and ginger pudding with toffee sauce rounds it all off nicely. Easy to find, this characterful pub has benefited from a wonderful refurb and there's space for everyone, from the pool room to the restaurant to the beautiful flagged bar with fire and wood-burning stove. There are five bedrooms too, the quietest at the back, which reflect the unfussy approach: natural colours and crisp ginghams; comfort and attention to quality make up for their size, though the King Room has an ante chamber should anyone snore! It is cheerful, hospitable, and breakfasts are worth waking up for. *Dragonfly Walk: a series of 3-12-mile walks around village of Long Compton. Stick to footpaths, close all gates behind you & have dogs on lead when close to livestock.*

Rooms	2 doubles, 1 twin: £95-£130.
	1 family room for 4: £115-£150.
	1 single: £60-£80.
Meals	Lunch & dinner £15-£20.
Closed	Christmas.
Treats	Home-cooked pig's ears & biscuits.

Lisa Phipps & Sarah Keightley
The Red Lion,
Main Street,
Long Compton, CV36 5JS

Tel	+44 (0)1608 684221
Email	info@redlion-longcompton.co.uk
Web	www.redlion-longcompton.co.uk

The Fuzzy Duck

In the rolling folds of the Cotswold countryside is this 18th-century coaching inn, polished to perfection by Tania, Adrian and their team. Beautiful fireplaces and gleaming tables, fine china and big sprays of wild flowers tell a tale of comfort and luxury, while the smiling staff are rightly proud of this gem of a pub. You dine like kings and queens in the sparkling bar, or in the clever conversion at the back, overlooking grounds that are part-orchard, part-walled-garden. Try Cotswold chicken breast with slow-cooked chorizo and white bean stew, or a splendid ploughman's with warm Scotch quail's egg. For pudding, try the zingy lemon posset, or treacle tart with orange scented milk ice. If you over-indulge, borrow wellies in your size for a bracing walk then back to your beautiful bed above the bar; rooms are sound-proofed and two have double loft beds (up very vertical ladders) for families. Best of all, the generous team has provided indulgent treats: lovely slippers; a nightcap tipple – come prepared to be spoiled. *Secure outside garden; lots of walks on doorstep. Some livestock nearby.*

Rooms	2 doubles: £110-£140.
	2 family rooms for 4: £160-£200.
Meals	Starters from £4.50. Mains from £9.95.
Closed	Never.
Treats	Biscuits, pig's ears, beds, blankets & advice on walks.

Tel	+44 (0)1608 682 635
Email	info@fuzzyduckarmscote.com
Web	www.fuzzyduckarmscote.com

The Manager
The Fuzzy Duck,
Ilmington Road,
Armscote, CV37 8DD

Brooks Country House

Led Zeppelin used to stay here when recording at studios nearby, and there's still a bit of a rock-star feel to the place. A big house in the country, a swimming pool in the kitchen garden and its own vineyard that produces wine for the restaurant... There's a rather good view, too, a clean sweep over ten miles of rolling country to rising mountains. The house once stood in 1,000 acres, it now has a mere 12, but the land beyond is owned by the National Trust and you can walk straight out, skirt a copse and find yourself at a 14th-century church. As for the hotel – smart, but relaxed, with down-to-earth Andrew and Carla at the helm. Expect an open fire in the sitting room, wood floors in the restaurant and cowhide rugs in a bar that opens onto a sun-trapping garden. Nicely priced rooms are scattered about, some grander, others smaller, all with good beds, warm colours and lovely bathrooms; and there's an apartment for four in the grounds if you want to look after yourselves. As for the food, it's earthy stuff; homemade soups, a local rib-eye, a sinful chocolate tart. Hard to beat. *Minimum stay: 2 nights at weekends. 15-acre garden & lovely walks; sheep in field so dogs on lead. Four big courtyard rooms with plenty of space.*

Rooms	14 twin/doubles, 6 four-posters: £79-£169. 2 suites for 2: £99-£169. 1 apartment for 4: £133-£250. 3 trucks for 2: £99-£139. Singles £89-£119. Extra bed £10-£20 p.p.p.n. Dogs £20. Max. 2.
Meals	Dinner £18-£24 (not Sundays). Sunday dinner from £19-£23.
Closed	Never.
Treats	Biscuits, basket with a snug blanket & toys.

Carla & Andrew Brooks
Brooks Country House,
Pengethley Park,
Ross-on-Wye, HR9 6LL

Tel   +44 (0)1989 730211
Email info@brookscountryhouse.com
Web   www.brookscountryhouse.com

The Stable & Barn, Cothill

The Lloyd family, sheep farmers here in the Black Mountains for generations, have lavished attention on their restoration of listed Barn, Stable and the sweetly simple Shepherd's Hut (let only with The Stable as it shares a bathroom). The result is a really successful mix of old: stone, slate, beams, china, general rusticity and retro pieces – and new: ultra-modern kitchens, bathrooms, heating and electronic devices – touches of fun, splashes of vibrant colour. Long, wild views from deeply comfortable, woody bedrooms will entice you out to those hills; return to soak in deep baths, then head down the wide oak stairs for a drink by the woodburning stove and dinner – perhaps prepared by Ali – though everything a cook could want is provided and this is a thoroughly foodie area. The Barn has the bigger garden, The Stable floods with light through the glazed doorway, the Hut stands between two ancient oaks. If you can tear yourself away, go to bookish Hay and to Abbey Dore for a concert, to Hereford market and to see the Cathedral and Mappa Mundi – a weekend is not enough! *Minimum stay: 3 nights. Large enclosed gardens; paths from door with woodland & 150 acres of farmland. Dogs on leads with sheep.*

Rooms	1 stable for 4, 1 barn for 8: £400-£1150 per week. Shepherd's Hut with Stable £40 p.n. for 2. Extra beds available. Deposit if bringing several dogs or children. Short breaks off peak.
Meals	Self-catering.
Closed	Never.
Treats	Basket, bowls, towels & treats. Outside taps & heated utility rooms for dogs to sleep in.

Tel	+44 (0)1981 550254
Email	cothillbarns@outlook.com
Web	www.cothillbarn.co.uk

Ali Lloyd
The Stable & Barn, Cothill,
Turnastone, Hereford, HR2 0RE

Drover's Rest

Through a tunnel of trees you'll find your meadow-dwelling safari tents – African in looks, but Welsh in spirit. Far enough away from each other to be private but neighbourly enough that you can easily borrow matches for the campfire. Your first tell-tale sign is the chimney of a log-burner popping out of the top of each tent and the rattan sofa with huge cushions on the porch. Beyond the farmhouse-worthy kitchen and living area padded out with sheepskins and cushions, there are two bedrooms, each with cast iron beds, Welsh blankets and sheepskin rugs. All tents have their own hot monsoon shower and flushing loo in a fully heated stable block, just a couple of minutes' walk from the tents and torches are provided for night time trips. The Hayloft barn is yours to share with other glampers and has WiFi, a café, a cocktail bar and its own farm shop. There's also a lounge with bean bags and movie screenings and a dining area for group suppers. Pizzas, curries and barbecues are served up on different days of the week but there's a barbecue outside each tent and a heavy-duty pot for cooking chillies and stews. *Walks direct from door. Dogs allowed in communal chill-out barn while you have dinner. Working farm so farm animals around.*

Rooms	7 safari tents for 4: from £75 per night. Dogs £20 per dog per stay. Max. 2; will come into contact with owners' dog.
Meals	Self-catering.
Closed	Never.
Treats	Water bowls, treats & advice on walks.

Canopy & Stars
Drover's Rest,
Llanycoed Farm,
Hay-on-Wye, HR3 6AG

Tel	+44 (0)117 204 7830
Email	enquiries@canopyandstars.co.uk
Web	www.canopyandstars.co.uk/droversrest

The Peren

Herons, kingfishers, badgers and weasels – just a few of the visitors to your glorious acre of wildflower meadow, the setting for the Peren, a 19th century restored barn. Owners Simon and Andrew have great green credentials. They run an organic smallholding nearby and have done what they can to make the barn eco-friendly while keeping it up to date and chic, including a ground source heat pump to keep you warm, with a wood-burning stove for back up. There's a part-canopied barbecue terrace overlooking the meadow for summer meals in the great outdoors. If you fancy spending a night under canvas you can pitch your tent in the meadow. Kids can run wild here, and in the evenings everyone can enjoy a bit of rabbit spotting or raid the supply of books and games under the stairs. *Minimum stay: 3 nights at weekends & in high season; 4 on weekdays. One-acre secure garden with lots of space to run around & explore. Walks from door down to river Wye. Hay-on-Wye is a very dog-friendly town to visit.*

Rooms	1 house for 5: £595-£1050 per week. Short breaks from £295. Dogs £15 per dog. Max. 2.
Meals	Self-catering.
Closed	Never.
Treats	A 'doggy bag' with towels, toys, food bowls & some locally made treats

Mobile +44 (0)7932 755515
Email info@theperen.com
Web www.theperen.com

Simon Forrester & Andrew Craven
The Peren,
Lower Wyeside, Clifford,
Hay-on-Wye, HR3 5EU

New Inn Brilley

A place of peace and beauty, where you can unwind and relax in one of New Inn Brilley's seven truly unique spaces, a fabulously ramshackle, retro, recycled camp in the hills above the stunning Welsh countryside. Choose from two wagons, two caravans, a roundhouse, a tabernacle or a cabin which each have their own rustic quirks, whether that be an outdoor bath or barrel tub to soak in after a long hike or decking to gaze across breath-taking views of mountains. The higgledy piggledy, bohemian nature is all part of the charm and owner Daphne can give you tips for roaming into the hills on foot, by bike or on horseback, find you a yoga class or just let you wander down to the stupa and calmly ponder your own spiritual journey. *Multitude of walks nearby & spectacular open spaces. Private corners for guests but not fence proof. Dogs to be kept under supervision due to livestock.*

Rooms	Wagons for 2: from £80. Cabin for 2: from £100. Tabernacle for 2: from £110. Roundhouse for 2: from £110. Caravan for 2: from £60. Prices per night. Dogs £20 per dog per stay. Max. 1 dog per cabin.
Meals	Self-catering.
Closed	January-March.
Treats	Bowl, treats and towel provided.

Canopy & Stars
New Inn Brilley,
Brilley,
Whitney-on-Wye, HR3 6HE

Tel	+44 (0)117 204 7830
Email	enquiries@canopyandstars.co.uk
Web	www.canopyandstars.co.uk/ newinnbrilley

Brook House Woods

Brook House Woods is home to Penny & Will's woodland wonderland and the Green Wood Workshop, with six woody spaces to choose from: hobbit hut, yurt, tree-tent and three tree cabins. The hobbit hut fits a surprising amount inside: king-size bed, fairy lights and wood-burner. Spot shooting stars, tucked up in bed in the colourful yurt under the trees. Goji, the tree tent is a spherical bedroom in the trees with a wood-burner and roof window above. The communal workshop kitchen offers cooking on an open fire or making pizzas in the cob barrel oven. The tree-cabins give elegance, simplicity and adventure in perfect balance: roll top tub on the deck, chaise longue, smoker and barbecue. There are plenty of on-site activities to get involved in: green wood working with Will, yoga with Penny or book in for tennis or a soak in the hot tub. Take a dip in the secret lake, wander along the river Frome, follow miles of trails. *Babies welcome. 350 acres of off-lead private footpaths through fields, forest & orchards; river paths. Map of Brook House walks – all ending up in a dog-friendly pub. Dog-friendly taxi service too.*

Rooms	1 Hobbit hut for 2: from £100. 3 treehouses for 2: from £155. 1 tree tent for 2 from: £105. 1 yurt for 2: from £90. Prices per night. £10 per dog per stay.
Meals	Self-catering.
Closed	Never.
Treats	Pond & little stream for paddling; a dog-stop in workshop where you can all snuggle by fire; a veranda where you can wash muddy hounds.

Tel	+44 (0)117 204 7830
Email	enquiries@canopyandstars.co.uk
Web	www.canopyandstars.co.uk/brookhousewoods

Canopy & Stars
Brook House Woods,
Brook House Farm, Avenbury Lane,
Bromyard, HR7 4LB

Lilla Stugan

Lilla Stugan, or 'little cottage', was inspired by the long summers Martin and Annika spent in their Swedish summer house. And what's not to love about a country that designates whole days to celebrating sugary cakes and buns? To top off these sweet credentials, the hut lives at the bottom of its very own apple orchard – a mini Moominvalley! – and you can try beekeeping or cider making, depending on the season. A private gate leads straight out onto the beautiful Knapp and Papermill Nature Reserve. In warmer months, the orchard is awash with daffodils, blossoming trees, long meadow grasses and rare orchids. Come autumn, the trees are heavy with bright red apples, pears and plums, ripe for picking and juicing. Wander

into the trees and you'll stumble across a huge fire pit, complete with a cooking pot to winch your bubbling stews up and down; you can order a dinner hamper – and breakfast one too. Strum the guitar or let the nearby weir and the crackle of the fire be your soundtrack. *Dogs free to roam in orchard; horses & chickens elsewhere on farm. Public footpaths. Mill Race & Leigh Brook for dog swims. Nature reserve with signed woodland walks.*

Rooms	Cabin for 2 (+2 children on a futon & fold out bed): from £100 per night. £10 per child per night. Dogs £20 per dog per stay. Max. usually 1 dog.
Meals	Self-catering.
Closed	November-March.
Treats	Basket, bowls, hose pipe & towels. Butchers within 10 mins' drive for meaty dog treats.

Canopy & Stars
Lilla Stugan,
Millham Farm, Millham Lane,
Alfrick, WR6 5HS

Tel	+44 (0)117 204 7830
Email	enquiries@canopyandstars.co.uk
Web	www.canopyandstars.co.uk/lillastugan

Cider Mill Cottage

If you want to get off the beaten track, this is the bucolic bolthole for you. A rustic road with beautiful Malvern views ends at a cluster of Victorian farm buildings amidst a sea of fields. Pleasant, organised owner Catherine – dogs in tow – welcomes you to a neat stone cottage opposite the main house. On the open plan ground floor, sofas cluster around a wood-burner, a small dining table tucked in beside them. The brick and terracotta floor is swathed in Persian rugs, but otherwise the house is decorated with a pared-back elegance, letting the venerable beams and walls sing. At the far end of the room, a Victorian mill wheel is cleverly incorporated into a stylish modern kitchen complete with Aga and welcoming goodies like wine, homemade jam, bread and milk. Up the spiral staircase – tricky for some – and you're in the eaves, with space for an armchair on the landing, a cosy double room warmed by the wood-burner flue, a sunny single room and a pristine modern bathroom beneath the beams. Outside, breakfast al fresco on your little patch of lawn, or roam Catherine's beautifully tended garden. *Children over 5 welcome. Fantastic paths to fields & woods with streams nearby. Large paddock for safe runs.*

Rooms	1 cottage for 3: £460-£700 per week.
	Short breaks available.
	Dogs £20 for 1 large dog or 2 small.
Meals	Pubs serving food nearby.
Closed	Rarely.
Treats	Cosy basket & box of treat biscuits.

Tel	+44 (0)1886 812156
Mobile	+44 (0)7590 073084
Email	info@cidermill-cottage.co.uk
Web	www.cidermill-cottage.co.uk/

Catherine Prindezis
Cider Mill Cottage,
Ayngstree,
Clifton Upon Teme, WR6 6DS

The Coach House

Way up a simple track, your stone-walled, stone-tiled hideaway was built almost entirely from reclaimed materials. Much of it crafted by Ellie, who will greet you on arrival and lives in a 16th century timber-framed house on the estate. Inside is open plan and easy and filled with fresh flowers. Recline on your leather chesterfield, toes directed at a wood-burner stacked with logs from the woods, or sit out on the veranda with Ellie's homemade cake or a glass of wine – there are magnificent views across open pastures to the Teme and Kyre valleys. Venture further to foodie Ludlow, book-lined Hay-on-Wye and the grand industrial heritage that is Ironbridge. Or you can take to the slow life on the steam railway, stride out on the Mortimer Trail, meander through local villages. Return to much tranquillity. *Seven acres of specially fenced land for carefree scampers & no roads for miles.*

Rooms	1 house for 2: £700 per week.
Meals	Self-catering.
Closed	Never.
Treats	Towels, bowl & treats.

Ellie Van Straaten
The Coach House,
Vine Lane, Kyre,
Tenbury Wells, WR15 8RL

Tel	+44 (0)1885 410208
Mobile	+44 (0)7725 972486
Email	ellie_vanstraaten@yahoo.co.uk
Web	www.a-country-break.co.uk

Long Cover Cottage

Stealing its name from the backdrop of ancient undisturbed woodland, the cottage and its surrounds make a natural family home – for both frazzled humans and local badgers. Winding your way up the long peaceful track to this converted stable, you catch glorious glimpses of the Teme and Kyre valleys; the setting is spectacular. On arrival, you're greeted by the delightful Ellie, whose grounds and beautifully tended English country garden you share. Generous windows flood rooms with light that bounces off polished elm floorboards; a woodburner and Aga keep things cosy, the kitchen is handcrafted, the views are long and bucolic. Upstairs, bedrooms are brass-bedded and floral, tucked under the eaves in that cottagey way. You get a handy loo and basin up here, and a sparkling bathroom with a roll top tub downstairs. Lucky children have seven acres to romp in, and a secret treehouse with hammocks and a barbecue for midnight feasts. Resting on the borders of three counties, this is prime walking country. Bustling Ledbury and Ludlow, England's Slow Food capital, are just a drive away. *Seven acres of specially fenced land for carefree scampers & no roads for miles.*

Rooms	1 cottage for 6: £900 per week.
Meals	Self-catering.
Closed	Never.
Treats	Towels, bowl & treats.

Tel	+44 (0)1885 410208
Mobile	+44 (0)7725 972486
Email	ellie_vanstraaten@yahoo.co.uk
Web	www.a-country-break.co.uk

Ellie Van Straaten
Long Cover Cottage,
Vine Lane, Kyre,
Tenbury Wells, WR15 8RL

Hop Pickers' House

Down winding country lanes in the depths of the Welsh Marches, an Elizabethan farmhouse sitting in nine acres and surrounded by attractive barns. The Hop Pickers' House sits at right angles to an open barn. Step in to find an airy feel, open-plan upstairs and down, with white walls, old beams, wooden floors and a charming mix of pretty china, comfy chairs, throws and jugs of flowers. The kitchen area is cosy and rustic with a painted dresser, pine table for four and wood-burner (plenty of logs); you'll find milk in the fridge, cake, jam and, of course, apple juice. Hop up painted stairs to a big four-poster with diaphanous drapes – be lulled to sleep by the hoot of an owl, the bleat of a lamb. Stroll through woodlands, wild flowers, fern gulley

and orchards; rest by a babbling brook. In a distant corner with a view of the setting sun is a makeshift barbecue. The owners are in the farm next door through a rose-strewn pergola but you'll feel very private. Lovers will purr with happiness here, walkers too, and cooks can stock up with food from famous Ludlow only 15 minutes away. A mouth-watering snug of a nest. *Lots of woodland walks & pretty brooks. 'Doggie' guest pack with dog-friendly places to eat, drink & walk.*

Rooms	1 cottage for 2: £510-£570 per week. Short breaks available.
Meals	Pubs/restaurants 2 miles.
Closed	Never.
Treats	Cosy blankets to snuggle up in, towels for drying off, bowls & poo bags provided.

Steven Hickling & Stephen Snead
Hop Pickers' House,
Berrington,
Tenbury Wells, WR15 8TJ

Mobile	+44 (0)7736 341906
Email	stephensnead@yahoo.co.uk
Web	www.brookfarmberrington.org

Lakeside Retreat

Off-piste drivers will delight in the approach – down a bumpy farm track, over an open field, across a ford and through grassy woodland. You land in a dreamy, bucolic setting with an arboretum and views over two deep water lakes (yes you may swim, yes you may use a little boat) with island, waterfalls, a small summerhouse that revolves, and a stream teeming with wildlife. A veranda and patio with table and chairs face south so you won't miss a thing; writers, artists and those clutching a large drink may take root here on less chilly days. Your wooden cabin is comfortable and very cosy: find one fresh and airy living/dining room with a fully formed kitchen area and plenty of good seating; glass doors open out to the terrace. The main bedroom has a giant bed with a pretty rose strewn bedspread and a cream rug; the bunk room is fine for adults or children but it's all so romantic you may want to farm them out! Owner Victoria, who lives nearby, leaves you jam from her damsons and raspberries, local apple juice, something baked, and fresh flowers. A gorgeous little watery retreat. *Children over 5 welcome. 15 acres of garden & woodland.*

Rooms	1 cabin for 4: £395-£795 per week. Weekly bookings (Fri-Fri) or 3 night weekends (Fri-Mon). Additional night's stays available. Dogs £30 per stay. Max. 2.
Meals	Self-catering.
Closed	Never.
Treats	Treats, blankets & advice on walks.

Tel	+44 (0)1299 270780
Email	vjorchard@gmail.com
Web	www.ludlowholidaylet.co.uk

Victoria Orchard
Lakeside Retreat,
Old Hall Farm, Milson,
Cleobury Mortimer, DY14 0BH

Old Downton Lodge

The last time anything really happened here was in 1067 when Edric the Wild got a bit shirty with invading Normans. Fast forward five hundred years and Old Downton is taking shape. It's a fine old building, a little like walking onto the set of Wolf Hall, with original timbers, mighty crossbeams and beautiful stone walls. It sits in pristine country. Pheasants strut, hills roll, woodlands sprawl along distant ridges; a stunning walk across it all takes you over to Ludlow. Back at the house Pippa and Willem look after you in great style. There's a lovely sitting room in the old dairy with a roaring fire, then a dining room in an 11th-century barn that resembles a medieval banqueting hall. In summer, life moves into the courtyard where you can eat, drink and make merry. Big bedrooms mix timber frames, stone walls, flagged floors and oak furniture, while bathrooms have robes and lashings of hot water. Back outside, follow the river Teme up to Downton Gorge for ferns, otters, Roman baths and bluebells in spring. Bring your Tesla – there are two chargers here. *Some bedrooms are dog-friendly; please ask. Lots of great walks from door. Dogs on lead in courtyard.*

Rooms	5 doubles, 2 twins, 2 four-posters: £155-£295. Dogs £15 per stay. Max. 2.
Meals	Dinner, 3-9 courses, from £50.
Closed	Christmas.
Treats	Water bowl & dog bin. Blankets on request.

Willem & Pippa Vlok
Old Downton Lodge,
Downton-on-the-Rock,
Ludlow, SY8 2HU

Tel	+44 (0)1568 771826
Email	bookings@olddowntonlodge.com
Web	www.olddowntonlodge.com

Timberstone Bed & Breakfast

The house is engaging – as are Tracey and Alex. Bedrooms are inviting – two snug under the eaves, two in the smart oak-floored extension – roll top baths, pretty fabrics, thick white cotton, beams galore... Or you can decamp to The Retreat, a wooden cabin in the garden warmed with a wood-burner. Tracey, once in catering, is a reflexologist – book a session, or sauna, in the garden studios; ask about 'gadget-free breaks' too. In the guest sitting/dining room find art, books, comfy sofas and doors onto the terrace. Breakfasts are good with croissants and local eggs and bacon; dinners are delicious too, or you can head off to Ludlow and its clutch of Michelin stars. *Large garden & good country walks from door & nearby.*

Rooms	3 doubles: £100-£150. 1 family room for 4: £110-£120. 1 cabin for 2: £100-£150. Singles £75-£98. Dogs £10 per dog per stay. Max. 2.
Meals	Dinner, 3 courses, £25. Pubs/restaurants 5 miles.
Closed	Rarely.
Treats	Bed, blanket, towels & treats. Dog walking & sitting if needed.

Tel	+44 (0)1584 823519
Mobile	+44 (0)7905 967263
Email	timberstone1@hotmail.com
Web	www.timberstoneludlow.co.uk

Tracey Baylis & Alex Read
Timberstone Bed & Breakfast,
Clee Stanton, Ludlow, SY8 3EL

Walcot Hall

A wonderful place for a holiday, with plenty of space for everybody. The big house, built for Clive of India, sits comfortably at the bottom of a long winding drive and the holiday homes radiate out from it: Berkeley, Plassey and Garden Flat are all warm and comfortable with original pictures and furniture, oodles of interesting books and generous free logs. Clive and Harold, tucked into a corner of the old brick stable yard, are cosy boltholes with pretty fabrics, colourful rugs and neat-as-a-pin kitchens. Garden House stands on its own with a private lawn in front and a south-facing terrace at the rear. All the downstairs rooms have large windows allowing light to pour in, underfloor heating keeps you cosy, the kitchen is large and the sitting room has

a wood-burner. You have the estate to stroll through, mature trees to admire, and if there is no wedding taking place, the arboretum and garden to wander at will – you can fish in the small pools too. Book a tour around the house if you're a party of 16. A slice of history in a lovely part of the world: borrow a bike to discover all its treasures. *Minimum stay: 2 nights weekend; 4 weekdays. Beautiful arboretum & grounds to explore; other people may be walking dogs & sometimes there are sheep. Mixture of secure & open gardens with cottages; please check.*

Rooms	3 cottages for 4, 1 cottage for 5, 1 cottage for 6: £450-£850 per week. 1 house for 10: £1450-£1750 per week. House: 2-night weekend stay/4-night midweek stay, £825-£925. Short breaks in cottages from £375.
Meals	Pubs/restaurants 15-minute walk.
Closed	Never.
Treats	Treats & water bowls.

The Reception Team
Walcot Hall,
Walcot, Lydbury North, SY7 8AZ

Tel	+44 (0)1588 680570
Email	enquiries@walcothall.com
Web	www.walcothall.com/shropshire-cottages

Walcot Hall

Lose yourself in the grounds of Walcot Hall – play croquet, go fishing, boating, biking, hiking and discover all the quirky treasures. There's the Dipping Shed, with stunning views of the Long Mynd, a rough outer shell and a beautifully decorated interior with a high, beamed ceiling. On a grassy hill, neighbours Buffalo Springfield Yurt with a great, fur-covered bed and Crazy horse Yurt with a big brass bed and sheep skins, share a modern loo in the former hen house and a gas-powered shower in the AA caravan, as well as spectacular views. After The Gold Rush, for the more adventurous, is perched high above two secluded fishermen pools, shares the loo and has a wood-burner, double and sofa bed. Deep in the arboretum and a 500-yard walk from the nearest parking sits The Chapel, a delightful airy bolthole, with subtle modern comforts and an organ you can play; curtains shield two separate beds from the fray. Then there's Green Glory, an authentic showman's caravan, The Wheelwright's Shop, a cavernous workshop cabin adorned with antiques and curiosities and Norbury Hall, a grand cabin, spacious through and through. *Plenty of walking, small pools to swim in, large arboretum to explore; dog-friendly pubs nearby. Sometimes livestock around estate.*

Rooms	2 cabins for 4: from £81. 1 cabin for 6: from £101. 1 wagon for 2: from £45. 2 yurts for 2: from £65. 1 yurt for 4: from £73. Prices per night. Extra space £15 p.p.p.n. Max 2-3 dogs.
Meals	Self-catering.
Closed	Never.
Treats	Walks, lots of space and many dog-loving staff!

Tel	+44 (0)117 204 7830
Email	enquiries@canopyandstars.co.uk
Web	www.canopyandstars.co.uk/walcothall

Canopy & Stars
Walcot Hall,
Walcot, Lydbury North, SY7 8AZ

The Castle Hotel

This thriving medieval market town sits amid some of the loveliest country in the land, a launch pad for walkers and cyclists alike, with Offa's Dyke, Long Mynd and the Kerry Ridgeway all close. After a day in the hills, roll back to this quirky hotel for a night of gentle carousing. You'll find heaps of country comforts: hearty food, impeccable ales, super rooms with honest prices. Downstairs, there's a coal fire in the pretty snug, oak panelling in the breakfast room, and Millie the short-haired dachshund who patrols the corridors with aplomb. Stylish bedrooms upstairs have all been refurbished. Expect good beds, warm colours, flat-screen TVs, an armchair if there's room. Some are up in the eaves, several have views of the Shropshire hills, two have baths in the room. Back downstairs you find the sort of food you'd want after a day in the hills, perhaps hot garlic prawns, beef and ale pie, sticky toffee pudding. Don't miss the hugely popular real ale festival in July, the beer drinker's equivalent of Glastonbury. The garden terrace, with long country views, is a fine spot for a sundowner. *Dogs welcome with you at table for meals in bar; let us know on booking, so we can allocate a dog-friendly table.*

Rooms	9 doubles, 1 twin: £95-£150. 2 family rooms for 4: £130-£155. Singles from £75. Dinner, B&B from £82.50 p.p. Extra beds for children £20.
Meals	Lunch from £4.50. Dinner, 3 courses, about £25.
Closed	Rarely.
Treats	Welcome Box in room including feeding mat, food bowl, towel, lead, treats & poo bags.

Henry & Rebecca Hunter
The Castle Hotel,
Bishops Castle, SY9 5BN

Tel	+44 (0)1588 638403
Email	stay@thecastlehotelbishopscastle.co.uk
Web	www.thecastlehotelbishopscastle.co.uk

The Shippen

An old stone shippen on a remote hillside in an AONB valley, with designer décor, delightful owners, and a glass-and-oak gable for heaven-sent views. No longer a cattle shed, this is one big living, sleeping and eating space with a south-facing decked veranda that gazes on Shropshire's sweet hills. Timbers have been re-used, the slate roof raised, and the stone floor replaced by pristine planks of oak. Not a building in sight, other than Jeannie and Paul's discreet farmhouse... just a sloping grass garden, a mini orchard and masses of wildlife. It's heaven for couples or families (there's a sofabed if you've little ones in tow), and perfect in every season; snuggle up by the the log-burner in winter and barbecue in summer. There's a filter for spring water, Freesat, Netflix, PlayStation, a wet room that takes a wheelchair, and a robot vacuum cleaner (a Sawday's first?!). Stroll the cobbled streets of Bishop's Castle and Shrewsbury, enjoy a local pint by the river, hike to the top of the Long Mynd. Then back to board games by the fire, bright starry skies, and owls that hoot you to sleep. *Minimum stay: 3 nights. Miles of woodland & fields for walking. Shropshire Way is right on doorstep or walk on lanes.*

Rooms	1 cottage for 2: £595-£780 per week.
	Extra bed/sofabed £10 p.p.p.n.
	Max. 2 dogs.
Meals	Pubs/restaurants 2.5 miles.
Closed	Never.
Treats	Biscuits, medium-sized bed, 2 bowls & towels.

Tel	+44 (0)1743 387873
Mobile	+44 (0)7747 115935
Email	jeannie@remote.online
Web	the-shippen.com

Jeannie McGillivray
The Shippen,
Little Wood House, Linley,
Bishop's Castle, SY9 5HP

Pen-y-Dyffryn Country Hotel

In a blissful valley lost to the world, a small country house that sparkles on the side of a peaceful hill. This is one of those lovely places where guests return again and again, mostly due to Audrey and Miles, who run a very happy ship. Outside, fields tumble down to a stream that marks the border with Wales. Daffodils erupt in spring, the lawns are scattered with deckchairs in summer, paths lead into the hills for fine walking. Lovely interiors are just the ticket: Laura Ashley wallpaper and an open fire in the quirky bar; colourful art and super food in the pretty restaurant; the daily papers and the odd chaise longue in the sitting room. Bedrooms hit the spot. Most have the view, one has a French sleigh bed, a couple have jacuzzi baths for two. Four lovely rooms outside are dog-friendly and have their own patios. You get warm colours, crisp linen, pretty fabrics and sparkling bathrooms. After a day in the hills come back for a good dinner, perhaps wild mushroom risotto, pan-fried wood pigeon, hot chocolate fondant with vanilla ice-cream. Offa's Dyke and Powis Castle are close. *Minimum stay: 2 nights at weekends. Secure garden; walking leaflets; 100-acre wood next to hotel. Dogs welcome in public areas until 6pm*

Rooms	8 doubles, 4 twins: £120-£190. Singles £90-£99. Dinner, B&B £99-£136 p.p. Extra bed/sofabed £35 p.p.p.n. Max. 2 dogs.
Meals	Light lunch by arrangement. Dinner £30-£37.
Closed	Rarely.
Treats	Doggy box in bedroom with towels & cloths, dog mat, lead, bowl, treats & poo bags.

Miles & Audrey Hunter
Pen-y-Dyffryn Country Hotel,
Rhydycroesau,
Oswestry, SY10 7JD

Tel	+44 (0)1691 653700
Email	stay@peny.co.uk
Web	www.peny.co.uk

Offa's Dyke Yurt

The two pod set up, spectacular views from the glass doors and complete privacy make Offa's Dyke Yurt a great place for any kind of escape. You can bring the family down and watch the kids play in your personal play park, or go it alone and lounge in the spacious yurt camp. The main living area is beautifully decorated with rich, glowing woods and soft fabrics and the big double bed is housed in a separate, but adjoined mini yurt, giving extra space and privacy. On the same soaring deck are your own gas-powered shower, flushing loo and the wood-store. There's also some outdoor furniture, the centrepiece of which, a big wooden chaise longue, is perfect for napping in front of the views of the rolling hills. As the name suggests, the yurt is rather well placed for the Offa's Dyke Path, with some hearty hiking to be done for about 180 miles in both directions and miles of world class mountain biking trails all around. You can also do courses in everything from fruit tree grafting to bench making and woodwork. Jo and Wilf are happy to take you badger spotting in an adjoining field after the chickens have settled. *Keep dogs under control as sheep may be in next field. River & plenty of walks. Own garden but dogs could get out; they can be secured with little trouble.*

Rooms	Yurt for 4 (+2 children): from £99 per night. Max. 2 dogs – please bring your own bedding and keep them off the furniture.
Meals	Self-catering.
Closed	Never.
Treats	Advice on walks.

Tel	+44 (0)117 204 7830
Email	enquiries@canopyandstars.co.uk
Web	www.canopyandstars.co.uk/offasdyke

Canopy & Stars
Offa's Dyke Yurt,
The Barn, Fron Uchaf,
Weston Rhyn, SY10 7NQ

North West

Another Place – The Lake, page 194

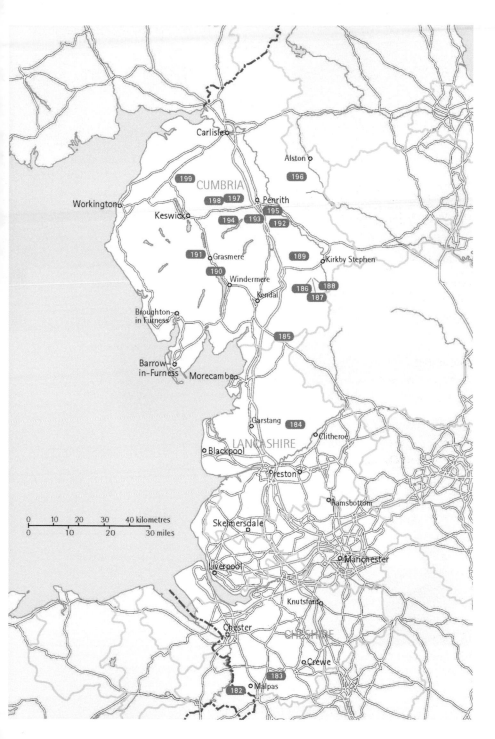

Mulsford Cottage

Delicious! Not just the food (Kate's a pro chef) but the sweet whitewashed cottage with its sunny conservatory and vintage interiors, and the green Cheshire countryside that bubble-wraps the place in rural peace. Chat – and laugh – the evening away over Kate's superb dinners, lounge by the fire, then sleep deeply in comfy bedrooms: cane beds, a bright red chair, a vintage desk. The double has a roll top bath, the twin a tiny shower-with-a-view. Wake for local bacon, sausages and honey and just-laid bantam eggs. Walk the 34-mile Sandstone Trail to Shropshire; Wales starts just past the hammock, at the bottom of the bird-filled garden. *Log fire to doze by. Large fenced garden, dense woodland, rivers to splash in & hours of fun chasing rabbits, but watch out for sheep.*

Rooms	1 double: £90. 1 family room for 3: £90-£115. Singles £65. Dogs £8 per night. Max. 2.
Meals	Dinner from £18. Pub 1.5 miles.
Closed	Rarely.
Treats	Bowls & towels for drying off.

Kate Dewhurst
Mulsford Cottage,
Mulsford, Sarn,
Malpas, SY14 7LP

Tel	+44 (0)1948 770414
Email	katedewhurst4@gmail.com
Web	www.mulsford-cottage.co.uk

The Cholmondeley Arms

As prim and proper as a Victorian schoolmistress on the outside, as stylish as Beau Brummell within: the sandblasted brick walls of this old school house rise to raftered, vaulted ceilings and large windows pull natural light into every corner. Shelves of gin hover above fat radiators, cartoons and photos nestle amongst old sporting paraphernalia, and oriental rugs sprawl beneath an auction lot of tables, pews and chairs. The glorious carved oak bar dominates the main hall and apart from the malted charms of Cholmondeley Best Bitter and other local cask ales, there are a staggering 366 varieties of ruinously good gin to discover, with the aid of a well-thumbed guide or one of the many charming staff. And when the dinner bell goes study the menus on antique blackboards or opt for sharing the amazing seafood trawler board followed by their legendary steak and kidney pie. Rooms in the old headmaster's house behind are calm and civilised with all the comfort you need. Seldom has going back to school been this much fun. *Land where a dog can exercise chasing a ball. Many walks nearby: the Sandstone Trail, Cholmondeley Castle Gardens, Beeston Castle.*

Rooms	5 doubles, 1 twin: £60-£110.
	Dogs £10 per stay. Max. 2 per room.
Meals	Lunch & dinner £7.25-£17.95.
	Sunday lunch £14.50.
Closed	Rarely.
Treats	Biscuits on bar, water bowls & Doggie Beer.
	Dog basket for dogs staying in rooms.

Tel	+44 (0)1829 720300
Email	info@cholmondeleyarms.co.uk
Web	www.cholmondeleyarms.co.uk

The Reception Team
The Cholmondeley Arms,
Wrenbury Road, Cholmondeley,
Malpas, SY14 8HN

The Inn at Whitewell

It is almost impossible to imagine a day when a better inn will grace the English landscape. Everything here is perfect. The inn sits just above the river Hodder, and doors in the bar lead onto a terrace where guests can enjoy five-mile views across parkland to rising fells. Inside, fires roar, newspapers wait, there are beams, sofas, maps and copies of Wisden. Bedrooms, some in the Coach House, are exemplary and come with real luxury, perhaps a peat fire, a lavish four-poster, a fabulous Victorian power shower. All have beautiful fabrics, top linen and gadgets galore; many have the marvellous view – you can fall asleep to the sound of the river. There are bar meals for those who want to watch their weight (the Whitewell fish pie is rightly

famous) or a restaurant for splendid food, so dig into seared scallops, Bowland lamb, a plate of local cheese (the Queen once popped in for lunch). Elsewhere, a wine shop in reception, seven miles of private fishing and countryside as good as any in the land. Magnificent. *River Hodder runs adjacent to inn & is a favourite for walkers, and their dogs of course! Dogs welcome throughout inn except main dining room.*

Rooms	17 doubles, 5 twin/doubles: £137-£270. 1 suite for 2: £235-£270. Singles £99-£218.
Meals	Bar meals from £8. Dinner £25-£35.
Closed	Never.
Treats	Beds, bowls & towels upon request.

Charles Bowman
The Inn at Whitewell,
Dunsop Road,
Whitewell, BB7 3AT

Tel	+44 (0)1200 448222
Email	reception@innatwhitewell.com
Web	www.innatwhitewell.com

The Sun Inn

This fine old inn sits between the Dales and the Lakes in an ancient market town, one of the prettiest in the north. It backs onto a churchyard, where wild flowers flourish, and on the far side you'll find 'the fairest view in England' to quote John Ruskin. Herons fish the river, lambs graze the fells, a vast sky hangs above. Turner came to paint it in 1825 and benches wait for those who want to linger. As for the Sun, it does what all good inns do, looks after you in style. It dates to 1670 and started life as a butcher's. Inside, there's lots of pretty old stuff – stone walls, rosewood panelling, wood-burners working overtime – then warm colours, fresh flowers and the daily papers. You'll find leather banquettes, local art and dining-room chairs from Cunard's Mauretania, so eat in style, perhaps goat's cheese with honey, hogget with onion jam, banana parfait with chocolate sorbet. Rooms have good beds, smart fabrics, robes in spotless bathrooms. Parking permits come with your room and can be used far and wide. Market day is Thursday, don't miss Sunday lunch. *Minimum stay: 2 nights on weekends. Dog-friendly area in restaurant. Kirkby Lonsdale is very dog-friendly. Easy walks to river Lune, Devil's Bridge, Casterton, Barbon. Homemade dog treats for sale.*

Rooms	9 doubles, 2 twin/doubles: £135-£189. Dinner, B&B from £90 p.p. Singles from £85. Extra beds £20. Dogs £20 per stay.
Meals	Lunch from £6. Dinner, £21-£34. Sunday lunch from £14.50. No food Mon lunch.
Closed	Never.
Treats	Bowl, mat, biscuits, towel & local walking map. Bowls & biscuits in bar. Dog shower outside.

Tel	+44 (0)15242 71965
Email	email@sun-inn.info
Web	www.sun-inn.info

Iain & Jenny Black
The Sun Inn,
6 Market Street,
Kirkby Lonsdale, LA6 2AU

The Farmhouse at A Corner of Eden

A lovely Georgian farmhouse, set in a glorious valley with infinite sky and distant Cumbrian hills. The wood, the stone, the honesty of the structure create an enveloping, peaceful retreat. Layered on to this lovely house is deep comfort and more than a touch of luxury. The hunting lodge-style sitting room has a log fire, antlers, woollen sofas and the beautiful beamed dining room has seating for a small crowd. Bedrooms sport original fireplaces, and have polished wooden floors, gorgeous wallpapers and spoiling fabrics. Both bathrooms are super stylish. Richard and Debbie are the loveliest hosts – they live in an adjacent barn and have thought of everything, generously leaving fluffy robes, thick towels, Barbours and wellies to borrow, an

honesty bar in the dairy and a welcome basket bursting with local goodies and champagne. The large range cooker will excite keen cooks and the not so keen can easily find their way to the pub across the fields or ask Debbie to arrange for caterers. Simply heaven. Take Angel Barn and Shepherd's Cottage, too, and come with friends. *Minimum stay: 3 nights at weekends. Walled garden, paths from door, river & woods nearby, open access land (sheep). Maps with walks highlighted. 3 local pubs allow dogs in bar area when eating.*

Rooms	1 cottage for 8: £995-£1495 per week. £750-£945 for a 3-night weekend or 4-night mid-week stay. Dogs welcome downstairs, £20 per dog per stay.
Meals	Pub 1 mile.
Closed	Never.
Treats	Welcome biscuit, water bowl & spare towels.

Debbie & Richard Greaves
The Farmhouse at A Corner of Eden,
Low Stennerskeugh, Ravenstonedale,
Kirkby Stephen, CA17 4LL

Tel	+44 (0)1539 623370
Mobile	+44 (0)7759 469059
Email	enquiries@acornerofeden.co.uk
Web	www.acornerofeden.co.uk

Shepherd's Cottage

A heavenly hideaway for couples in a glorious corner of the world, coddled between the Lakes and the Dales. You approach through a charming walled garden, then straight into the kitchen with its flagged floor, red Aga, lovely beams and glorious view. Snuggle by the wood-burner (logs on the house) in the beamed sitting room with your very generous welcome basket: champagne, locally made chocolates, homemade bread and cake, all you need for breakfast, and a mini honesty bar with beers, wines and spirits. Upstairs to your oak beamed bedroom and bathroom: the handmade king-size bed is spoiling (with choice of pillows), so is the bathroom with ruby red roll top, thick white towels, robes and large shower. Debbie's creative flair makes the whole place sparkle, and outside you get another red roll top, front and back gardens to follow the sunshine. Walk across fields to the pub for supper, head back for a cosy night in. Great for couples who want privacy, but you can also take other properties – The Shepherd's Cottage and The Farmhouse are attached, Angel Barn and helpful owners are nearby. *Walled garden, paths from door, river & woods nearby; open access land (sheep). Maps with walks highlighted. Three local pubs allow dogs in bar when eating.*

Rooms	1 cottage for 2: £825-£1050 per week. 3-night weekend or 4-night mid-week break, £495-£595. Children under 10 in 'Little Room' £25. Dogs welcome downstairs; £20 per dog per stay.
Meals	Self-catering.
Closed	Never.
Treats	Welcome biscuit, water bowl & spare towels.

Tel	+44 (0)1539 623370
Mobile	+44 (0)7759 469059
Email	enquiries@acornerofeden.co.uk
Web	www.acornerofeden.co.uk/shepherds-cottage

Debbie & Richard Greaves
Shepherd's Cottage,
Low Stennerskeugh, Ravestonedale,
Kirkby Stephen, CA17 4LL

The Burton

Selina's gorgeous showman's wagon dates back to 1940 and was originally pulled by four horses. These days it sits behind the farmhouse with views up Clouds Fell and a fire pit in the garden for starry nights. It's a brilliant feat of interior engineering with a Nordic, chalet feel. You get everything you need wrapped up in oodles of rustic chic: rugs on wood floors, chairs at a pretty table and a wood-burner to keep you cosy. Find books and flowers too, and a welcoming tipple waiting for you. A sweet little kitchen bar comes with a microwave and a hob, and a tiny shower room does the trick in style. The bed is fabulous: lovely linen, a good mattress and drawers below. There's a decked terrace at the front, then a drying room, a

fridge/freezer and piles of logs in the shed behind, home to the boiler that assures hot showers. Selina is happy to take delivery of supplies before you arrive, but she also manages a lovely local inn, so a slap-up meal is on hand if you don't want to cook. Great walking to be had straight from the door; return to your romantic space, get yourself a cup of tea and be glad you're here. *Surrounded by livestock so advise dogs on leads, but many different walks all within a 4-mile radius: woodland, riverside and fells.*

Rooms	Wagon for 2: from £95 per night. Dogs £10 per dog per stay. Max. 1.
Meals	Self-catering.
Closed	Never.
Treats	Wonderful walks from door onto the Cumbrian fells.

Canopy & Stars
The Burton,
Stennerskeugh, Ravenstonedale,
Kirkby Stephen, CA17 4LL

Tel	+44 (0)117 204 7830
Email	enquiries@canopyandstars.co.uk
Web	www.canopyandstars.co.uk/theburton

Brownber Hall

Peter and Amanda, London escapees keen on cycling and walking, have stylishly restored this big old house, adding contemporary touches and all the comforts. The atmosphere is relaxed and sociable, there's an honesty bar with local craft beers and excellent wines, plenty of space to chill, and heaps of bedrooms with deeply comfortable beds to choose from. The rooms at the front have the views. Breakfast tables have white cloths and wild flower posies; wake to homemade granola, sausages, bacon, sourdough toast and great coffee. Join the Coast to Coast path by foot or bike, hop on the wonderfully scenic Settle to Carlisle railway. *Lots of glorious walks from door. 2 dog-friendly rooms, 1 downstairs.*

Rooms	4 doubles, 2 twin/doubles: £90-£130. 1 suite for 2: £130-£180. 1 single: £60-£70. Cot £10. Extra bed £15 per night breakfast included. Dogs £5.
Meals	Dinner for walkers available by arrangement. Pub/restaurants 5 miles.
Closed	Christmas.
Treats	Water bowls & towels for muddy dogs.

Tel	+44 (0)1539 623208
Mobile	+44 (0)7412 504765
Email	peter@brownberhall.co.uk
Web	www.brownberhall.co.uk

Peter & Amanda
Brownber Hall,
Newbiggin-on-Lune,
Kirkby Stephen, CA17 4NX

Rothay Manor Hotel

This tranquil 1820s country house has retained much of its original character, and is surrounded by mature gardens with no immediate neighbours so feels private. Jamie and Jenna run the place along with their team of friendly staff, and always try to greet each guest personally. Bedrooms are comfortable and generous in size, and all include seating areas – one room has a hot tub. This is the kind of place where dogs aren't just tolerated but welcomed, and there are several dog-friendly rooms with wooden floors and private garden areas. Settle next to a roaring fire in the lounge with a good book and a drink from the bar, head to the Brathay Lounge for a light lunch or casual dinner, or treat yourself to a lavish

afternoon tea or a tasting menu in the restaurant, perhaps ham hock terrine, venison cottage pie followed by sticky toffee pudding or a selection of cheeses. Ambleside is a 10-minute walk for a wide selection of shops, restaurants and art galleries, and Lake Windermere is just a short stroll further. *Minimum stay: 2 nights at weekends. Eight rooms dog-friendly, all with external access or small enclosed courtyard. Gardens & masses of walks from the door; lake swims.*

Rooms	16 twin/doubles: £155-£375. 2 suites: £260-£350. 1 single: £155. Dogs £20 per dog per stay. Max. 2.
Meals	Dinner, 2 courses, £49; 3 courses, £55. Tasting menu, 5 courses £65. Afternoon tea £21.50.
Closed	Rarely.
Treats	Advice on walks.

The Reception Team
Rothay Manor Hotel,
Rothay Bridge,
Ambleside LA22 0EH

Tel	+44 (0)1539 433605
Email	hotel@rothaymanor.co.uk
Web	www.rothaymanor.co.uk

Lancrigg

There's nothing stuffy about this rambling old house on a hillside bang in the middle of the Lake District. A friendly informality pervades the place, so everyone will feel completely at home, from families with young ones to lone walkers. You can drink and snack in the cosy and stylish Poet's Bar, once the old library, or get down to more serious eating in the dining room. This is where the hotel's chef creates imaginative feasts, inspired by vintage recipes, using the very best of local, seasonal ingredients. Simon and his friendly staff look after you well. While the kids run wild in the woodland playground, relax in the sitting room by the fire, drink in those outstanding views, and tell yourself you're going to go for a bracing walk soon. Wordsworth found this house an inspiring place to stay, and so will you. *Minimum stay: 2 nights at weekends. Lancrigg is set within the fells so there's a bounty of great walks. Owners should be aware that red squirrels, deer & fell sheep are in the grounds.*

Rooms	5 doubles, 3 twins, 2 family rooms for 4: £79-£220. Extra beds £30-£45 p.p.p.n. Dogs £15 per dog per night.
Meals	Breakfast £8-£12. Lunch from £12.95. Dinner à la carte, 4 courses, £39.95.
Closed	15 January to early February.
Treats	Basket, towel & a pouch with treats.

Tel	+44 (0)1539 435317
Email	info@lancrigg.co.uk
Web	www.lancrigg.co.uk

Alison Drury
Lancrigg,
Easedale Road,
Grasmere, LA22 9QN

Steele's Mill

There's been a working grain mill here since 1327; this one was built in the 1800s. Fragments of the past remain: staircases and floors of oak grown on the estate, grinding stones set into the floor, and the old apple-wood cogs encased in glass. There's a lovely approach to this stunning conversion, a hugely comfortable retreat for four, with the master bedroom positioned grandly at the top, and below the tiny twin. Cook just-caught brown trout from the river Lyvennet on a shiny black Rangemaster, dine at a handmade oak table furnished with welcoming flowers and a bottle of wine, lounge on a leather sofa by the gas wood-burner, idle with a book on the balcony. By day, venture out on the snaking road past fields of cattle to

King's Meaburn village, to Appleby for delis, pubs and a country fair in summer, to Lowther Castle for those seeking gothic revival grandeur. Nature is embraced indoors, too: the mill has a hidden bat loft with an aperture only accessible to the pipistrelle! Colours are cream and duck-egg blue melting into pale oak, mattresses are superb, shower heads drench you and the peace is supreme. *Minimum stay: 3 nights; 7 in high season. Secure garden, woodland walks & safe rivers.*

Rooms	1 house for 4 : £600-£920 per week. Dogs 1 free; 2nd £30 per stay. Max. 3.
Meals	Self-catering.
Closed	Never.
Treats	Advice on walks.

Karen Addison
Steele's Mill,
King's Meaburn, Penrith, CA10 3BU

Tel	+44 (0)1931 714017
Mobile	+44 (0)7831 865749
Email	karenaddison@karenaddison.co.uk
Web	www.steelesmill.co.uk

Askham Hall

Askham is a dream, one of the loveliest houses in the Lakes. It's a Grade I-listed manor house with a 12th-century peel tower, but grand as it is, Charlie grew up here and it retrains the feel of home, making it a delightfully informal base. Expect contemporary art and open fires, a beautiful drawing room with an honesty bar, a small spa with an outdoor pool, then a café for lunch and gardens that open to the public. The hall sits in 40 acres of prime Cumbrian grazing land with paths that follow a river into glorious parkland. It's all part of the Lowther estate, where Charlie rears his own meat for Richard Swale's kitchen. As for the food, it's out of this world, ambrosial stuff that makes you want to move in permanently. You might find Askham pork cheek and barbecued hock, rough fell lamb with wild garlic risotto, Yorkshire rhubarb tart with brown butter ice cream; a kitchen garden and two polytunnels provide much for the table. Chic bedrooms have a cool country-house style (Prince Philip loved his). Some are vast, one has a tented bathroom, others have views to Knipe Scar. One of the best. *Dogs welcome in most areas, but not main restaurant. Fields, woods & river walks. Riverside loop & pool for dips; short walk to Askham Fell.*

Rooms	11 twin/doubles: £150-£260. 4 suites for 2: £250-£320. Extra bed/sofabed £35 p.p.p.n. Dogs £15 per stay. Max. 3.
Meals	Lunch from £9. Dinner, 3 courses, £50. 5-course tasting menu £65.
Closed	Sun & Mon. Jan & early Feb.
Treats	Welcome basket with treat, map of local walks & doggy bag.
Tel	+44 (0)1931 712350
Email	enquiries@askhamhall.co.uk
Web	www.askhamhall.co.uk

Charlie Lowther
Askham Hall,
Askham, CA10 2PF

Another Place – The Lake

This is a fantastic contemporary renovation of a Lakeland country house hotel. It sits on Ullswater in 18 beautiful acres that roll down to the lake shore. Both hotel and water offer lots to do. You can paddle board on the lake, jump in for a swim, or set off to explore in a kayak. If that sounds too energetic, head back to the hotel for sofas to sink into and an indoor 20-metre pool where walls of glass frame the view and adults reign after 6pm. The main building dates to 1714 and comes with ornate ceilings, marble fireplaces, the odd panelled wall. You'll find an airy restaurant for super food, then sofas and banquettes in The Living Space, a child-friendly place to stop and eat, play games by the fire in the library, or slip onto the sun-trapping terrace where views shoot across the lake to mountains soaring beyond. There's a gym, a hot tub, a sauna and treatment rooms, and forest school for kids. Rooms have fine beds, the best linen, robes in smart bathrooms. Most have the view, some have baths that look the right way. There's a kitchen garden, a croquet lawn, and wellies at the front door, too. *Lake District National Park & Ullswater are at bottom of grounds. You can eat with your dog in The Living Space. Certain bedrooms are dog-friendly.*

Rooms	28 twin/doubles: £170-£205. 6 suites for 2, 6 suites for 5: £285-£385. Singles from £120. Extra bed from £40. Dogs £15 per night; £5 for second dog. Max. 2.
Meals	Lunch from £7. Dinner, 3 courses, £40.
Closed	Never.
Treats	Acres of tracks & trails to explore.

Alison Mathewson
Another Place – The Lake,
Watermillock, Penrith, CA11 0LP

Tel   +44 (0)1768 486442
Email life@another.place
Web   www.another.place/the-lake

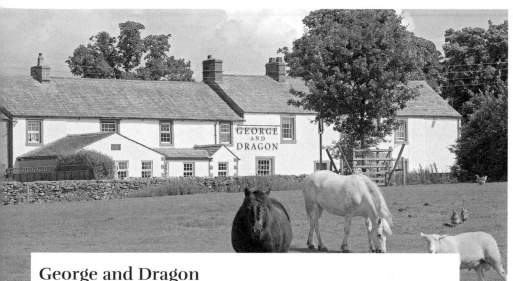

George and Dragon

Charlie Lowther has found a new head chef, award-winning Gareth Webster, who does perfect justice to the slow-grow breeds of beef, pork and lamb produced on the Lowther Estate – and you'll find lovely wines to match. Ales and cheeses are local, berries and mushrooms are foraged, vegetables are home-grown. Our twice-baked cheese soufflé with a hint of spinach was divine. As for the long low coaching inn, it's been beautifully restored by craftsmen using wood, slate and stone, and painted in colours in tune with the period. Bare wooden tables, comfy sofas, intimate alcoves and crackling fires make this a delightful place to dine and unwind; old prints and archive images tell stories of the 800-year-old estate's history. Outside is plenty of seating and a lawned play area beneath fruit trees. Upstairs are 11 bedrooms of varying sizes (some small, some large and some above the bar), perfectly decorated in classic country style. Carpeting is Cumbrian wool, beds are new, ornaments come with Lowther history, showers are walk-in, baths (there are two) are roll top, and breakfast is fresh and delicious. *Dogs welcome in the bar dining area but not main restaurant. Woodland & riverside walks nearby; walks up Askham Fell.*

Rooms	11 twin/doubles: £100-£160. Singles £85-£119. Extra bed/sofabed £25 p.p.p.n. Dogs £10 per stay. Max. 3.
Meals	Lunch & dinner from £12. Sunday lunch from £12.95.
Closed	26 December.
Treats	Welcome pack with treat, map of local walks & a doggy bag.

Tel	+44 (0)1768 865381
Email	enquiries@georgeanddragonclifton.co.uk
Web	www.georgeanddragonclifton.co.uk

Charlie Lowther
George and Dragon,
Clifton, Penrith, CA10 2ER

Edenhall

A grand estate on the doorstep of the Lake District with two secluded hideaways. Located on a private stretch of the river Eamont, The Lodge is frontier living at its finest. Find comfy armchairs around a wood-burner and sliding doors that open to a veranda and summer breezes. You can catch trout for your supper, cook it up on the four-hob gas stove, then relax in the hot tub. The Bothy at High Barn sits on a hill of Eden Hall Estate, affording it incredible views. The space has a hip but homely feel, with art prints and eclectic furniture, including a huge hand-carved bed, all set off by a floor reclaimed from a sports hall. Choose between heading to the firepit for toasted marshmallows or jumping into the hot tub. Sandwiched right

between the Pennines – an Area of Outstanding Natural Beauty – and The Lake District, Edenhall is your drop-off to hiking, biking and all sorts of adventure. You can take the Ullswater steamers, drop in to the Lakes Distillery or The Shepherd's Inn makes for a great start or end point for hikes in the Eden Valley and only a couple of miles' walk away. *Very secluded area with no traffic. Lots of walks from door & further afield: great yomping territory for you & your dog.*

Rooms	Cabin for 6: from £270 per night. Bothy for 2 from £165 per night. No charge for 1 dog, £30 per dog per stay for 2+.
Meals	Self-catering.
Closed	Never.
Treats	Two doggie bowls and dog treats.

Canopy & Stars
Edenhall,
Penrith, CA11 8ST

Tel	+44 (0)117 204 7830
Email	enquiries@canopyandstars.co.uk
Web	www.canopyandstars.co.uk/edenhall

Johnby Hall

You are ensconced in the quieter part of the Lakes and have independence in this Elizabethan manor. Once a fortified Pele tower, it's a fascinating historic house yet very much a lived-in family home with a wonderful atmosphere. The airy bedrooms have a sitting room each with books, children's videos and squashy sofas. Beds have patchwork quilts, windows have stone mullions and all is peaceful. Henry gives you sturdy breakfasts in the great hall: sausages and bacon from the free-range pigs, eggs from the hens and jams from the orchard. Children will have fun – animals to feed, garden toys galore and woods to roam – and dogs are very welcome too. *Please keep dogs who aren't trustworthy with chickens under control in the garden; sheep fields nearby too.*

Rooms	1 twin/double: £135. 1 family room: £135-£165. Singles £95. Extra bed/sofabed £20 per person per night. Extra child £15. Under-5s free.
Meals	Supper, 2 courses, £22.50. Pub 1 mile.
Closed	Rarely.
Treats	Acres of garden & woodland sniffs; one room has an enclosed garden that's dog-proof for most breeds!

Tel	+44 (0)1768 483257
Email	bookings@johnbyhall.com
Web	www.johnbyhall.co.uk

Henry & Anna Howard
Johnby Hall,
Johnby, Penrith, CA11 0UU

Scales Plantation

High in the wilds of the North Lakes, in the woods around Scales Farm, Tabitha and Rob Wilson have created a selection of fabulous boltholes. Three shepherd's hut camps with timber kitchens are set in semicircular clearings on the edge of the forest; there's the Herdwick bell tent and cabin camp too. The sites are sheltered and peaceful, with views out towards Bowscale Fell and Mount Skiddaw. As part of the regeneration of the woodland, the once thick canopy has been thinned to allow wildlife such as the resident red squirrels to flourish. The camps have already come to feel like natural extensions of the Lake District, with beautiful walks across the fells on your doorstep. You can get trail advice or hire bikes just

down the road and head into the hills, then come back to the rustic comfort of the hut and your toasty woodburner. Groceries can even be supplied by your hosts: simply choose from the list of supplies in advance and they'll be waiting on your arrival. *The whole of the Lake District on the doorstep for dogs to drag their owners around! Keep dogs on leads when sheep are about.*

Rooms	3 shepherd's huts for 4: from £75. Camp for 4: from £95. Prices per night. Max. 2 dogs; speak to owner.
Meals	Self-catering.
Closed	Never.
Treats	Advice on walks and dog-friendly activities. Local pubs are dog-friendly.

Canopy & Stars
Scales Plantation,
Scales Farm, Berrier,
Penrith, CA11 0XE

Tel	+44 (0)117 204 7830
Email	enquiries@canopyandstars.co.uk
Web	www.canopyandstars.co.uk/scalesplantation

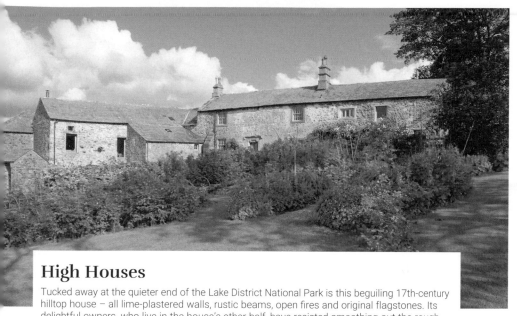

High Houses

Tucked away at the quieter end of the Lake District National Park is this beguiling 17th-century hilltop house – all lime-plastered walls, rustic beams, open fires and original flagstones. Its delightful owners, who live in the house's other half, have resisted smoothing out the rough edges; 1920s graffiti still adorns the stable dividers. The hardships of country living have, however, been banished: find lovely new pink and soft-green 'pineapple' covers on sitting room chairs, delicious bed linen and towels, hand-made soaps and piping hot radiators. Bedrooms may prompt some tough decisions – do you choose the room with the roll top bath (semi en suite) and the cockloft for kids, or the four-poster with the sofabed and the log fire? The farmhouse kitchen is cosy with Aga, big fridge and gadgets aplenty, but reluctant cooks can book Jill's homemade meals in advance. Beautiful views reach out from every fine sash window to wildlife-rich farmland beyond – 350 private acres, yours to explore. Venture further and you reach the Lakes and the Solway Plain. Heaven for sybarites and walkers. *Great place for walking with your dog: totally surrounded by fields, bridlepath behind house & no traffic.*

Rooms	1 house for 6: £700-£900 per week. 3-night stay at weekends in low season only, £550. 4-night stay on weekdays, £550. Max. 3 dogs.
Meals	Self-catering.
Closed	Never.
Treats	Water bowl & perfect walks from door.

Tel	+44 (0)1697 371549
Mobile	+44 (0)7929 397273
Email	enquiries@highhouses.co.uk
Web	www.highhouses.co.uk

Jill Green
High Houses,
Snittlegarth, Ireby,
Wigton, CA7 1HE

Yorkshire

The Traddock, page 205

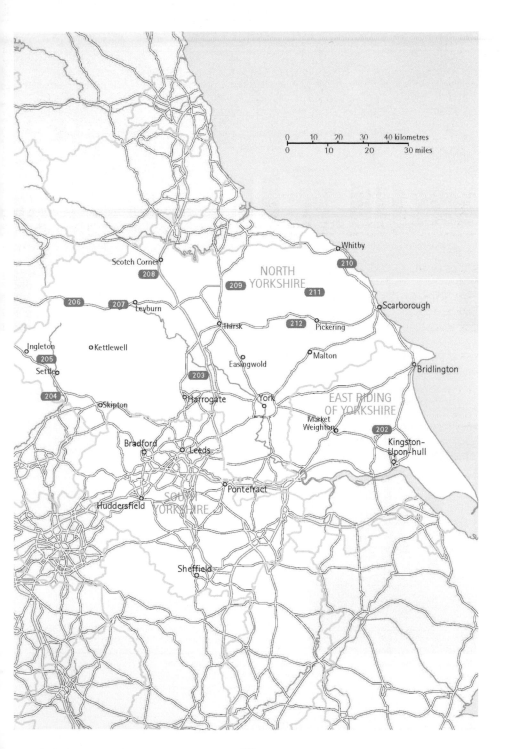

Tickton Grange

This fine Georgian manor house surrounded by four acres of formal gardens, parklands and fields was once the home of wealthy landowners – King Edward VIII used to play cards here – and is now a family-run hotel. Feel pampered by meticulous attention to detail: dinner that looks like a work of art served on specially commissioned and hand-painted Royal Crown Derby china; drinks afterwards in the stylish library; dressing gowns, slippers and eye masks in your room, plus handmade truffles on your pillow. Start the day with breakfast – scrambled eggs and local-cured salmon, croissants, freshly squeezed juices and specially blended coffee. Visit Beverley or Hull, join the Hockney trail, return for afternoon tea that could put the Ritz to shame – dainty cakes and scones with champagne or a G&T – the bar has 45 varieties. *Garden; 12 acres of fields; woodland. Dogs welcome off lead, but area not fully fenced. Yorkshire Wolds nearby; Hornsea beach 10 miles; Beverley Westwood, common land, 4 miles (freely grazing cattle).*

Rooms	17 doubles, 1 twin/double, 1 twin: £120-£150. 2 suites for 2: £150. Dogs £15 per night. Max. 2 per room. 4 dog-friendly rooms in The Granary.
Meals	Lunch from £9.95. Dinner, 2-3 courses, £32.50-£39.50.
Closed	Never.
Treats	Bowls, treats, cosy beds and Bert, a field spaniel, is always looking for a friend to play with.

The Reservations Team		**Tel**	+44 (0)1964 543666
Tickton Grange,		**Email**	info@ticktongrange.co.uk
Main Street,		**Web**	www.ticktongrange.co.uk
Tickton, HU17 9SH			

Lodge Cottages

Two sweet escapes for two. One is tucked next to Rick and Sue's house in a quiet village, with charming roses-and-hollyhocks exterior; inside it's romantic with low beams and sheepskin rugs. Step straight into the low-beamed sitting room (tall folk beware) with soft colours, bright gingham armchair and cream wood-burner. There's a smart kitchen, a table-for-two and upstairs a dove-grey bedroom with soft rugs on painted floorboards. The other is a little loft conversion at the bottom of the garden. A secret path lined with espaliered apple trees and tubs of flowers takes you to a dinky private courtyard. Walk through a glass door into a contemporary space: an open plan dining area and kitchen with upcycled furniture, pretty porcelain plates and a soft grey colour scheme enlivened with zingy limes and pinks. Vases burst with fresh flowers and skylights let in the light. Upstairs to your cosy double and funky bathroom. Rick is a chef and it shows: for lazy suppers he can prepare meals to re-heat or you can slip next door to the pub. Ripon Cathedral and Harrogate are nearby or take bracing walks on the North York Moors. *Plenty of wonderful walks locally & very dog-friendly pub next door.*

Rooms	2 cottages for 2: £450-£600 per week. Short breaks available. Pet fees may apply.
Meals	Dinner, 3 courses, £25.
Closed	Never.
Treats	Advice on walks & a lovely nature reserve just 2 minutes away

Tel	+44 (0)1423 340700
Email	info@lodgecottages.co.uk
Web	www.lodgecottages.co.uk

Sue & Rick Hodgson
Lodge Cottages,
1 Lodge Cottage,
Main Street, Staveley

Gamekeepers Cottage & Cross Cottage

Gorgeous countryside in this neck of the woods, rolling and lush, with a posse of sheep round every corner. The house, cottages and six acres of orchard and paddock stand on their own, with heart-stopping views. Warm smiling Louise lives in the main house, keeps hens, ducks and geese and is passionate about North Yorkshire. Two stunning cottages – one new, though you'd never know it – with rug-cosy, stone-flagged sitting rooms and kitchens to love. The style is an enticing mix of modern and vintage: smartly upholstered wing chairs, a squishy old chesterfield, a fine pine cupboard. Gamekeepers Cottage has two bedrooms downstairs and a master up top. We loved the ground-floor double bedroom, calming and

cosy, but the top suite is a wow, with three separate spaces and a French-style bed. Cross Cottage has two charming ground-floor bedrooms. Snuggle up by the wood-burner for a cosy night in; in summer, drift onto the patio with furniture, barbecue and views. As for pubs, you're spoilt: the Coach & Horses at Bolton by Bowland, the legendary Inn at Whitewell, the Spread Eagle at Sawley, down the road. *Minimum stay: 2 nights on weekdays; 7 in high season. Secure garden and dog-specific walks; livestock at property so dogs on leads.*

Rooms	1 cottage for 4, 1 cottage for 6: £399-£1199 per week. Short breaks available October-March from £199. Dogs £30 per stay. Max. 2.
Meals	Self-catering.
Closed	Rarely.
Treats	Blankets, throws, treats & bowls. Dog tags with our phone number; hose for cleaning muddy paws & towels for drying off.

Louise & Stephen McAneny
Gamekeepers Cottage & Cross Cottage,
Wigglesworth House, Becks Brow,
Wigglesworth, BD23 4SA

Tel	+44 (0)1729 840168
Email	info@wigglesworthhouseandcottages.co.uk
Web	www.wigglesworthhouseandcottages.co.uk

The Traddock

A northern outpost of country-house charm, beautiful inside and out. It's a family affair and those looking for a friendly base from which to explore the Dales will find it here. You enter through the drawing room – crackling fire, pretty art, the daily papers, cavernous sofas. Potter about and find polished wood in the dining room, panelled walls in the breakfast room, then William Morris wallpaper in the sitting room bar, where you can sip a pint of Skipton ale while playing Scrabble. Bedrooms are gorgeous, some coolly contemporary, others warmly traditional. The stars of the show are the new suites – sand-blasted timbers, lovely big sofas, stunning free-standing baths – but all are charming, with chic fabrics, warm colours, comfy beds and the odd claw-foot bath. Downstairs, a white-washed sitting room opens onto the garden for afternoon tea, while delicious food waits in the restaurant, perhaps seafood chowder, braised lamb shank, apple and calvados mousse. Walks start at the front door, there are cycle tracks, even caves to explore (one is bigger than St Paul's). Unbeatable. *Minimum stay: 2 nights at weekends March-November. Walks from door in Yorkshire Dales National Park.*

Rooms	8 doubles, 1 twin/double: £95-£165. 2 family rooms for 4: £95-£175. 2 suites for 2: £180-£235. Extra bed £25 p.p.p.n. Dogs £5. Max. 1-2 per room.
Meals	Lunch from £9.50. Dinner, 3 courses, £30. Picnics from £7.50. Afternoon tea from £15.95.
Closed	Never.
Treats	Towels & advice on walks.

Tel	+44 (0)1524 251224
Email	info@thetraddock.co.uk
Web	www.thetraddock.co.uk

Paul Reynolds
The Traddock,
Austwick, Settle, LA2 8BY

Mill Fosse Cottage

Follow the babbling Mill Race to a quiet corner of Hawes to find this beautifully converted piece of Wensleydale history. The old Mill Fosse Cottage, with its blend of quirky touches, thick stone walls, flagged floors and exposed beams, is a snug, stylish retreat. Within a couple of minutes, you're in the heart of Hawes. Visit the Wensleydale Creamery and Museum, browse the antique shops or have a lazy lunch by the river. The Dales are ready to be explored, or you can take the short walk to Hardraw Falls and the pub next door. Two people can spread out a bit here. Cook in the sociable kitchen (there are stools for chatterers), eat in the dining hall then relax in the upstairs sitting room in front of the wood-burner.

Minimum stay: 3 nights at weekends & in high season; 4 on weekdays. No garden but plenty of walks from the cottage and access to the Pennine Way. Great sniffs and streams to splash in. Dogs will love it – just watch out for sheep in fields.

Rooms	1 cottage for 2: £600-£800 per week. Dogs £15. Max 2.
Meals	Self-catering.
Closed	Never.
Treats	Towels, poo bags, bowl & biscuits.

Aisling Anderson
Mill Fosse Cottage,
Chapel Street, Hawes, DL8 3QG

Mobile	+44 (0)7710 943614
Email	aisling@millfossecottage.co.uk
Web	www.millfossecottage.co.uk

Stow House

Past ancient stone walls and fields of lambs you reach sleepy Aysgarth and this dignified rectory. Step inside to find – Shoreditch pizzazz! Sarah and Phil have swapped the world of London advertising for a dream house in the Dales; she does cocktails, he does breakfasts and their take on Victoriana is inspiring. Floors, banisters and sash windows have been restored, stairs carpeted in plush red, sofas covered in zinging velvet. Bathrooms are wow, bedrooms are soothing and the papier-mâché hare's head above the bar says it all. A stroll down the hill are the Aysgarth Falls, beloved of Ruskin, Wordsworth and Turner. *Minimum stay: 2 nights at weekends. Magnificent walks & big garden. Keep dogs on lead when walking through livestock.*

Rooms	6 doubles: £110-£175. 1 family room for 3: £175. Extra bed/sofabed £10-£20 p.p.p.n. Max. 1 dog.
Meals	Pubs/restaurants 5-minute walk.
Closed	Rarely.
Treats	Raw beef bones from butcher & towels.

Tel	+44 (0)1969 663635
Email	info@stowhouse.co.uk
Web	www.stowhouse.co.uk

Sarah & Phil Bucknall
Stow House,
Aysgarth, Leyburn, DL8 3SR

The Mollycroft

The Mollycroft is a 1940s showman's living van, restored to gleaming glory and as eccentric as the people who once toured in it. Inside, a combination of dark wood and bright yellow and green décor creates a lively but homely feel. There are sofas in both the living room and the bunk room, which doubles as the kitchen, so you have plenty of space for lazy loafing in this tumbling, spacious wagon. You're far from the '40s in comforts: gas hobs and fridge in the kitchen, mains power and WiFi bring things up-to-date. Next to the Mollycroft is a fire pit complete with cooking gear, and the compost loo and outdoor shower are both a walk away (you're still camping, after all). With no other guests around, it's ideal for families or groups looking for peace, though the three-foot high deck makes it unsuitable for toddlers. The grounds hold rare bamboo gardens, a lake, and your host Greville has converted a chapel to display his modern art collection. Head off into the stunning Yorkshire Dales; don't miss the enormous Sunday market at Catterick racecourse – or the races, or course. *Secure garden, woodland and lakes. Dogs must be kept on lead.*

Rooms	Wagon for 4: from £100 per night. Max. 2 dogs.
Meals	Self-catering.
Closed	November-March.
Treats	A lake for swimming, lovely walks on site & contained 2-acre bamboo garden where dogs can roam off the lead.

Canopy & Stars
The Mollycroft,
Saint Paulinus, Brough Park,
Tunstall, DL10 7PJ

Tel	+44 (0)117 204 7830
Email	enquiries@canopyandstars.co.uk
Web	www.canopyandstars.co.uk/themollycroft

A Place in the Pines

Matt is the brains behind these forest hideaways. He scoured the mountains of Switzerland in search of canvas-topped inspiration. He found that nothing quite beats waking up in the forest to the smell of stovetop coffee and bacon, with a day of trudging unknown lands ahead. And, lucky for you, he also scribbled down hot baths and homemade sloe gin on his list of must-haves. Easy to get to, not far off the main road, the four safari tents – all about 60 metres apart – each have their own personality. The super-stoves inside don't stop at keeping the whole family warm all night, they can slow cook a joint at the same time! It doesn't have to be Easter for an egg hunt here: you can collect your breakfast from the hens most mornings or pick up duck eggs from the honesty box by the pond. Say hello to the sheep, pigs and ponies in the next field. Hop over the fence to explore the glorious Yorkshire Moors. If you go in August, you can glimpse local farmers battling it out for the title of longest pod of sugar peas or heaviest courgette at the famous Osmotherley show. *Site fenced off & away from roads. North Yorkshire Moors, streams for dogs to paddle in; advice on walks; local pubs all dog-friendly. Dogs on leads in some areas.*

Rooms	4 safari tents for 5: £120 per night. Dogs £10 per dog per stay. Max. 2.
Meals	Self-catering.
Closed	November-March.
Treats	Advice on walks & dog-friendly pubs.

Tel	+44 (0)117 204 7830
Email	enquiries@canopyandstars.co.uk
Web	www.canopyandstars.co.uk/aplaceinthepines

Canopy & Stars
A Place in the Pines,
Keepers Cottage,
Thimbleby, DL6 3PY

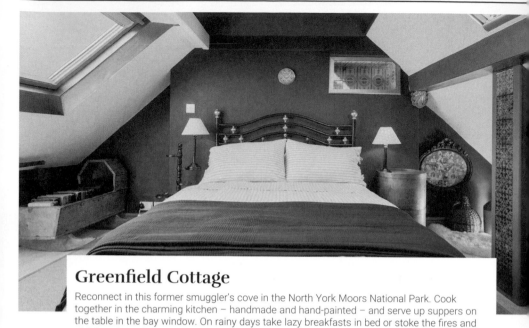

Greenfield Cottage

Reconnect in this former smuggler's cove in the North York Moors National Park. Cook together in the charming kitchen – handmade and hand-painted – and serve up suppers on the table in the bay window. On rainy days take lazy breakfasts in bed or stoke the fires and sink into the sofas with books and games. Bedrooms are beautifully outfitted in antiques. When the sun shines you'll find a little bench on the front path for your morning coffee – greeting the locals as they go. Martin and Diana have left you the essentials – add to them with dressed crab from the fishmonger or scones from the tea room. Check the tide and amble to Ravenscar's wild seal colony across the wide stretch of sand or bring bikes to pedal part of the Coast to Coast route which starts nearby. *Minimum stay: 3 nights. Open woodland starts at end of cottage path. The village is dog-friendly with all pubs & most cafés & shops allowing dogs. No dog restrictions on four-mile beach all year round.*

Rooms	1 cottage for 4: £495-£695 per week. Dogs £20 per dog per stay. Max. 2.
Meals	Self-catering.
Closed	Never.
Treats	Dog bowls, poo bags, towels, throws for sofas & jar of treats. Wicker baskets (bring some bedding – own scent is important) & a cosy place by wood-burner. Sleeping crate on request.

Martin & Diana Decent
Greenfield Cottage,
Plane Tree Street,
Robin Hood's Bay, YO22 4SX

Mobile	+44 (0)7900 127252
Email	decentartist@btinternet.com
Web	www.greenfieldcottage.co.uk

The Hayloft at Flamborough Rigg

On and on the road goes, deeper into the woods until the single track stops at an 1820s farmhouse surrounded by open fields. The gravelled drive crunches nicely under the tyres and the kitchen sports a hamper of local goodies (and, on occasion, home-brewed elderflower champagne!). Philip and Caroline love making guests feel at home and you may freely roam their super big garden with orchard, vegetable patch, loungers and barbecue. You can head off for a long walk over the rolling North Yorkshire Moors and come back to deep comfort. Snuggle up with a book in front of the wood-burner, watch a DVD, play a round of cards at the chunky table. There are quirky touches like old Singer sewing machines as table bases, a shelf of vintage china in the well-thought out kitchen/diner, and modern art on the walls. The bedrooms feel light and fresh with local oak furniture and cheerful cushions. Jump in the car for a trip to the coast or wander round the charming market town of Helmsley. The Hayloft feels as though it's in the middle of nowhere and yet moors, dales and the sea are wonderfully close. *Short breaks available. Large fully enclosed garden.*

Rooms	1 barn for 4: £595-£695 per week.
Meals	Self-catering.
Closed	Rarely.
Treats	A guide to local dog-friendly pubs & beaches.

Tel	+44 (0)1751 475263	**Philip & Caroline Jackson**
Email	enquiries@flamboroughriggcottage.co.uk	The Hayloft at Flamborough Rigg,
Web	www.thehayloftatflamboroughrigg.co.uk	Middlehead Road,
		Stape, Pickering

Little Garth

In the gentle foothills of the North York Moors, four miles from the market town of Kirkbymoorside, lies Normanby, an ancient settlement blessed with a Norman church and a trout stream. And, tucked behind the village street, through the picket gate, this immaculate little cottage. Having swapped a farmhouse in the Lakes for Little Garth, Pippa has poured love into its revival. Now all is light, warm and cosy inside, with plenty of pretty things to catch the eye: old paintings, quirky pots, cheerful rugs on polished flagged floors. Fresh flowers glow on old pine tops, cotton-covered armchairs are deep and comfortable, and a super, bright, light kitchen with all the kit opens to a very private rose and honeysuckle garden. After a day's roaming the sheep-speckled moors, bliss to snuggle down here. Light the candles, throw another log on the fire, pop the cork, or stroll to the pub for a drink. For eating out, Pippa recommends The Sun Inn at Normanby, a short walk. Return to sweetly floral bedrooms with gleaming white woodwork and generously clad beds. A lovely, very comfy hideaway. *Minimum stay: 3 nights. Secure garden.*

Rooms	1 house for 5: £320-£700 per week. Max. 2 dogs.
Meals	Self-catering.
Closed	Never.
Treats	Dog bowl.

Pippa Galloway
Little Garth,
Normanby, Sinnington, YO62 6RJ

Tel	+44 (0)1904 431876
Email	p.galloway@talk21.com
Web	www.holidaycottage-normanby.co.uk

North East

Rose & Crown, page 216

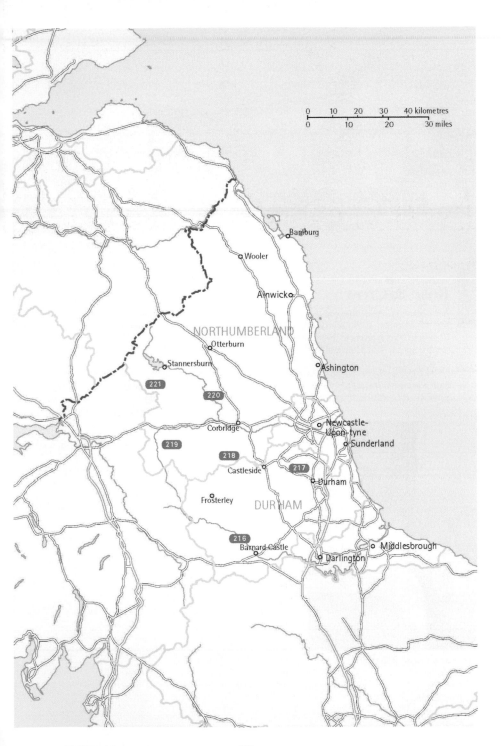

0 10 20 30 40 kilometres
0 10 20 30 miles

Bamburg

Wooler

Alnwick

NORTHUMBERLAND

Otterburn

Stannersburn

Ashington

221

220

Corbridge

Newcastle-
Upon-tyne

Sunderland

219

218

Castleside

217

Durham

Frosterley

DURHAM

216

Barnard Castle

Middlesbrough

Darlington

Rose & Crown

Romaldkirk is one of those lovely villages where little has changed in 200 years. It sits peacefully in the north Pennines, lost to the world and without great need of it. As for the Rose & Crown, it dates to 1733 and stands on the village green next to a Saxon church. Roses ramble across stone walls at the front, so grab a pint of local ale, then sit in the sun and watch life pass by. Inside, you can roast away in front of a fire in the wonderfully old-school bar while reading the Teesdale Mercury. There's a peaceful sitting room for afternoon tea, then a panelled restaurant for excellent food, perhaps local Raby Estate venison pie followed by white chocolate panna cotta and pistachio ice cream. Thomas and Cheryl bought the place in 2012 and have been spending money on it ever since: it has never looked better. Stylish rooms – some in the main house, others out back, a couple in a cottage next door – have warm colours, comfy beds, Bose sound systems and super bathrooms. Don't miss High Force waterfall, the magnificent Bowes Museum or the sausage sandwich at lunch. *Great walks from door, village green next to inn & river nearby.*

Rooms	7 doubles, 3 twins: £115-£160. 2 suites for 2: £180-£200. 1 cottage for 4: £115-£200. Singles £95. Dinner, B&B from £79 p.p. Max. 2 dogs.
Meals	Lunch from £10.50. Dinner, 3 courses, from £27. Sunday lunch £19.50.
Closed	23-27 December and one week in January.
Treats	Beds, towels & locally made treats.

Thomas & Cheryl Robinson
Rose & Crown,
Romaldkirk,
Barnard Castle, DL12 9EB

Tel	+44 (0)1833 650213
Email	hotel@rose-and-crown.co.uk
Web	www.rose-and-crown.co.uk

Burnhopeside Hall

It's peaceful, traditional, pristine, and nothing is too much trouble for Christine. Welcome to a listed Georgian house on a 475-acre estate near Durham, its elegant sitting rooms furnished with pictures and photos, log fires and big sofas, billiards and a baby grand, and great sash windows with garden and woodland views. Resident springer spaniels Max and Barney love all dogs, so bring yours; stroll the magnificent lawns, cycle alongside the river. Breakfast? Eggs from the hens, bacon from the pigs, honey and fruits from the walled garden: a perfect start to the day. Enormous beds, luxurious linen and fresh flowers await your return. *Lots of river and woodland walks, with a safe garden well away from the road (off-lead is no problem).*

Rooms	6 doubles: £100-£120.
	1 apartment for 6: £100-£150. Singles £70-£85.
Meals	Pubs/restaurants 4 miles.
Closed	Rarely.
Treats	Acres of dog-friendly garden & farmland to explore & friendly resident dog Max to play with.

Tel	+44 (0)1207 520222
Email	harmerchristine@hotmail.com
Web	www.burnhopeside-hall.co.uk

Christine Hewitt
Burnhopeside Hall,
Durham Road,
Lanchester, DH7 0TL

Lord Crewe Arms at Blanchland

Originally the abbot's lodge and kitchens (and its garden the cloisters), the Lord Crewe Arms has become a Grade II*-listed inn. The village, in a sheep-clad valley on the moors' edge, was built with stone from the abbey's ruins. Inside: ancient flags, inglenook fireplaces, fortress walls and a classy country décor. Public areas range from lofty to intimate and the atmospheric bar is in the vaulted crypt. With a head chef from Mark Hix's 'stable', the robust modern British menu includes steaks, chops and spit-roasted meats, fresh crab salad and ruby beets. Puddings hark back to ancient times: sea buckthorn posset, rhubarb fumble. Wines include great burgundies and clarets, ales range from Allendale's Golden Plover to Nel's Best from High House Farm, and there are water bowls for dogs in the garden. If you stay, you're in for a treat. Most bedrooms are divided between The Angel, a simple, beautiful, listed ex-inn across the way, and the former tied cottages. Some rooms have exposed stone walls and real fires, all have soft carpets, fine fabrics, divine beds and deep baths. *Rivers to jump in. Sheep in fields so dogs to be kept on leads.*

Rooms	19 doubles: £119-£192. 1 suite for 2: £144-£212. 1 family room for 4: £189-£252. Dogs £10. Max. 2.
Meals	Lunch & dinner from £12.75. Sunday lunch, 2-3 courses, £18-£24.
Closed	Rarely.
Treats	Bed, towel, bowl & suggested walks.

Tommy Mark
Lord Crewe Arms at Blanchland,
The Square, Blanchland, DH8 9SP

Tel +44 (0)1434 677100
Email enquiries@lordcrewearmsblanchland.co.uk
Web www.lordcrewearmsblanchland.co.uk

The Waiting Room

Staward Station had trains puffing in and out for over 80 years. It closed in 1950 along with the traditional waiting room now owned by Allan and Alison, who live nearby. You'll be sleeping in the old ticket office, and in fact the original ticket hatch is still in use, opening onto the reading room (although morning cups of tea might be more appreciated than tickets these days). It's also a bit cosier than it used to be, with new double glazing on the replica south-facing windows and with insulation material used by NASA lining the roof. There's still the main entrance from the platform, leading into the sitting room, and if you go through the fully-equipped kitchen you'll find another door leading out the back to your private courtyard garden. The old stone railway bridge is just at the end of the platform, and from the top you can see over the tree tops down into Staward gorge and across to Hadrian's Wall – perfect for planning your walking route through the surrounding countryside. A good one to start with is the John Martin trail, a ten mile off-road walk that you can join just at the bottom of the garden. *Secure area of garden; woodland. Advice on dog-friendly walks away from farm stock. (No bitches in season.)*

Rooms	Cabin for 4: from £83 per night. Dogs £25 per dog per stay; multiple dogs may be brought by arrangement, please call to discuss.
Meals	Self-catering.
Closed	Never.
Treats	Leads, bowls, furniture throws & poo bags.

Tel	+44 (0)117 204 7830
Email	enquiries@canopyandstars.co.uk
Web	www.canopyandstars.co.uk/thewaitingroom

Canopy & Stars
The Waiting Room,
Staward Station, Langley upon Tyne,
Hexham, NE47 5NR

Middle & East Cottages, Southlands Farm

You'll fall in love with this rugged county, for its beauty and its space; no crowds, no traffic jams, no rush. Stay in a 19th-century byre and a granary (the original feeding troughs stand outside, spilling flowers in summer), immaculately converted, alongside two others, in an eco-friendly way. Solar panels heat the water, the logs are on the house, electricity comes from renewable sources. Step into East Cottage to find a light modern space with soaring ceilings, tiles warm underfoot, bright rugs and cushions and a wood-burning stove. The kitchen glows at the other end: hand-built Shaker-style units, granite tops, an old pine dresser with plenty of china, a table for lazy breakfasts; owner Dee delivers a sizzling full English if you want, all local and seasonal. Up the spiral stairs are super bedrooms with buttermilk walls, wooden floors, pastel-striped blankets and exquisite beds; bathrooms are dazzling white, the twin has a wet room, the towels are thick and white. You can walk to a superb pub; or take a sundowner to the patio, and choose a home-cooked supper from the honesty freezer. *North Tyne river walks, a stream to splash in and a public footpath right by the gate.*

Rooms	1 cottage for 2, 1 cottage for 4: £360-£800 per week. Dogs £30 per stay. Max. 2.
Meals	Self-catering.
Closed	Never.
Treats	Drying room, towels & Bonedrybed dog bed. Advice on walks, & hose pipe area for muddy paws. Birthday cakes on request & 37 acres to explore.

Charles & Dee McGowan
Middle & East Cottages,
Southlands Farm,
Gunnerton, Hexham, NE48 4EA

Tel	+44 (0)1434 681464
Mobile	+44 (0)7876 455620 / +44 (0)7900 271455
Email	dee@southlandsfarmcottages.co.uk
Web	www.southlandsfarmcottages.co.uk

Sky Den

The Sky Den was built by William Hardie Designs with George Clarke during the second series of his Amazing Spaces programme. It's composed of three different shapes which blend together the best of outdoors and indoors, taking in everything from the red squirrels in the trees around you to the sweeping river below. The square is the central point and your main living space, with glass doors opening onto a wide balcony with captivating views over the river. Inside, George has created an impressively versatile space, with a functional kitchen in a clutter-phobe's paradise of fold-away furniture (including two single beds) and wet room. Then there's the circle, a simple viewpoint of corrugated iron, where you can have a picnic and brew up a cuppa over the wood-burning stove. Finally the triangle is the loft space of your already lofty suite, accessed by steps from the outside deck. In good weather open the whole roof for an unobstructed view of the Northumberland Dark Skies. You're in the Kielder Water & Forest Park so wildlife lovers and adventure-seeking families will be happy. Bring warm clothes! *Maps of area provided. Please note only assistance dogs are allowed in centre building.*

Rooms	Treehouse for 4: from £160 per night. Dogs £50 per dog per stay. Max. 1.
Meals	Self-catering.
Closed	Never.
Treats	Bowls & advice on walks through forest & along Lakeside Way.

Tel	+44 (0)117 204 7830
Email	enquiries@canopyandstars.co.uk
Web	www.canopyandstars.co.uk/skyden

Canopy & Stars
Sky Den,
Calvert Trust, Kielder,
Hexham, NE48 1BS

Wales

Banceithin, page 240

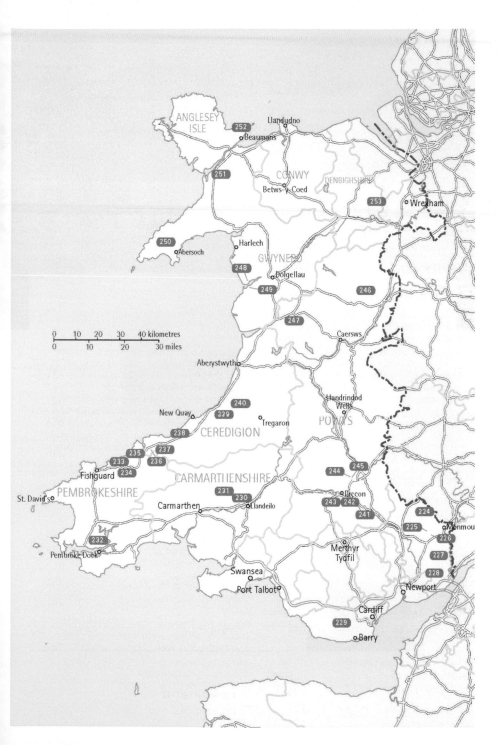

The Bell at Skenfrith

The position here is magical: an ancient stone bridge, a river snaking through the valley, glorious hills rising beyond, cows grazing in lush fields. It's a perfect spot, not least because providence blessed it with this chic little inn. Inside, you find a locals' bar for the odd game of rugby, sofas in front of a wood-burner in the sitting room, then an airy restaurant for some very good food. In summer, doors fly open and life spills onto a stone terrace with views of hill and wood – a fine spot for lunch in the sun. Elegant country-house bedrooms brim with light. Some are beamed, most are big, you'll find padded bedheads, Farrow & Ball colours, perhaps a walnut bed or a claw-foot bath in your room. Those at the front have river views, those at the back look onto the hills, some have sofas, all have robes in excellent bathrooms. Seven circular walks start at the front door with maps to show you the way. Delicious food awaits your return, perhaps Welsh rarebit with a poached egg, braised beef brisket with dauphinoise potatoes, apple doughnuts with toffee sauce and mulled cider. *Minimum stay: 2 nights at weekends. Secure garden; circular walks from door. Beware of sheep & cows.*

Rooms	5 doubles, 3 twin/doubles, 3 four-posters: £150-£250. Singles £90. Dogs £20. Max. 2.
Meals	Lunch from £5.95. Sunday lunch from £14.95. Dinner, 3 courses, around £38.
Closed	Rarely.
Treats	Dog parlour & towels. Treats for well-behaved dogs.

Richard Ireton & Sarah Hudson
The Bell at Skenfrith,
Skenfrith, Abergavenny, NP7 8UH

Tel	+44 (0)1600 750235
Email	enquiries@skenfrith.co.uk
Web	www.skenfrith.co.uk

Woodlands Farm

Woodlands Farm is all about creating an experience. Join life on the farm collecting eggs and feeding hens or leave the horsebox and bothy behind to visit Areas of Outstanding Natural Beauty nearby. Spend your days hanging out at the farm and ignoring modern life, chatting to Craig and Charles about their crafts, their farm and their parties, taking some pottery lessons, or ranging through the valley to explore Tintern Abbey, canoe down the Wye and tramp through the Forest of Dean. The bright, warm and very Stripy Bothy, will be waiting for you when you get home. *Two very friendly dogs on site. Each unit has acre of private ground for dogs to run around in. Farmland site so all visiting dogs must be well behaved. Many woodland walks around with streams to play in.*

Rooms	Bothy for 2: from £105 per night.
	Horsebox for 2: from £90 per night.
	Dogs £20 per dog per stay. Max. 1 obedient dog.
Meals	Self-catering.
Closed	Never.
Treats	Dog treats, dog blankets or towels if required.

Tel	+44 (0)117 204 7830
Email	enquiries@canopyandstars.co.uk
Web	www.canopyandstars.co.uk/
	woodlandsfarm

Canopy & Stars
Woodlands Farm,
Penrhos, NP15 2LE

Old-Lands

Send the children off to the Forest School; buy your produce from the honesty shop: sausages, bramble chutney, apple juice from the farm. Immersed in wildlife and rolling hills, this grand gothic house is home to the Bosanquet family, whose love of sustainable farming is inspiring. They offer a cottage in the stables, an apartment in the West Wing, and a barn conversion for two, with a little loft den (or bell tent) for children and grand-children. All ages love it here. Raglan Castle is a 10-minute drive, the Forest of Dean half an hour, and the Beacons are just beyond. This is a foodie area so book lunch at The Bell at Skenfrith (about 10 miles), tour the vineyards of Ancre Hill (seven miles), and visit the Chapel in Abergavenny (12 miles). Then back for a stroll down the yew-tree walk, and a row on the wildlife-rich lake. *Minimum stay: 2 nights at weekends; 4 on weekdays; 7 in high season. Lovely lake for chasing balls & masses of land to roam – watch out for livestock. Secure garden in one cottage.*

Rooms	1 apartment for 5: £400-£800. 1 barn for 4: £350-£790. 1 cottage for 5: £400-£850. Prices per week. Dogs £20 per dog per stay.
Meals	Self-catering.
Closed	Never.
Treats	Towels for drying off after lake swimming.

Clare Bosanquet
Old-Lands,
Dingestow Court,
Dingestow, NP25 4DY

Tel	+44 (0)1600 740141
Email	clarebosanquet@gmail.com
Web	www.old-lands.co.uk

The Chickenshed

The Chickenshed completely belies its name, which makes for extra wonderment when you approach the stunning red cedar, glass and stainless steel structure. Put your shoes in the boot room and pad barefoot across the heated polished concrete floor. Owner Sue will show you round and explain how some of the space-age kitchen gadgets work. This is the place to truly enjoy cooking a feast. The floor to ceiling glass across the expansive open-plan living area creates a dramatic connection to the beautiful Wye Valley. The cabin's agricultural roots, like the corrugated roof and chunky wooden cladding, are kept soft and modern with striking greens, asymmetrical windows, and lights which appear to float around the glulam beams. Outside there are two private acres where the kids, big or small, can play safely, and a wood to wander through and gaze up at canopies of ancient trees. When you're sitting around the crackling flames of fire pit on the paved terrace with the bats flapping above, and some sizzling steaks cooking... you'll see you don't have to do much to make days and evenings here perfectly atmospheric. *Surrounding area paradise for dogs. Large secure garden, field & woods beyond; safe for dogs to be off-lead for miles. Local guide, OS maps and walking books available.*

Rooms	Cabin for 8: from £210 per night. Discounts may be available for groups of 2-4. Dogs. £25 per dog per stay. Max 2.
Meals	Self-catering.
Closed	Never.
Treats	Outside tap & blankets for drying muddy paws. Dog bed & crate available. Sue & Nick have 2 active collies & are always happy to advise.

Tel	+44 (0)117 204 7830
Email	enquiries@canopyandstars.co.uk
Web	www.canopyandstars.co.uk/thechickenshed

Canopy & Stars
The Chickenshed,
Parkhouse,
Trellech, NP25 4PU

Little Idyll

You'll be greeted by wildlife and livestock galore here. Birds, muntjac deer, alpacas, potbellied and kunekune pigs, ducks, chickens, turkeys... and a lively, curious pony in the sloping field next door, which you'll climb up to reach Little Idyll. Sharon's dogs are likely to pad up and say hello too – they're always excited to meet new people. Then hop into a wonderfully crafted shepherd's hut, decorated in subtle colours that complement the larch and oak panelling and worktops. Every comfort has been considered, from the bed occupying one whole end of the hut, to the nifty kitchen and the en suite compost loo; you can order a breakfast hamper too. Having retired from the Police Force, Sharon settled here to pursue her other dream of creating the perfect holiday

spot and it's easy to see why she chose it: the view is breathtaking. The decking area with the fire bowl is like a front row seat at a fabulous show, with the countryside stretching out across the Wye Valley and as far as the Cotswolds on a clear day. Head out for scenic walks and historic castles, canoeing, hiking and biking through the hills. *Enclosed garden; adjacent fields. Dogs on leads until they reach hut & when walking through fields. Footpaths from hut; woodland walks a short drive; advice on walks. Dog-friendly pubs nearby; two vets within 10-minute drive.*

Rooms	Shepherd's hut for 2: from £90 per night. Up to 2 horses £15 per night in paddock (hay & water provided). Dogs £20 per dog per stay. Max. 1 small/medium dog.
Meals	Self-catering.
Closed	Never.
Treats	Welcome pack with biscuits. Blanket & throws for furniture so you can cuddle up.

Canopy & Stars	**Tel** +44 (0)117 204 7830
Little Idyll,	**Email** enquiries@canopyandstars.co.uk
Maybee Cottage, Usk Road,	**Web** www.canopyandstars.co.uk/littleidyll
Shirenewton, NP16 6TZ	

Tŷ Cerrig

Come for silent nights and stargazing at these woodland retreats. Bwncath cabin is packed with sheep's wool insulation and has big French doors for flinging open onto the private deck when the sun comes up. It's built for spending time together with little pockets of places to gather around: the farmhouse table for lazy breakfasts, leather sofa and chairs around the wood-burner for playing board games, fire pit and picnic table outside for barbecues and drinks. Gwdihw the shepherd's hut has a goose feather duvet on a clever fold down bed, wood-burning stove and bunks for little ones: talk about shepherd's delight! Both have a kitchen with all you need, hot shower and flushing loo. Make sure you keep an eye on the battery monitor to check your power usage or you might be reading your bedtime stories by torchlight. The spaces are about 100 metres apart, but the meadow is the only thing you'll be sharing. Pick up a map or guide and pack a picnic before you set off on adventures: beautiful long walks around the Vale of Glamorgan, kite-flying on the beach, and Cardiff is just half hour away. *Over 25 acres of woodland on site to run around in. Close to dog-friendly beaches and numerous dog-friendly pubs.*

Rooms	Cabin for 2 (+2 adults/children in twin room): from £105 per night. £10 p.p.p.n. Shepherd's hut for 4: from £90 per night. Travel cot & Moses basket available. Max. 1 dog in shepherd's hut, 2 in cabin.
Meals	Self-catering.
Closed	November-February.
Treats	Towels, advice on walks & dog-friendly pubs.

Tel	+44 (0)117 204 7830
Email	enquiries@canopyandstars.co.uk
Web	www.canopyandstars.co.uk/tycerrig

Canopy & Stars
Tŷ Cerrig,
Maerdy Newydd,
Bonvilston, CF5 6TR

The Log House Studio

You may well be greeted by the ever-exuberant Charlie Brown, terrier and proprietor of Cwm Farm. Well, technically that's Tim, who lives with Charlie in the cottage across the field, and whose paintings festoon the walls of this raised, Swedish-style log cabin built from local timber. Step inside and you'll find an open-plan space, complete with artists' easel and desk, a comfortable double bed and a wood-burner to keep things cosy whatever the weather throws at you. Everything you might need for coffee brewing or sausage frying is also on hand and Charlie will be delighted to assist. The mezzanine level, reached by wooden ladder, provides space either for extra guests or just to read a book. The private compost loo and wonderfully

hot, gas-powered shower are down a few steps. Although secluded, you'll never feel too alone here; there are cows and sheep in the fields, and from time to time you'll hear the odd barking from the kennels next door too. The surrounding countryside offers plenty of walks, some of Wales' best mountain biking trails, and a whole selection of ruined castles to explore. *The fields are mostly fenced from livestock next door. Resident dog Charlie Brown welcomes well-behaved friends.*

Rooms	Cabin for 2 (+2 adults/children on sofabed or mezzanine; bring own bedding): from £100 per night. £20 p.p.p.n. Dogs £10 per dog per stay. Max. 2.
Meals	Self-catering.
Closed	Never.
Treats	Advice on walks & water bowl provided.

Canopy & Stars
The Log House Studio,
Cwm Farm, Capel Isaac,
Llandeilo, SA19 7UE

Tel	+44 (0)117 204 7830
Email	enquiries@canopyandstars.co.uk
Web	www.canopyandstars.co.uk/loghouse

Tŷ Mawr Country Hotel

Pretty rooms, attractive prices and delicious food make this welcoming country house hard to resist. It sits in a very peaceful spot. You drive over hills, drop into the village, then wash up at this 16th-century stone house that comes in soft yellow. Outside, a sun-trapping terrace laps against a trim lawn, which in turn drops into a passing river. Gentle eccentricities abound: croquet hoops take odd diversions, a seat has been chiselled into a tree trunk, there's boules for those who play. Inside, original stone walls and low beamed ceilings give a warm country feel. There are fires everywhere – one in the attractive sitting room that overlooks the garden, another in the dining room that burns on both sides. Excellent bedrooms, two of which are on the ground floor. You get big beds, warm colours, crisp linen, good bathrooms. Some have sofas, all are dog-friendly, three overlook the garden. Back downstairs, the bar doubles as reception, while Welsh art on the walls is for sale. Steve's cooking is the final treat, perhaps Cardigan Bay scallops, organic Welsh beef, calvados and cinnamon rice pudding. Top stuff. *Over 10s welcome. Dogs welcome in sitting room & bar.*

Rooms	3 doubles, 3 twin/doubles: £115-£130. Singles £80.
Meals	Dinner £25-£30.
Closed	Rarely.
Treats	Biscuits, beds, bowls, towels, leads & advice on walks.

Tel	+44 (0)1267 202332
Email	info@wales-country-hotel.co.uk
Web	www.wales-country-hotel.co.uk

Annabel & Steve Thomas
Tŷ Mawr Country Hotel,
Brechfa, SA32 7RA

Cwtch Camping

The Welsh camping experience has been given a thoroughly contemporary spin by Beth, creator of the Cwtch (meaning a cuddle or a snug place, in Welsh). The three handcrafted timber pods are a short walk through the trees from where you park your car, or a scenic cycle from local stations. Light pours through French doors, chunky brocante finds distinguish the interiors and a real double bed is bliss after a day in the fresh air. The cabins share a kitchen, shower and WC, but are privately sited with their own deck and picnic table. Local eggs, fresh bread and organic milk are among the goodies in your welcome hamper and Beth can supply extras for your private barbecue if you ask in advance. The Cwtch stands firm in all seasons in the midst of Pembrokeshire's natural beauty: follow the riverbank walk to a nature reserve teeming with bird life – and a family of otters – or take a boat trip to the island of Skomer. Camping has never been cosier! *Many dog-friendly pubs, restaurants and cafés nearby. Advice on the beaches without dog restrictions given.*

Rooms	2 pods for 2: from £72 per night. 1 pod for 4: from £79 per night. Max. 2 dogs.
Meals	Self-catering.
Closed	November-March.
Treats	Biscuits, towels, walking advice and 3 acres of woodland where dogs can run around off the lead.

Canopy & Stars
Cwtch Camping,
12 Vale Court,
Houghton, SA73 1NQ

Tel	+44 (0)117 204 7830
Email	enquiries@canopyandstars.co.uk
Web	www.canopyandstars.co.uk/cwtchcamping

Llys Meddyg

This beautiful small hotel has a little bit of everything: chic bedrooms that pack a punch, a cellar bar for cocktails before dinner, a stylish restaurant for delicious local food. In summer you decant into the garden, where a café/bistro opens up for coffee and cake or pizza from a wood-fired oven. There's a smokehouse out here, too, then a yurt tucked away around the corner that comes with a wood-burner and a hot tub. It's an intimate place, where staff stop to chat, locals pop in for a coffee, and you can take home a jar of quince jelly made by Ed's mum. Food lies at the heart of the affair and you eat in a stylish restaurant with Welsh art on the walls, perhaps home-smoked salmon, slow-cook lamb, caramelised pear with blue-cheese ice cream. Beautiful bedrooms are scattered about. Those in the main house have cool colours, vast beds and fancy bathrooms. Those in the mews have a rustic feel and garden views; all have fluffy robes. Pembrokeshire's coastal path waits for windswept cliffs and sandy beaches. Don't miss St Davids or the Preseli Hills. *Minimum stay: 2 nights at weekends. Estuary path, long sandy beach with dunes, mountain walks – all from door; maps to borrow. Lovely garden.*

Rooms	8 doubles: £100-£180. 1 yurt for 2: £100-£120. Singles from £85. Dogs £15 per stay; 3 dog-friendly rooms.
Meals	Lunch from £7. Dinner from £14.
Closed	Rarely.
Treats	Dog bowls & outside hose. There is always a sausage at breakfast.

Tel	+44 (0)1239 820008
Email	info@llysmeddyg.com
Web	www.llysmeddyg.com

Louise & Edward Sykes
Llys Meddyg,
East Street,
Newport, SA42 0SY

The Tudor Kitchen

You're in the oldest part of the house and your bedroom used to be the dairy – the thick and ancient beams above you still have their original kitchen hooks. On dank or rainy days with the wood piled high by the burner, soft sofas, books and games, it will be deliciously cosy here. The wildlife is bountiful, deep in the Pembrokeshire Coast National Park – not only birds but foxes, badgers and otters too. Daniel and Jemma are creating a wildlife meadow which you can see from your sitting room. Join the rugged coastal path which explodes with wild flowers in spring, drive to Newport (five minutes) for a wonderful wide beach with estuary and good food shops. If you don't want to cook, then walk down to the Salutation Inn in the village or drive to The Old Sailors in Dinas Cross for lobster and fresh fish caught in the bay. The night skies are star-filled when there's no cloud and owls will hoot you to sleep. *Minimum stay: 2 nights at weekends. Plenty of walking from door. Sheep in nearby field so dogs on lead.*

Rooms	1 studio for 2: £347-£420 per week. Short breaks available. Dogs £30 per stay. Max. 1 medium dog.
Meals	Self-catering.
Closed	Never.
Treats	Biscuits & hot & cold outside taps for muddy paws.

Daniel & Jemma Slade-Davies
The Tudor Kitchen,
Felindre Farchog,
Newport, SA41 3XG

Tel   +44 (0)1239 820768
Email daniel_davies@icloud.com
Web   www.thetudorkitchen.co.uk

The Old Vicarage

Owners Megan and Jaap fell instantly in love with this patch of rural bliss and, now that carpenter Jaap has crafted every inch of this lovely space, you can too. Although Douglas and Birch and Cedar and Birch are nominally shepherd's huts, the cosy bed, tiled shower room and wood-burner warmed lounge are quite a bit more comfortable than most would have had when out tending the flock. There's also a hammock for lying back and watching the stars, plus seating outside for al fresco evening meals. Megan, who is always cooking and pretty great at it, will leave you a few basic ingredients (including eggs from their hens) and can give you tips on picking up more great local produce. If you don't feel like cooking at either end of the day, she can even whip up a memorable dinner or breakfast with a bit of notice, served in The Old Vicarage just up the garden. *Dog-friendly beaches, restaurants and pubs close by. Acre of enclosed garden and two beautiful sandy beaches within a short drive.*

Rooms	2 shepherd's hut for 2: from £110 per night. Dogs £15 per dog per stay. Max. 2 dogs.
Meals	Self-catering.
Closed	Never.
Treats	Bed, bowls, Pooch&Mutt treats, biodegradable poo bags, advice on walks & big secure garden.

Tel	+44 (0)117 204 7830
Email	enquiries@canopyandstars.co.uk
Web	www.canopyandstars.co.uk/ theoldvicarage

Canopy & Stars
The Old Vicarage House & Huts,
Moylegrove, SA43 3BN

Den by the Stream

If you ever built a den in the woods as a child, then this place is probably what you were imagining while you did it. Tree branches frame the four-poster bed and lead up to another branch covered with fairy lights as a chandelier. The brook provides a natural soundtrack and is a hunting ground for otters that live downstream, with resident badgers and a host of wildlife found in the surrounding woods. You can explore adventurous cooking over the fire pit by the fallen oak or on the Cobb oven, but there's also a hob indoors for quick cups of tea. The cupboard under the cabin is full of blankets that you can take to the circular stargazing platform, staying snug as you gently push yourself round, following the wheel of the night sky.

The Den is completely separate from the rest of estate and no livestock are on the premises. Quarter acre of land and 3 acre field so dogs can run. Woodland walk with streams to splash in.

Rooms	Cabin for 2: from £95 per night. Dogs £10 per dog per stay. Max. 2.
Meals	Self-catering.
Closed	Never.
Treats	Dog covers so dogs can still get up for a cuddle, towel, water bowl and water troughs in both fields. Running stream which dogs love during the heat of the summer.

Canopy & Stars	
Den by the Stream,	
Garden Cottage,	
Llangoedmor, SA43 2LB	

Tel	+44 (0)117 204 7830
Email	enquiries@canopyandstars.co.uk
Web	www.canopyandstars.co.uk/denbythestream

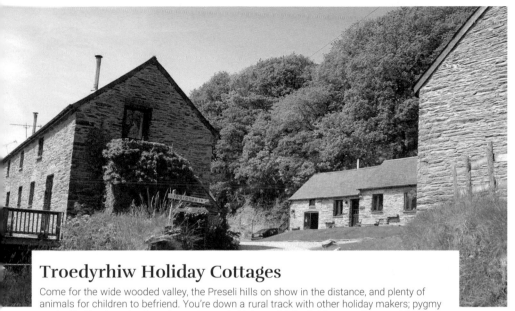

Troedyrhiw Holiday Cottages

Come for the wide wooded valley, the Preseli hills on show in the distance, and plenty of animals for children to befriend. You're down a rural track with other holiday makers; pygmy goats, Shetland ponies, kune kune pigs and chickens dot the fields around you and the owners (who will greet you) live on site should you need them. All the sitting rooms have wood-burners (logs are on the house), local art on the walls and comfy sofas and chairs; kitchens and bathrooms are modern (if slightly small) but fine for holiday needs. Bedrooms are spotless and bright— you'll sleep well, away from traffic noise. Each cottage has its own small garden or tranche of decking, plus barbecue and furniture so you can spill out for summertime meals and games. Fields lead down to the wide stream, perfect for welly (or barefoot in summer) splashing, and woodland walks. You're only a mile away from the nearest pub and shops and there are wide safe beaches for picnics and swimming; also walking, birdwatching, rugged mountain biking. Shopaholics will enjoy Cardigan, an appealing Welsh estuary town. *Woodland walks, streams to jump in, hills to walk up & coast path to explore.*

Rooms	1 cottage for 1, 1 cottage for 3, 1 cottage for 4, 1 cottage for 6, 1 cottage for 8: £495-£1750 per week. Short breaks available. Dogs £20. Max. 2.
Meals	Self-catering.
Closed	Never.
Treats	Advice on walks & dog-friendly beaches.

Tel	+44 (0)1239 811564	**Rob & Michelle Silcox**
Email	info@troedyrhiw.com	Troedyrhiw Holiday Cottages,
Web	www.troedyrhiw.com	Penparc,
		Cardigan, SA43 2AE

Locke's Cottage

It's difficult to know what to call the charming building sitting on the side of the Hoffnant Valley – downstairs, thick stone walls give away this former barn's agricultural past, while the timber upper level with oak tree 'growing' through the centre has a distinctly cabin-like feel. In wonderfully thrifty style, many of the materials used in this unusual creation are recycled; floors and window sills have been cleverly fashioned from scaffold boards used during the renovation, the double-ended bath sits on a cradle handmade from reclaimed wood and the pan rack in the large downstairs kitchen was once an old meat spit retrieved from somewhere in the grounds. Big windows along the front look down over the valley, and double doors lead from the upstairs living area onto an open balcony. You're so close to the sea that you can hear waves breaking when the wind is right. You have easy access onto the coastal path: follow the headland round to beautifully sandy West Wales beaches. Owners Kathryn and Geoff recommend the beach at Llangrannog for a great pub and unbeatable homemade ice cream from the beachside café. *Huge network of tracks, paths and hills to explore; 2 beaches within 1.5 miles, both dog-friendly all year round. Nearly all the surrounding pubs welcome dogs too.*

Rooms	Cabin for 2 (+3 adults/children on double sofabed & single sofabed): from £99 per night. £10 p.p.p.n. Dogs £10 per dog per stay. Max. 2.
Meals	Self-catering.
Closed	Never.
Treats	Towels for drying, feeding and water bowls, poo bags, nice dog biscuits and guided walks.

Canopy & Stars
Locke's Cottage,
Troed Rhiw Fawr,
Brynhoffnant, SA44 6EF

Tel	+44 (0)117 204 7830
Email	enquiries@canopyandstars.co.uk
Web	www.canopyandstars.co.uk/lockescottage

One Cat Farm

In the wild meadows of a quiet valley live one cat, two owners, Jessie and Lyndon, and four grass-roofed dens, lovingly crafted by Lyndon. Helyg Den is pitched right by the pond so wildlife lovers, this one's for you. Next along is Celyg Den followed by Derwen Den, both overlooking the pond and a great spot for sunsets – and Onnen Den, pitched at the top. The grassy exteriors aren't the only thing Nordic here – the dens are simple and cosy inside and the flexible layout make them a perfect fit for families and couples. There is a double bed and two single beds, which stow away as a sofa. Once a home for saddlebacks, The Pig Shed is now a warm communal barn, a two-minute walk away from the dens, with a kitchen and a big dining table where you can get to know your fellow glampers. The hot showers and flushing loo are next door. Seek out the twin wood-fired outdoor baths for an evening of stargazing or dunking the muddy littles after a day of adventures. With beaches and mountains both nearby, it's a perfect base for fishing, walking, horse riding and surfing. *Surrounded by working farmland so dogs must be kept on leads on site. Numerous walks from doorstep and nearby; beaches are close.*

Rooms	4 cabins for 2 (+2 adults/children on 2 single beds): from £75 per night. £10 p.p.p.n. Dogs £15 per dog per stay. Max. 2 small or 1 large.
Meals	Self-catering.
Closed	Never.
Treats	Water bowl & advice on walks.

Tel	+44 (0)117 204 7830
Email	enquiries@canopyandstars.co.uk
Web	www.canopyandstars.co.uk/onecatfarm

Canopy & Stars
One Cat Farm,
Bronfre Fach,
Ciliau Aeron, SA48 7PT

Banceithin

David and Philippa, who live in the farmhouse opposite, are deeply embedded in their eco-friendly patch so you know you're in Wales at these two cottages filled with Welsh art, Welsh blankets (from Jane Beck no less) and a 'bible' to guide you to all the super things to do. Each has a private garden and shares a games room complete with table tennis and dart board. The ten-acre farm includes orchard, veg beds, bees, pigs and owl boxes. Children will love it and you can buy homemade pies and sausages, farm eggs, veg and honey. Walk out into unspoilt countryside, cycle quiet lanes (there is secure storage) or drive to the coast with a picnic for long beaches and fine sand. Find the sundown spot complete with blankets and corkscrew and settle in while the children dip in the pond and build dens under the treehouse. *Minimum stay: 2 nights; 7 in high season. Enclosed garden. Keep on lead outside garden due to pets, free-range chickens & sheep roaming in fields. Evening dog-sitting available.*

Rooms	1 cottage for 2, 1 cottage for 6: £275-£880 per week. Short breaks available. Max. 2 medium/large or 3 small dogs.
Meals	Self-catering.
Closed	Never.
Treats	Homemade biscuits, guide with vet details, walks, dog-friendly pubs. Towels, blankets for the sofa, poo bags & scoop.

David & Philippa Pickworth
Banceithin,
Bethania, Llanon, SY23 5NP

Tel	+44 (0)1974 272559
Mobile	+44 (0)7794 738403
Email	escape@banceithin.com
Web	www.banceithin.com

B

Powys

Ty'r Chanter

Warmth, colour, children and activity: this house is huge fun. Tiggy welcomes you like family; help collect eggs, feed the lambs, drop your shoes by the fire. The farmhouse and barn are stylishly relaxed; deep sofas, tartan throws, heaps of books, long convivial table; views to the Brecon Beacons and Black Mountains are inspiring. Bedrooms are soft, simple sanctuaries with Jo Malone bathroom treats. The children's room zings with murals; toys, kids' sitting room, sandpit – it's child heaven. Walk, fish, canoe, book-browse in Hay or stroll the estate. Homemade cakes and whisky to help yourself to: fine hospitality and Tiggy is wonderful. *River to swim & large field to run in. But lots of livestock around – & mind the chickens!*

Rooms	3 doubles: £100. 1 children's twin: £20 per child. Singles £55.
Meals	Packed lunch £8. Pub 1 mile.
Closed	Rarely.
Treats	Sausages for breakfast, towels, bowls & walks.

Tel	+44 (0)1874 731144
Mobile	+44 (0)7802 387004
Email	tiggy@tyrchanter.com
Web	www.tyrchanter.com

Tiggy Pettifer
Ty'r Chanter,
Gliffaes, Crickhowell, NP8 1RL

The Old Store House

If a spick and span house gives you pleasure, read no further. Peter has filled his home mostly with books, but chickens and swans might wander in too. Things are moved out of the way rather than put away, there are no hard and fast breakfast times and guests are welcome to use the kitchen. Bedrooms are large, light and comfy with sofas and armchairs; two have wood fires and the room at the top has exterior stone steps and a door that stays open all summer – fledgling swallows might sit on the beam between flying practices. The sitting room is cosy with a big fire, the lived-in conservatory looks across the valley... come and go as you please. *Canal at bottom of garden, 30 miles of fenced-in towpath for instant walks. Dogs need to be on a lead in garden if inclined to eat chickens!*

Rooms	3 doubles, 1 twin: £90. Singles £45.
Meals	Packed lunch £4. Pub/restaurant 0.75 miles.
Closed	Rarely.
Treats	Blankets, towels, dog sitting, walk advice – & food if you've forgotten to bring some.

Peter Evans
The Old Store House,
Llanfrynach,
Brecon, LD3 7LJ

Tel	+44 (0)1874 665499
Email	oldstorehouse@btconnect.com
Web	www.theoldstorehouse.co.uk

Danyfan Carriage

Danyfan Carriage is the latest project of Emma and Stevie, who fled London for the country life a few years ago. They found a perfect spot to make their home, and also the perfect place for a little glamping. The railway wagon, as far as they know, is an early 20th-century artefact. In converting it they have kept as much of the original work as possible, adding only what will complement the period feel, with a grand wicker-headboarded bed and a burnished walnut wardrobe. The whole site is completely off-grid, with a cleverly designed (piping hot!) gas shower and washing-up area, plus a separate compost loo, just steps from the carriage. Being off-grid doesn't have to mean hardship: the wood-burner keeps you beautifully warm, the bed is a wonder of mountainous soft pillows. Lanterns and torches give a soft light, and the gas hobs make cooking easy. Your corner of the garden is sheltered, with mountain views and a rushing stream. Walks through the Brecon Beacons National Park stretch out from the door and wildlife and nature surround you. *Large garden, owners' dog (lives next door) to play with, and wonderful walks up in the mountains. Livestock in neighbouring fields.*

Rooms	Train carriage for 2: from £80 per night. Max. 1 dog.
Meals	Self-catering.
Closed	Never.
Treats	Biscuits, leads, bowls & advice on walks.

Tel	+44 (0)117 204 7830
Email	enquiries@canopyandstars.co.uk
Web	www.canopyandstars.co.uk/danyfan

Canopy & Stars
Danyfan Carriage,
Danyfan, Cwmgwdi,
Brecon, LD3 8LG

The Dome at Argoed

The Geodome at Argoed is a friendly competition between the inside and the outside for the title of most impressive view. Outside, the Brecon Beacons reach away from the hilltop site, stretching in misty folds for miles. Inside, intense scouring of antique shops and auctions has resulted in a lavish version of frontier style, all furs and blankets and dark wooden furniture. The two are brought together by the clear picture window that spans five whole metres of the eight metre space, as well as the sofa and the bed, both perfect places to snuggle and watch the sun set on the hills. You'll also get pretty good views from Ty Bach, the little house behind the dome which houses the shower and loo, but the best way to enjoy the stunning scenery has to be while soaking in the wood-fired hot tub.

Amazing walks on the doorstep; occasionally sheep in the adjacent fields. Dogs not allowed on furniture or bed.

Rooms	Geodome for 2: from £100 per night. Dogs £20 per dog per stay. Max. 2 dogs.
Meals	Self-catering.
Closed	November-March
Treats	Welcome pack of towel, poop bags and treats.

Canopy & Stars
The Dome at Argoed ,
Argoed Barns, Talachddu,
Brecon, LD3 0UG

Tel	+44 (0)117 204 7830
Email	enquiries@canopyandstars.co.uk
Web	www.canopyandstars.co.uk/thedome

The Felin Fach Griffin

Quirky, homespun, colourful: feel like you're staying in the home of a fashionable old friend, with bright art splashed on the walls and pretty bedrooms (some fresh from a spruce up) decked out in antiques. Bring four-legged friends to run around the grassy beer garden, where you can enjoy al fresco lunches. They take food and drink seriously here. Supper is served in the white-walled restaurant, with stock pots simmering on an Aga and a little shop selling homemade piccalilli. Much of what you eat comes from a half-acre kitchen garden, with meat and game from the hills around you, plus a full vegan spread. Breakfast is leisurely: read the morning papers, make your own toast, choose the full Welsh works. A road passes outside, but quietly at night, while lanes lead into the hills. Come to walk, ride, bike, canoe. Hay is close for books galore.
Large garden with plenty of space to run around & local rivers for swimming. Stunning walks in Brecon Beacons.

Rooms	3 doubles, 3 twin/doubles: £140-£207. 1 family room for 3: £175-£232. Singles £110-£137. Extra bed £25 p.p.p.n.
Meals	Lunch from £15. Dinner, 3 courses, from £25-£30. Sunday lunch from £12.50.
Closed	4 days in January.
Treats	Biscuits, blanket, towels, advice on walks, poo bags, dog bowls – & very friendly staff.

Tel	+44 (0)1874 620111
Email	enquiries@felinfachgriffin.co.uk
Web	www.felinfachgriffin.co.uk

Charles & Edmund Inkin
The Felin Fach Griffin,
Felin Fach, Brecon, LD3 0UB

The Sleepout

The good solid bones of this little cabin were affectionately crafted by botanist Rachel and tree surgeon Mike, whose warm welcomes feel totally relaxed and unscripted. Down a rough track and through wonderful wilderness, you'll find The Sleepout; a cosy cabin where a wooden ladder leads from the small sitting area up to a sleeping den. We love the magic of climbing up to the little nook and, other than a bunch of sweet peas, a welcome basket and a pile of logs for the wood burner, there are no knick-knacks to crowd up the sleeping space; just a bed, pale wool throws, and the stars. Without neighbours close by, the windows are left naked and you don't feel like you are inside at all, but rather staring into the Milky Way, or floating along with the clouds. It doesn't hurt that you're perched slap bang in the midst of the Welsh valleys either. Who wouldn't want to spend time up there? *Woodlands for walks directly beside the cabin, a large river to jump in and a dog-friendly local pub serving good food and beer. Sheep in neighbouring fields so please keep dogs on leads.*

Rooms	Cabin for 2: from £95 per night. Space for 2 children from £10 per child per night. Dogs £20 per dog per stay. Max 2.
Meals	Self-catering.
Closed	Never.
Treats	Advice on walks & maps in cabin. Biscuits, towel, basket, bowl & poop scoop.

Canopy & Stars
The Sleepout,
Sunnylea,
Meifod, SY22 6YA

Tel	+44 (0)117 204 7830
Email	enquiries@canopyandstars.co.uk
Web	www.canopyandstars.co.uk/thesleepout

Beudy Banc

Six handmade and upcycled cabins surrounded by some of the best biking trails and beaches, wooded bridleways and ancient drovers' roads. Caban Cilfa first is the most compact with a double bed, kitchen and bathroom all built in. Caban Coch, crafted from an old hay trailer, has a wood-burning stove, kitchen/dining area with a full-sized cooker, sink and storage, next to a sleeping area and the wet room with a shower. Cylindrical Caban Crwn has a ladder which leads up to the mezzanine bed and a lounge area downstairs. The compact compost loo and shower unit are through a hidden door. Caban Copa is framed by a domed ceiling, glass doors and porthole windows – a sofa sits by the wood-burner, opposite the kitchen and hidden behind Is an ensuite compost loo. Up the ladder is your cosy bedroom for the night. Caban Cader and Caban Cadno sit at the top of the hill – their walls festooned with collected treasures. Each has a living area with a double sofabed, a dining area, kitchen and a sleeping loft above with double bed. Calling all mud-seekers, adventurers and off-roaders, Beudy Banc has the quirky cabin just for you! *Children & babies welcome. Nearby stream; marked walking routes on the farm.*

Rooms	5 Cabins for 2: from £75 per night. Space for 1 adult/child at £10 p.p.p.n. Dogs £10 per dog per stay. Max. 1.
Meals	Self-catering.
Closed	Never.
Treats	Water bowl & tether. Maps & routes for walks around farm, local footpaths & bridleways.

Tel	+44 (0)117 204 7830
Email	enquiries@canopyandstars.co.uk
Web	www.canopyandstars.co.uk/beudybanc

Canopy & Stars
Beudy Banc ,
Cwm Llywi Uchaf Farm, Abercegir,
Machynlleth, SY20 8NP

The Slate Shed at Graig Wen

Sarah and conservationist John spent months travelling in a camper looking for their own special place and found this lovely old Welsh slate cutting mill... captivated by acres of wild woods and stunning views. You'll feel at ease as soon as you step into their eclectic modern home with its reclaimed slate and wood, cosy wood-burners, books, games, snug bedrooms (one downstairs) and superb bathrooms. Breakfast communally on local eggs and sausages, honey from the mountainside, homemade bread and granola. Hike or bike the Mawddach Trail, climb Cadair Idris, wonder at the views... and John's chocolate brownies. *Minimum stay: 2 nights at weekends & in high season. Children over 10 welcome. Dogs welcome in rooms & at breakfast. Advice on dog-friendly walks, beaches, places to eat & visit; doggie day care while guests take the train up Snowdon or visit Portmeirion.*

Rooms	4 doubles, 1 twin/double: £80-£130. Singles £65. Dogs £10 per dog per stay. Max. 2.
Meals	Packed lunch £7.50. Pub 5 miles.
Closed	5 November-14 February.
Treats	Treats, towels and throws for muddy paws, and wonderful walks from the doorstep.

Sarah Heyworth
The Slate Shed at Graig Wen,
Arthog, LL39 1YP

Tel	+44 (0)1341 250482
Email	hello@graigwen.co.uk
Web	www.slateshed.co.uk

Coes Faen Lodge

Effortless simplicity is the key to this new spa B&B. A glass and rock entrance, a hallway suffused with light: this Victorian lodge on the edge of Mawddach Estuary has been stunningly, meticulously revived. Bedrooms are cocoons of sleek opulence, bathrooms are rich in slate and stone, and detailing is sublime: mood lighting, hands-free technology, pearlescent tiles that reflect the light. Choose a sauna smelling of cedar or a rooftop hot tub and terrace... Richard and Sara have Welsh roots and love both place and landscape. Acres of woodland garden await behind; breakfasts and dinners are original and exquisite. *Rooms have terrace with direct access to 20 acres of walled woodland gardens.*

Rooms	6 doubles: £165-£275.
	Dogs £15 per stay. Max. 2.
Meals	Dinner from £35. Pubs/restaurants 0.5 miles.
Closed	Rarely.
Treats	Bed, blankets, biscuits, outside hot water shower, shampoo & towels.

Tel	+44 (0)1341 281632
Email	richard@coesfaen.com
Web	www.coesfaen.co.uk

Richard & Sara Parry-Jones
Coes Faen Lodge,
Coes Faen, Abermaw, LL42 1TE

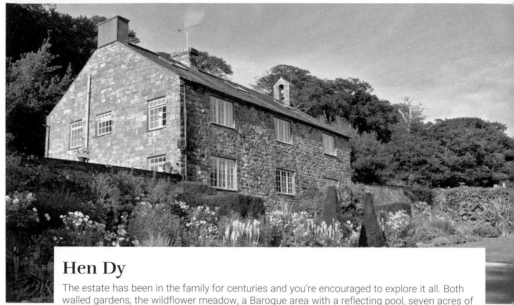

Hen Dy

The estate has been in the family for centuries and you're encouraged to explore it all. Both walled gardens, the wildflower meadow, a Baroque area with a reflecting pool, seven acres of ancient woodland... Help yourself to herbs, meander around the mile-long circular woodland walk. For ball games you have your own patch. Hen Dy is the oldest house on the estate and was the gardeners' bothy and laundry, with a bell tower that announced mealtimes. Now there's a sunny sitting room with books, games and a large fireplace – estate logs are left for you. Upstairs big bedrooms overlook the gardens which are lovely – ablaze with rhododendrons and azaleas in spring with views down to lake, pastures, woodland and sea. In season a trug of estate fruit and vegetables will arrive on the doorstep. Abersoch is three miles down the road and you're surrounded by some of the most glorious countryside in north Wales. *Woodland for walks and ponds to jump in. Occasionally cattle in park so keep dogs out of there if asked.*

Rooms	1 house for 7: £850-£1500 per week. Short breaks: Fri-Sun £450; 3 nights £650; 4 nights £800. Max. 4 dogs.
Meals	Pubs/restaurants 10-minute drive.
Closed	September-December.
Treats	Biscuits, special bowls & mat, towels & wonderful, traffic-free dog walks on estate.

Karen Morgan
Hen Dy,
Nanhoron, LL53 8DL

Tel	+44 (0)1758 730610
Email	karen.morgan@nanhoron.com
Web	www.nanhoronestate.co.uk

Plas Dinas Country House

The family home of Lord Snowdon dates to the 1600s and stands in 15 rural acres with an avenue of oak sweeping you up to the house. Princess Margaret often stayed and much of what fills the house belongs to the family: striking chandeliers, oils by the score, gilt-framed mirrors – an Aladdin's cave of beautiful things. There's a baby grand piano in the drawing room, where you find a roaring fire and an honesty bar, but potter about and find masses of memorabilia framed on the walls (make sure you visit the private dining room). Bedrooms – some with views across fields to the sea – mix a graceful past with modern design. You get four-posters, period colours, bold wallpapers, a sofa if there's room. A cute room in the eaves has mountain views, all have hot-water bottles, Apple TVs and excellent bathrooms, some with showers, others with free-standing baths. Good food waits in the restaurant, perhaps fishcakes with lime and ginger, lamb shank with a rosemary jus, chocolate tart with white chocolate ice-cream. Snowdon is close, as you'd expect, so bring walking boots and mountain bikes. *Minimum say: 2 nights on bank holiday weekends. 15 acres of grounds. 3 dog-friendly rooms.*

Rooms	3 doubles, 5 twin/doubles: £109-£169. 2 suites for 2: £159-£249. Extra beds £50. Dogs £10 per night. Max. 2.
Meals	Dinner, 3 courses, £25-£35.
Closed	23-27 December.
Treats	Advice on dog-friendly dining, biscuits, towel, poo bags & suggestions for walks.

Tel	+44 (0)1286 830214
Email	info@plasdinas.co.uk
Web	www.plasdinas.co.uk

Neil Baines & Marco Soares
Plas Dinas Country House,
Bontnewydd, Caernarfon, LL54 7YF

Wonderfully Wild

The safari tent lodges at Wonderfully Wild are a classic safari style with plenty of added Welshness, including slate hearths from local quarries and warm woollen rugs in the spacious living areas, not to mention the mountain views of Snowdonia from the outside decks. Derw, at one end of the field (and closest to the car park), is Welsh for Oak, and then there's Castan (Conker), Onnen (Ash) and Jacmor (Sycamore) at the far end. As well as the private showers, toilets and fully-equipped kitchens in each one, owners Victoria and Robin have toured the auctions to fill the lodges with quality upcycled furniture. You're surrounded by 200 acres of fields, woodland and streams – the nearest borders the field where you'll be staying. The

Telor Tour cycle route borders another side of the field and is a great way to explore this beautiful corner of Anglesey by bike. It's a short drive to a choice of beaches, and just 40 minutes' walk to take you to the seaside town of Beaumaris – perfect for a day out. A big chest of board games and then comfy beds to come back to in the evening. *Fields and woodland to walk in, streams to play in; safe environment.*

Rooms	4 safari tents for 6: from £110 per night. Dogs £20 per dog per per stay. Max. 1 big dog or 2 small dogs.
Meals	Self-catering.
Closed	November-March.
Treats	Advice on dog-friendly pubs, beaches & days out.

Canopy & Stars
Wonderfully Wild,
Cichle Farm, Beaumaris, LL58 8PS

Tel	+44 (0)117 204 7830
Email	enquiries@canopyandstars.co.uk
Web	www.canopyandstars.co.uk/wonderfullywild

Copse Camp

Margaret and Jenny have created a wonderfully rustic spot in their own homespun style. The treehouse is wallpapered in Beano magazines, with hessian potato sacks repurposed for cushions and blinds – though you'll find only the finest crisp bed linen and fluffy towels. Feel at one with the wood in your cosy bed in the roof, with the gentle creaking of timber to lull you to sleep, a different view from each window and a pot belly stove to warm you. Cross the rope bridge to stoke the fires for s'mores and camp cooking in the Dutch oven, or use the practical kitchen for more adventurous suppers. Wash up to views of the moors – you're off-grid, but there's hot and cold running water straight from the hills (plus a great shower and a compost loo). Everything on camp is yours to use, including a gypsy caravan which doubles as both dining room and second bedroom. On a quiet lane you're miles from traffic and modern disruptions. *Situated beside Llandegla Forest with walking trails, visitor centre and cafe. Dog-friendly pubs within walking distance. 330 acres of open moorland. Carpeted bridge with artificial turf on entrance. Fenced field with two streams for dogs to run around.*

Rooms	Treehouse for 2: from £80 per night. Extra space for 4: £20 per night. Dogs £10 per dog per stay. 3 dogs max.
Meals	Self-catering.
Closed	November-March.
Treats	Towels, blankets, water bowl, poo bags, bottle of dog beer & natural dog treats. Books with dog-friendly walks. A welcome board with dog's name.

Tel	+44 (0)117 204 7830
Email	enquiries@canopyandstars.co.uk
Web	www.canopyandstars.co.uk/copsecamp

Canopy & Stars
Copse Camp,
Faraway, Llandegla, LL11 3BG

Scotland

The Meikleour Arms, page 262

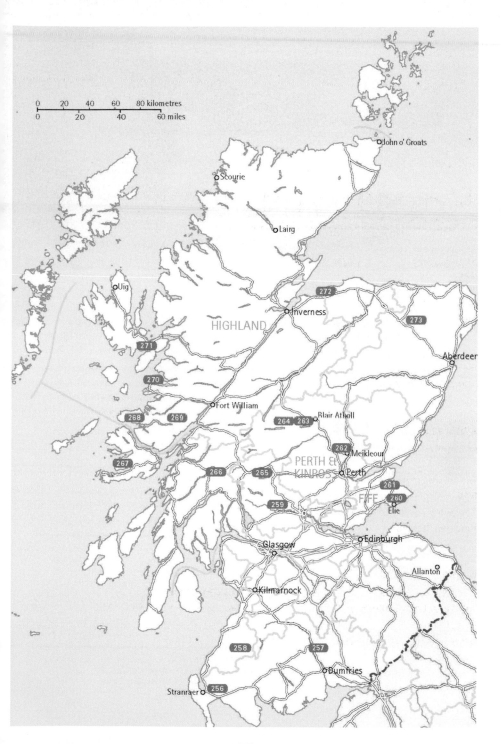

Lochinch Castle Cottages

On an isthmus hugged by freshwater lochs is one of Scotland's finest gardens with the dreamy ruins of Castle Kennedy at one end and Lochinch Castle, the family home of the Stairs (they've been here for generations) at the other. With 75 acres to roam, all ages will be happy here; walks ramble off in all directions. Explore land sculptures built in the 1730s; spot geese, herons, maybe an osprey, red squirrels and otters too. There are mesmerising displays of rhododendrons, azaleas and embothrium, and the ancient Monkey Puzzle Avenue is a treat. Find three charming properties. Chauffeur's, on the top floor of a two-storey Victorian carriage house, has pretty French chateau style turrets, an open fire, long views, a large kitchen and

three beautifully restful bedrooms. Balker Lodge, originally a gate house, is a cleverly revived bolthole for two. Ice House is a single-storey cottage with two pretty bedrooms, a log-burner in the sitting room and a pristine kitchen. All have their own private outside space, splendid welcome baskets with delicious cakes, and you get the run of the gardens. Why not take a guided tour with head gardener, John, who's worked here for 25 years! *Minimum stay: 3 nights. Great walks in acres of gardens & beautiful countryside.*

Rooms	1 apartment for 6: £400-£825. 1 cottage for 4: £380-£695. 1 house for 2: £360-£550. Prices per week. £15 booking fee; £45 deposit; £15 charge per dog per week; max 2.
Meals	Breakfast £12-£13. Dinner £12.
Closed	Never.
Treats	Baskets, large comfortable rooms & advice on walks.

Emily Stair
Lochinch Castle Cottages,
Lochinch Castle, Stranraer, DG9 8RT

Tel	+44 (0)1776 702024
Email	housekeeping@lochinchcastle.com
Web	www.castlekennedygardens.com/holiday-cottages/

Trigony House Hotel & Garden Spa

A welcoming family-run hotel with good food and nicely priced rooms. There's a small spa in the garden, too, with rather good views from the hot tub. The house dates to 1700 and comes with Japanese oak panelling in the hall, a wood-burner in the sitting room and an open fire in the dining room, where doors open onto the terrace for dinner in summer. Adam cooks lovely rustic fare, perhaps prawns with coconut and coriander, saddle of roe venison, rhubarb and hazelnut crumble; a small, organic kitchen garden provides for the table in summer. Bedrooms – some big, some smaller – have warm colours, crisp linen, good beds and spotless bathrooms. A couple are dog-friendly, those at the back have the view, the suite opens onto a private garden. As for the spa, there's a treatment room, a sauna and a hot tub, so plenty of scope to recuperate after a day walking the Southern Upland Way or discovering the spectacular country between Moniaive and the Galloway Forest, a lost world of huge beauty you'll have to yourself. Don't miss Drumlanrig Castle for its gardens, walking trails and mountain bike tracks. *Beautiful walks. Well-behaved dogs welcome in lounge & bar.*

Rooms	4 doubles, 4 twin/doubles: £120-£140. 1 suite for 2: £165. Singles £90-£120. Extra beds £15. Dogs £9.
Meals	Lunch from £7.50. Afternoon tea £15. Dinner £25-£35.
Closed	24-26 December.
Treats	Poo bags, map of local dog-friendly walks, bag of treats & blanket/bed.

Tel	+44 (0)1848 331211
Email	trigonyhotel@googlemail.com
Web	www.trigonyhotel.co.uk

Adam & Jan Moore
Trigony House Hotel & Garden Spa,
Closeburn, Thornhill, DG3 5EZ

Alton Albany Farm

Discover Ayrshire... pine forests, hills and wild beauty. Alasdair and Andrea (sculptor/garden photographer) are generous hosts who love having you to stay – your visit starts with tea, coffee and cake. There's an arty vibe with their work on display; the dining room brims with garden books and games; large bedrooms have cosy lamps and more books. Big breakfasts by a log fire are a treat, perhaps with haggis, garden fruit, homemade bread; hearty dinners too. Rich in wildlife and orchids the garden has a rambling charm, the salmon-filled river Stinchar runs past and dogs are welcome – resident Daisy, Clover and Tansy are friendly. *Minimum stay: 2 nights. Path round two-acre garden; burn running through orchard which water-loving dogs are free to romp in; riverside walks; field for exercise & ball throwing, if no livestock.*

Rooms	1 double; 1 double, 1 twin, sharing bath, let to same party only: £115. Singles £75. Dogs max. usually 2.
Meals	Dinner £17.95. Pubs/restaurants 10 miles.
Closed	Rarely.
Treats	Treat on arrival. Biscuits for every taste; cocktail sausages for the pernickety! Hose, bowl, basket of towels, toys, balls & launcher.

Andrea & Alasdair Currie
Alton Albany Farm,
Barr, Girvan, KA26 0TL

Tel	+44 (0)1465 861148
Mobile	+44 (0)7881 908764
Email	alasdair@gardenexposures.co.uk
Web	www.altonalbanyfarm.com

Ben Lomond

A fusion of Kyrgyz design and local materials, there are three yurts here but Ben Lomond is the only one to welcome your canine friend. All three yurts have a homely, earthy feel, with thick rugs, rough tapestries and wood-burning stoves adding comfort. Ben Ledi and Ben Lomond yurts share the woodland just a little way on from Stuc a'Chroin yurt. In each is a double bed, a double futon, and a single 'sleep over' for a child. From the boardwalk leading to the communal kitchen are impressive views across Flanders Moss National Nature Reserve. Arts and crafts courses aplenty too, from willow crafting to Japanese block printing and yoga. There's an abundance of local produce, including veg from the kitchen garden, steaks for the barbecue, local eggs and homemade bread. With all this and the beauty of the Trossachs National Park to explore, you won't be short of ways to create a memorable stay. And for those furry friends looking to curl up beside the wood-burner, blankets are provided for extra comfort. *Working farm so dogs on leads on farm, but there are no animals in the vicinity of the yurt. Lots of space for a run in the woodland around the yurt.*

Rooms	Yurt for 4: from £101 per night (+1 child on sleepover mat). £10 p.p.p.n. Dogs £30 per dog per stay. Max. 1.
Meals	Self-catering.
Closed	November-March.
Treats	Bowls, bed, towel and toothbrush treat! Advice on walks.

Tel	+44 (0)117 204 7830
Email	enquiries@canopyandstars.co.uk
Web	www.canopyandstars.co.uk/ben-lomond

Canopy & Stars
Ben Lomond,
West Moss-side Organic Farm and
Centre, Thornhill, FK8 3QJ

Catchpenny Safari Lodges

Catchpenny Safari Lodges sit on a remote curve of the coast to the north of the firth, basking in glittering sea views and surrounded by incredible wildlife. Dolphins and seals are regularly seen and even humpback whales have been spotted. The tranquil setting is beautiful, but just 500m away is the award-winning Ardross Farm Shop, where you can stock up on local produce. A couple of miles along the scenic Fife Coastal Path are the upmarket shops and eateries of Elie and in the other direction St Monans, with the trail's 117 miles stretching round the coast as far as the Firth of Tay. Each lodge is wonderfully crafted, from the warm central wood-burner and the sofa, to the king-sized beds, well-equipped kitchens and piping hot showers in the en suite bathrooms. Cracking open the games basket, grabbing a drink from the fridge and taking to the screened suntrap deck is the perfect end to a day of wilderness exploring and the simple pleasures of rural peace. When the sun has set over the water, light the fire and gather round as the stars fill the unspoilt skies. *Direct access onto the Fife Coastal Path, 117 miles of coastal walks and deserted beaches around Fife's historic coastline.*

Rooms	Safari tents for 6: from £94 per night. Dogs £10 per dog per stay. Max. 2.
Meals	Self-catering.
Closed	November-March.
Treats	Dog bowls & biscuits.

Canopy & Stars
Catchpenny Safari Lodges,
Ardross, Elie, KY9 1EU

Tel	+44 (0)117 204 7830
Email	enquiries@canopyandstars.co.uk
Web	www.canopyandstars.co.uk/catchpenny

Kincaple Stables

The tap-tap of woodpeckers and singsong of birds are the soundtrack to a stay at Kincaple, a quaint hamlet three miles from St Andrews. The cottages, former stables, rest in the pretty, sheltered courtyard of Kincaple House, next to the Coach House where Claudia lives – her friendly terriers and cat may wander over to see you. She has an eye for colour: subtle tones of grey-blue, honey and buttermilk are sparked by vases of flowers; in the living and dining room, a cream sofa curves around a stylish wood-burner and a bleached solid oak table seats four. It's all top quality. Find Villeroy & Bosch, Le Creuset and Siemens in the kitchen – small, square, with a stable door to the courtyard and well-stocked wine cooler – and Molton Brown in the bathroom. The main bedroom is flooded with light; the second bedroom has a zip-link bed. Well-travelled Claudia is passionate about this beautiful area of Scotland where she and her three daughters have settled. There are beaches, birds and golfing to enjoy, as well as ancient St Andrews with its university, vast cathedral and many fine shops and restaurants. *Minimum stay: 3 nights; 7 in high season. Plenty of walks including 'Chariots of Fire' beach. Quiet grounds to roam, but some unfenced land.*

Rooms	2 cottages for 4: £625-£895 per week. Up to £795 during the Golf Open. 3-night short break: £95 per night. Dogs welcome in one cottage.
Meals	Self-catering.
Closed	Rarely.
Treats	Blankets & towels to get dry after the sea.

Mobile	+44 (0)7780 695960
Email	cdaventry@me.com
Web	www.kincaplestables.com

Claudia Daventry
Kincaple Stables,
Coach House, Kincaple,
St Andrews, KY16 9SH

The Meikleour Arms

With their own ale, over twenty malts and a bevvy of artisan gins, you'll find a toast for every occasion at this lovely inn where bedroom names (Flahaut, Hortense, Lansdowne) reflect the French and Scottish ancestry of the owners. Much of the food in the restaurant comes from the estate – vegetables and herbs grown in the walled garden, scallops hand-dived on the west coast and venison from the Meikleour Forest. You can also sample some quirky finds from the less well known vineyards in Bordeaux. Walk to the river for a morning's fishing on the Tay – book a fly-fishing lesson with the head ghillie. Spot ospreys, otters, kingfishers. The Blairgowrie Golf Course is a five-mile drive, while three others are within 30 miles. Book a tour of a couple of whisky distilleries too – Blair Athol and Edradour are in Pitlochry. Scone Palace, Glamis and Balmoral are all within reach. You stay in the 19th-century coaching inn or the cottages in the grounds – a short drive or walk from the inn. The cottages have small kitchens, but you can wander over for breakfast in the restaurant each morning. *Minimum stay in cottages: 2 nights. Each cottage has fenced little garden. Path from beer garden into wood; river Tay walk with shingle beach. Map of walks on website.*

Rooms	10 doubles, 1 twin/double: £100-£130. 2 cottages for 2, 2 cottages for 4, 1 cottage for 6: £110-£225. A laundered dog bed £15 per stay.
Meals	Light bites about £8. Lunch & dinner à la carte, 2 courses, about £20.
Closed	Never.
Treats	Treats at bar, bowl of water, hose outside. Socialise in pub restaurant, sleep by fire in winter.

Claire Mercer Nairne	**Tel** +44 (0)1250 883206
The Meikleour Arms,	**Email** contact@meikleourarms.co.uk
Meikleour, PH2 6EB	**Web** www.meikleourarms.co.uk

The Inn at Loch Tummel

You weave through the forest, then arrive at this 200-year-old inn to find views of field, hill, loch and sky. It's a magical spot, with a small garden to the front that drinks it all in. As for the inn, Alice and Jade rescued it from neglect, poured in love and money and now it shines. Interiors mix contemporary flair with Highland charm, the very definition of rustic chic. You'll find a cool little bar, painted beams and a wood-burner in the restaurant, then a first-floor sitting room with fat sofas, books and games, goatskin rugs and Jade's guitar. Bedrooms are a treat: chic fabrics, beautiful beds, cool colours, woollen throws. Some are big, none are small, one is dog friendly, most have the view. All have good art, decanters of whisky and spotless bathrooms, some with walk-in showers. By day you explore the hills, whizz down mountain bike trails or climb Schiehallion, the local munro. At night you return for delicious food, perhaps calamari with chilli and lemon, rack of local lamb, an espresso brownie with beetroot meringue. Queen's View, up the road, has one of the best views in Scotland. *Children over 5 welcome. Lochside walks; Allean Forest, a few minutes' drive.*

Rooms	2 doubles, 4 twin/doubles: £95-£140. Dogs £10. Max. 2 per room.
Meals	Dinner with wine £27.
Closed	Rarely.
Treats	Biscuits, water bowls, hose for muddy dogs.

Tel	+44 (0)1882 634317
Email	info@theinnatlochtummel.com
Web	www.theinnatlochtummel.com

Alice & Jade Calliva
The Inn at Loch Tummel,
Queens View,
Strathtummel, PH16 5RP

Rose Cottage, Dunalastair Estate

You feel relaxed the moment you've pulled off your wellies in the little rustic porch (draped with, you've guessed it, roses in summer) and stepped inside this neat-as-a-pin stone cottage on the sprawling Dunalastair Estate. You'll find a tray of tea and Border biscuits on the table – soak up the warmth from the kitchen's Ray burn as you check out the other welcome goodies. The light, clean, practical decor is comfortable rather than showy, ideal for children; bad weather boredom can be kept at bay with games, books and satellite TV. Climb Schiehallion, one of the easier Munros which stands proud within sight of the cottage; enjoy a game of tennis (rackets and balls provided); head off on estate walks right from the door –

through fields of cattle and sheep and edging the Dunalastiar Loch, where you can fish for trout for free. By day keep a look out for deer and red squirrels, and eagles swooping overhead; at night the lack of light pollution means the stars are magical when skies are clear. *Minimum stay: 3 nights; 7 in high season. Secure garden & a loch to swim in. Working farm so dogs on leads near livestock.*

Rooms	1 cottage for 5: £527-£763 per week. Dogs £16 per week. Max. 2.
Meals	Restaurants 5-minute drive.
Closed	Never.
Treats	Treats, water bowls & advice on walks.

Beatrice Tainsh
Rose Cottage, Dunalastair Estate,
Kinloch Rannoch, PH16 5PD

Tel +44 (0)1882 632491
Email cottages@dunalastair.com
Web www.dunalastair.com/Rose-Cottage

Mhor

Monachyle Mhor, boutique hotel run by the Lewis family is also home to two Highland hideouts. Pilot Panther is a classic 1950s showman's wagon originally built by The Coventry Steel Company, once renowned as the finest wagon makers in the country. Off the main living and sleeping area, which also has the oven and grill, is the double bunk room and the views from every window are of the spectacular loch. The Ferry Waiting Room is made up of a lost and found ferry terminal and bothy. Whilst the waiting room has become a cosy bedroom with a double bed and two bunks, the bothy houses a small kitchen – both with incredible views. Hot showers and flushing loos can be found in the courtyard of the hotel, shared with other guests.

The great walking and stunning views around the long loch will help you work up an appetite for dinner that's worthy of Monachlye Mhor, an award-winning pilgrimage for Scottish foodies. The family that run the restaurant also manage the farm, which ensures that a good supply of very local produce goes onto the amazing menus – take your pick from take away ingredients or eat-in goodies. *In the middle of a glen with plenty of countryside walks & rivers to jump in. Sheep in some fields where dogs need to be kept on lead.*

Rooms	Wagon for 4: from £125 per night. Cabin for 4: from £140 per night. Dogs £20 per dog per stay, payable on checkout. Max. 2.
Meals	Dinner and breakfast at the hotel must be pre-booked with reception prior to arrival.
Closed	Never.
Treats	Advice on walks & dog sitting available.

Tel	+44 (0)117 204 7830
Email	enquiries@canopyandstars.co.uk
Web	www.canopyandstars.co.uk/mhor

Canopy & Stars
Mhor,
Balquhidder, Lochearnhead, FK19 8PQ

Blue Cottage

Only one other house shares this road and it is invisible from the cottage. A glimpse of a Highland cow in the field way below is a silent but welcome sign of farm life and the hooting owl and fox are the only noises you'll hear as night falls. A blue velvet sofa and wood-burner make the living room the cosy hub of the home and just a glimpse of the kitchen will spark a passion for cooking. One bathroom is en suite to the master bedroom; the other is off the hall, past the twin room and contains a roll top cast iron tub. Pampering continues with a welcome hamper of local treats and beers. Help yourself to the fishing rods in the hall, bikes in the shed along with two sets of golf clubs and trolleys and even a blow up kayak! Oh yes, and

binoculars and bird book on the window sill, with a bird box within range. Even a leather bound sketch book if you felt artistically inclined. The Loch Awe boatyard is an easy stroll away, where you can hire a rowing boat or simply watch the fishermen at work from the jetty. *Garden open space; quiet road behind. Wilds of Argyll & banks of Loch Awe: miles of wonderful walks on doorstep; books & OS maps. Dog-friendly pub 2-minute walk.*

Rooms	Cabin for 4: from £109 per night. Dogs £15 per dog per stay. Max. 1 medium or 2 small dogs.
Meals	Self-catering.
Closed	Never.
Treats	Food (James Wellbeloved & Lily's), sometimes local homemade biscuits. Poo bags, 'tick' remover tool, bed, blankets for furniture so you can snuggle up. Outside standing water pipe too.

Canopy & Stars
Blue Cottage,
Ardbrecknish,
Dalmally, PA33 1BH

Tel	+44 (0)117 204 7830
Email	enquiries@canopyandstars.co.uk
Web	www.canopyandstars.co.uk/bluecottage

Tiroran House

The setting is magnificent – 17 acres of gardens rolling down to Loch Scridian. Otters and dolphins pass through, buzzards and eagles glide above, red deer visit the garden. As for this 1850 shooting lodge, you'll be hard pressed to find a more comfortable island base. There are fires in the drawing rooms, fresh flowers everywhere, games to be played, books to be read. Airy bedrooms hit the spot: crisp linen, beautiful fabrics, the odd chaise longue; some have watery views, all have silence guaranteed. You eat in a smart dining room with much of the delicious food from the island or waters around it, perhaps mussel and oyster broth, saddle of lamb with carrot purée, chocolate torte with vanilla ice cream. Wander to the Whitetail Coffee Shop for afternoon tea. You're bang in the middle of Mull with lots to do: Tobermory, the prettiest town in the Hebrides; Calgary and its magical beach; day trips to Iona and its famous monastery; cruises to Staffa and Fingal's Cave. If you want to be more independent there are two self-catering cottages in the grounds. *Gardens to walk through, enclosed fields, woodland walks beside a burn, private beach: dog paradise!*

Rooms	5 doubles, 5 twin/doubles: £175-£220.
Meals	Dinner, 4 courses, £48.
Closed	Rarely.
Treats	Dog biscuits.

Tel	+44 (0)1681 705232
Email	info@tiroran.com
Web	www.tiroran.com

Laurence & Katie Mackay
Tiroran House,
Tiroran,
Isle of Mull, PA69 6ES

Aspen Lodge

Your stone and timber lodge on the little-known Ardnamurchan Peninsula has a hillside setting and views from every window – use the telescope to spot red deer, golden eagles and the elusive Scottish wildcat if you're lucky. Downstairs is cosy with an open fire and plenty of books; teenagers will like the snug upstairs with an Xbox and a popcorn machine. You'll find a minibar and a welcome hamper which includes homemade jam, cake, wine and Scottish shortbread, and the kitchen is stocked with all you need. In summer, barbecue your supper in the garden and marvel at the stars on clear nights. You can walk and cycle from the door, launch a kayak into the sea loch opposite the garden or set off with a picnic for a day on the

beach, just a five-minute drive. There are other beaches and good restaurants – plus shops selling basics – within half an hour's drive, and you may spot minke whales, dolphins or puffins on summer boat tours of the loch. *Minimum stay: 7 nights; 3 in low season. Large, open garden with streams. All sorts of walks: beach, woodland, loch-side, heath. Dogs allowed on beaches all year round; some parts of the peninsula have grazing cattle and sheep.*

Rooms	1 house for 6: £1050-£1450 per week. Dogs free for 1 dog; £50 per stay for 2. Max. usually 1.
Meals	Pub/restaurant 25-minute drive.
Closed	Occasionally in January.
Treats	Beds, bowls, towels, biscuits & poo bags.

Samantha Davis
Aspen Lodge,
Acharacle, PH36 4JG

Mobile +44 (0)7717 820828
Email hello@aspenlodgescotland.co.uk
Web www.aspenlodgescotland.co.uk

Kilcamb Lodge Hotel & Restaurant

Another stunning West Coast setting with Loch Sunart at the end of the garden and Glas Bheinn rising beyond. Kilcamb – a barracks during the Jacobite uprising – is a perfect base. There's a smart drawing room with an open fire, an elegant dining room for super food, a cool little brasserie for a spot of lunch, then a handful of deeply indulging rooms. A 12-acre garden rolls down to the water, where you might spot otters and seals. Ducks and geese fly overhead, if you're lucky you'll see eagles. Back inside, you'll find a whisky bar that does a good line in gin, then driftwood lamps, fresh flowers, good books and local art. You can eat in the restaurant or the brasserie, either a five-course tasting menu or something simpler, perhaps hand-dived scallops, Highland lamb, raspberry bavarois with champagne sorbet. Bedrooms have a country-house feel, some with a contemporary twist. You'll find warm colours, smart fabrics and excellent beds. One has a balcony, most have the view, all have spotless bathrooms, some with separate showers. Don't miss Ardnamurchan or Sanna Bay at the end of the road. *11 acres of safe loch front garden. Dog sitting available*

Rooms	2 doubles, 6 twin/doubles: £220-£380. 2 suites for 2: £300-£435. 1 family room for 4: £390-£435. All prices include dinner. Dogs £12; £20 for 2.
Meals	Lunch from £7.50. Sunday lunch £25.
Closed	Jan & 1st 2 weeks in Dec. Ltd opening Nov & Feb.
Treats	Towel, blanket (covers bed for moments when dogs need a cuddle), bowl & mat; all in package with welcome letter. Breakfast sausage too!

Tel	+44 (0)1967 402257
Email	enquiries@kilcamblodge.co.uk
Web	www.kilcamblodge.co.uk

David & Sally Ruthven-Fox
Kilcamb Lodge Hotel & Restaurant,
Strontian, Argyll, PH36 4HY

Knoydart Hide

Not content with one gorgeous house high on the hill, Jackie and Ian have put up another and it's every bit as lovely. The only difference is size – this is a magical bolthole for two, perfect for honeymoons or just a blissful time away. Inside, walls of glass open onto a decked terrace, where you can soak in a hot tub while screened from the world by pine trees. Inside, there's a contemporary wood-burner in the sitting room, a kitchen with ample cooking stuff, a lovely big bed that looks out to sea, then a bathroom that's hard to beat with a double-ended bath, a walk-in power shower and an infrared sauna. You'll find all you'd want – fancy TV and DVD player, robes to pad about in, a bottle of prosecco on arrival – even the lawn is special, sown with 32 species of wild flower, the same turf as Olympic Park. If you don't want to cook, a chef can do it for you – lazy breakfasts, afternoon tea, seafood barbecues. Further afield, the wonders of Knoydart: wild orchids, sea eagles, mountains to climb. You can kayak, cruise the sea loch or do nothing. Stars fill the night sky, the Northern Lights come in winter. *Forest trails & woodland walks on doorstep, including three Munros. Long sandy beach & shoreline 100m away.*

Rooms	1 house for 2: £1450-£1875 per week. Extra beds £50-£75 per child per night. Short breaks available. Dogs £30 per stay. Max. 2.
Meals	Self-catering.
Closed	Never.
Treats	Bowls, extra towels for beachy paws, treat & advice on local walks.

Ian & Jackie Robertson
Knoydart Hide,
Inverie, Knoydart, PH41 4PL

Tel	+44 (0)1687 460012
Email	stay@knoydarthide.co.uk
Web	www.knoydarthide.co.uk

Skye Shepherd Huts

It's no great coincidence that Skye Shepherd Huts can be shortened to 'SSH!'. It's so peaceful here. A home, a henhouse, two donkeys and a pair of matching shepherd's huts make up Janet's characterful croft, which she tends to fervently. It's on the edge of the small village of Heaste so the neighbours are fairly (but not intrusively) close. The views, however, are nothing short of wild and immense, with the mountains on one side and the Isle of Rum on the other. Bothan Beilag is the more easily accessible of the two huts, while Bothan Buidheag is further back into the croft where Gilbert and George the donkeys hang out. There's a communal firepit in the ruins of a wee house between the huts and a shared summerhouse with a microwave. A continental breakfast is included or you can opt for a cooked breakfast for a fiver per person. The Big Shed, a well-equipped, open plan kitchen and lounge area is available for a small charge, if you want to self-cater. The huts themselves have their own kettle and a fold down table perfect for a dinner for two or board games. The bed is a comfy double and the hot shower and flushing loo are about 75 yards away in the main house. *Lots of beaches and walks but dogs must be kept on lead in village as surrounded by livestock and sheep.*

Rooms	Shepherd's huts for 2: from £80 per night. Dogs £10 per dog per stay. Max. 2.
Meals	Self-catering.
Closed	Never.
Treats	Homemade biscuits, towels, blankets, food, bowls, outside tap for dog washing, shampoo & even a spare lead are provided. Dog sitting available for a dog charity donation

Tel	+44 (0)117 204 7830
Email	enquiries@canopyandstars.co.uk
Web	www.canopyandstars.co.uk/ skyeshepherdhuts

Canopy & Stars
Skye Shepherd Huts,
1 Heaste, By Broadford,
Isle of Skye, IV49 9BN

Culbin Edge

This modern eco-cabin, in a stunning part of Scotland, sits at the top of a bank looking down over rough grazing that leads into a beautiful pine forest. Beyond the forest is the sea and you can reach the Sands and salt flats by foot in a couple of hours by following a wooded trail. Striking floor to ceiling windows make the most of these wonderfully wild surroundings with views stretching out over open farmland and towards the hills of Dava Moor. The sleek design continues inside but warm oak, comfy old armchairs and plenty of blankets and cushions keep the space cosy (not to mention the walk in shower and heated towel rails!). *Great forest walks on doorstep and lovely nearby beaches. Farm animals in fields at certain times of the year so dogs to be kept under control.*

Rooms	Cabin for 4: from £105 per night. Space for 2 adults from £10 per adult per night sleeping in own tent. Private hot tub £40 per stay.
Meals	Self-catering.
Closed	Never.
Treats	Towels, biscuits on arrival, bowls & feeding mat.

Canopy & Stars
Culbin Edge,
Brodie, IV36 2TE

Tel	+44 (0)117 204 7830
Email	enquiries@canopyandstars.co.uk
Web	www.canopyandstars.co.uk/culbinedge

Boutique Farm Bothies

Two upcycled bothies hidden away on a working farm in stunning rural Aberdeenshire, where Jane and James grow malting barley. They also breed sheep and grow strawberries, which you'll find tucked into your welcome hamper alongside homemade strawberry jam and Scottish treats. Barley Bothy's exterior is traditional, corrugated tin, and a veranda down its full length has an outside bike wash and storage for wet boots after those long countryside walks, perhaps up Bennachie or on the famous Malt Whisky Trail. Wool insulation, a log-burning range cooker and a vintage wood-burner will keep you warm in even Aberdeenshire winters. The two king-size cupboard beds have stargazing windows, as does the bathroom, which comes with a luxurious roll top bath as well as a vintage loo. The Sheep Shed is easily recognised by its tin shell and huge windows framed in red. Inside, there are more pops of colour in the kitchen, a comfy sofa, wood-burner and a ladder leading up to the mezzanine bedroom. There's a flushing loo and a tin trough bath too! Whichever bothy you choose, there's a private wood-fired hot tub and clear starry skies waiting for you. *Stream nearby & walks from door. Fabulous dog-friendly beaches: Sandend and Cullen. Hill walks on Bennachie. Dogs to be kept on leads on farm. Please keep dogs off beds.*

Rooms	2 Bothies for 2: from £115 per night (+2 adults/children on extra cupboard double bed) £15 p.p.p.n. Dogs £10 per dog per stay. Max. 2/3.
Meals	Self-catering.
Closed	Never.
Treats	Dog sleepover pack! Includes gravy bones, towel, blanket for sofa, bed, bowls & lead.

Tel	+44 (0)117 204 7830
Email	enquiries@canopyandstars.co.uk
Web	www.canopyandstars.co.uk/ boutiquefarmbothies

Canopy & Stars
Boutique Farm Bothies,
Newton of Begshill, Drumblade,
Huntly, AB54 6BJ

The Inn at Whitewell, page 184

Dog-friendly pubs

The Royal Oak, page 285

The Halsetown Inn

Built by a Victorian philanthropist in 1831 this inn has impeccable eco credentials and has won awards for its efforts. Inside, comfort and character abound with a choice of cosy corners, two open fires, an old Cornish range, and deep red walls. Tuck into the likes of pan-fried scallops with caramelised cauliflower and apple, followed by slow roasted pork belly with black pudding and cheddar hash brown, spring greens, cider gravy and onion rings. Leave room for puddings, especially rosewater panna cotta with pistachio biscotti. Vegetarians are well-served, children have their own menu, and special Wine and Dine evenings draw a happy crowd. You can walk from St Ives if the spirit moves you, then sit at the bar with a pint of Doom Bar or Skinner's ale or even a Cornish gin or a pastis! A pub with huge soul and great character. *Large field where dogs can run around & let off steam.*

Meals	Starters from £3.
	Lunch & dinner from £11.
Closed	Rarely.
Treats	Treats & water bowls.

Julia & Stuart Knight	**Tel**	+44 (0)1736 795583
The Halsetown Inn,	**Email**	info@halsetowninn.co.uk
Halestown, St Ives, TR26 3NA	**Web**	www.halsetowninn.co.uk

The Sheppey Inn

A funky country pub, one of the best in the west. Its exterior gives no hint of the wonders within – part cider house, part cool hotel. Low beamed ceilings in the bar, high white walls in the barn. There are cute booths, David Hockney prints, 50s retro furniture, the odd guitar waiting to be played. Music matters here: fantastic jazz, blues and funk bubbles away nicely, while a small stage hosts the odd travelling band. Local ales, scrumptious ciders, Belgian beers and lovely wines all wait, as does super food. Try a splendid fish stew (lobster bisque, fresh mussels) or Somerset beef with Yorkshire pudding and red wine gravy. In summer, life decants onto a long decked terrace that hangs above the little river; otters pass, fields stretch out beyond. Glastonbury and the Somerset Levels wait.
Out of this world. *Dogs are welcome in bar.*

Meals	Starters from £6.50. Mains from £13.50.
Closed	Never.
Treats	Dog treats & beer.

Tel	+44 (0)1458 831594
Email	hi@thesheppey.co.uk
Web	www.thesheppey.co.uk

Mark Hey & Liz Chamberlain
The Sheppey Inn,
Lower Godney, Wells, BA5 1RZ

Bird in Hand

The Bird in Hand is an unassuming little pub on Long Ashton's high street. Enter the bar, sparkling and new, for a pint of Gem or the guest ale of the week; turn right for plain tables and deep blue-grey walls. Owner Toby Gritten is as excited about foraged ingredients as he is about "heritage vegetables, forgotten cuts and wild fish", and his sentiments are echoed by those of head chef Sylvester and manager Dominic. Elegant dishes are served on white plates by friendly staff – chargrilled tenderstem broccoli, soft boiled duck egg, Berkswell cheese; haunch of wild venison, juniper, carrots, fondant potato; figgy pudding, stout and toffee sauce, cinnamon ice cream. Come on Sunday for champagne rhubarb fizz and a choice of two roasts, or gnocchi with artichokes and salsify. The food is satisfying, unshowy and steeped in flavour. *On Bristol cycle network which is a great walk with a dog. Two pub dogs, Minnie & Scooby.*

Meals	Lunch & dinner from £9. Sunday lunch from £12.50.
Closed	Open all day (from 12pm).
Treats	Water bowls always available.

Liz Pursey
Bird in Hand,
17 Weston Road,
Long Ashton, BS41 9LA

Tel	+44 (0)1275 395222
Email	info@bird-in-hand.co.uk
Web	www.bird-in-hand.co.uk

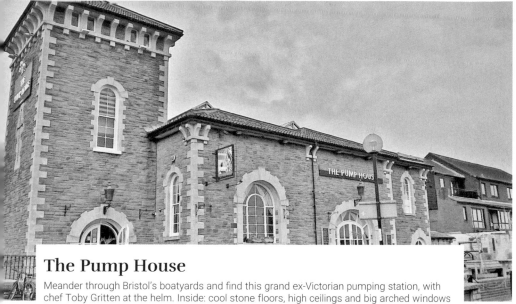

The Pump House

Meander through Bristol's boatyards and find this grand ex-Victorian pumping station, with chef Toby Gritten at the helm. Inside: cool stone floors, high ceilings and big arched windows frame gorgeous harbour views. Local guest beers and ales abound behind the bar, but it's the gins that really pack a punch: there are over 400! Just ask the cool, young bar staff to guide your choosing. Upstairs it's both formal and fun; foodies travel far and wide to sample the tasting menu. Try seared Brixham scallops with sweetcorn and chicken wings, belly of suckling pig pork with apples, leeks and coco beans, then finish with a Tahitian vanilla brûlée. In summer, catch some rays out on the lavender-framed courtyard, tuck into a hearty ploughman's, watch the boats sail past, and see how many famous landmarks you can spot. The SS Great Britain and M Shed are close. *On the Bristol cycle network which is a great walk with a dog. Two pub dogs, Minnie & Scooby.*

Meals	Starters from £5. Mains from £15.
Closed	Rarely.
Treats	Water bowls always available.

Tel	+44 (0)117 927 2229
Email	info@the-pumphouse.com
Web	www.the-pumphouse.com

Toby Gritten
The Pump House,
Merchants Road, Hotwells,
Bristol, BS8 4PZ

The Boot

In the pretty village of Berwick St James in the Till valley, sits this 'real British inn' where Giles and Cathy are working a quiet magic with food, ales and happy locals. The striking building – 17th-century Grade II listed, with flint and limestone bands – was once owned by Lord Malmesbury and later home to a boot and shoemaker who gave it its name. Inside, it's richly atmospheric, and very welcoming. You can sit snugly at the fireside with a ploughman's and a pint, or bring the family for Sunday lunch. Lush gardens, great Wadworth beers and proper pub food cooked with passion draws visitors and walkers. Tuck into lavender and cider roast ham with eggs and home-cut wedges, or Barnsley chop with bubble and squeak; for the more adventurous, try crab, whisky and sweetcorn risotto. Children welcome. *Secure garden and lovely walks nearby for an after-lunch stroll with your dog.*

Meals	Light lunches from £6. Mains from £13.
Closed	Rarely.
Treats	Dog biscuits for our four-legged guests & a bowl outside. Their owners get mints with their bills.

Giles & Cathy Dickinson
The Boot,
High Street, Berwick St James,
Salisbury, SP3 4TN

Tel	+44 (0)1722 790243
Email	cathy@theboot.pub
Web	www.theboot.pub

Noah's Ark

In an idyllic setting – beside village pond and churchyard, overlooking a cricket green – the Ark restores faith in the future of the English country pub. In Henry and Amy's hands, this old village boozer has become a place of charm; no more darts, but a surprise at every turn. From bar to cosy dining areas – and one barn-like room – are beams, parquet flooring, open fires, traditional country furniture and a sprinkling of modern leather. The kitchen's insistence on good-quality (local, seasonal) produce results in a roll-call of British dishes; come evening, the simple bar menu is bolstered by such dishes as confit duck leg with celeriac mash, pickled braised red cabbage and parsnip crisps. A cottagey garden to the side and picnic tables out front complete the very pleasing package. *Dogs are very welcome in bar. Miles of wonderful walks from door, as well as on nearby Blackdown.*

Meals	Bar meals from £6. Mains from £12.50. Sunday lunch, 3 courses, £30.
Closed	Rarely.
Treats	Dog treats on the bar; water bowls throughout the pub. Book a table with dogs & there'll be a plate of dog biscuits waiting when you arrive. Great walks around village too.

Tel	+44 (0)1428 707346
Email	amy@noahsarkinn.co.uk
Web	www.noahsarkinn.co.uk

Amy Whitmore & Henry Coghlan
Noah's Ark,
Lurgashall, Petworth, GU28 9ET

The Three Crowns

Landlord Tim Skinner's bonhomie helps to keep the customers coming at this convenient and convivial roadside pub. Exposed brick walls, parquet flooring and wooden beams give an old-time feel but it's bright and welcoming in the summer, cosy by the fire on cooler days. Relax in a comfy chair for afternoon tea, dine from wooden tables, or settle down beneath a heater on the large terrace to the rear. Local ingredients are used in innovative ways for the international and seasonal menu: chicken satay and Thai spiced crab; Sussex smoked haddock, seafood platter or Portobello mushroom burger. Sunday roasts come with their own mini versions for children. For grown-up tipples, try the Crown Inn Glory or guest ales. The gin menu – with nutmeg, with hibiscus, with grains of paradise – rather hits the spot. *In the quintessential village of Wisborough Green & set in the South Downs Nationsl park with many beautiful walks.*

Meals	Starters from £7. Dinner from £10.
Closed	Rarely.
Treats	Water bowl and dog bed in bar, and doggy menu featuring biscuits and treats.

Tim Skinner
The Three Crowns,
Billingshurst Road,
Wisborough Green, RH14 0DX

Tel	+44 (0)1403 700239
Email	info@thethreecrownsinn.com
Web	www.thethreecrownsinn.com

The Crown

Just a short stroll up from the beach, this old corner boozer oozes artful charm and hipster-cool. Décor is shabby-chic, the mood is laid-back, and the craft beer list is curated by an expert palate. With Tess and Andrew at the helm, the Crown celebrates fantastic local produce and menus bristle with local artisan producers: freshly caught fish, vegetables from a walled garden, and homemade bread by Emmanuel Hadjiandreou. Enjoy a pint of Romney Marsh Best with a beer-battered fish finger sandwich, or go the whole hog and tuck into venison cottage pie, roast vegetables and seasonal greens. Community spirit rings throughout and everyone is welcome, including the dog. Anything goes, from haircuts in the snug, monthly quizzes and board games to regular events such as storytelling and craft groups. *Near to bottom of East Hill country park, & close to beach. Dogs are allowed inside & outside.*

Meals	Starters £4-£9. Mains £10-£16.
Closed	Rarely.
Treats	Biscuits, water bowls – & a friendly welcome!

Tel	+44 (0)1424 465100
Email	hello@thecrownhastings.co.uk
Web	www.thecrownhastings.co.uk

Tess Eaton & Andrew Swan
The Crown,
64-66 All Saints Street,
Hastings, TN34 3BN

The White Horse

In tiny Hedgerley village is a perfectly preserved slice of unspoiled pubbery. Whitewashed brick, horseshoes and cartwheels peer from shrubbery and window baskets, illuminated by ancient gas lamps on both street and façade. Inside, exposed wood is overlaid by carpet, while endless beams and supports for low ceilings are festooned with artefacts. As a serious ale house, seven ever-changing beers are drawn direct from cask and served via a hatch, the selection rotating on a seasonal basis. Food is from a pre deep-fryer age with ploughman's, quiches, cold meats and baps displayed at a chilled counter alongside the odd hot option of chunky lamb broth or maybe pheasant Wellington. A busy garden and marquee are a treat in summer – and house an aviary of finches. *Large garden & plenty of fields & woods for walking; bird sanctuary nearby.*

Meals	Lunch £6-£10. No food in evenings.
Closed	Rarely.
Treats	Biscuits, bowls of water & open fires to snooze by.

Kevin Brooker
The White Horse,
Village Lane, Hedgerley,
Slough, SL2 3UY

Tel   +44 (0)1753 643225
Web   www.thewhitehorsehedgerley.co.uk

The Royal Oak

The old whitewashed cottage stands in a hamlet on the edge of the common – hard to believe that Marlow is just a mile away. It's a thriving dining pub (and sister pub to the Alford Arms, Herts). Beyond the terrace is a stylish open-plan bar, cheerful with cream-coloured walls, fresh flowers, rug-strewn boards, cushioned pews and crackling log fires. Order a pint of local Rebellion and check out the daily chalkboard or printed menu. You might start with breaded Cornish fishcake slider, mashed peas and tartar sauce before tucking into slow-cooked breaded lamb croquettes with sticky braised red cabbage, creamy mash and mint, saving room for lemon posset with hedgerow fruits and brandy snap cream. The sprawling gardens are perfect for a summer game of table tennis on the lawn. Book the posh teepee for a grand outdoor party. *Just down the road from beautiful Marlow Common. Dogs welcome in the bar.*

Meals	Lunch & dinner £12.75-£26.25
Closed	Rarely.
Treats	Huge garden to run around. Biscuits on bar, water bowls outside & large map by front door. Lovely circular walk on iFootpath.

Tel	+44 (0)1628 488611
Email	info@royaloakmarlow.co.uk
Web	www.royaloakmarlow.co.uk

David & Becky Salisbury
The Royal Oak,
Frieth Road, Bovingdon Green,
Marlow, SL7 2JF

The Alford Arms

It isn't easy to find, so come armed with precise directions before you set out! In a hamlet enfolded by acres of National Trust common land, David and Becky Salisbury's gastropub is worth any number of missed turns. Inside are two interlinked rooms, bright and airy, with soft colours, scrubbed pine tables, wooden and tile floors. Food is taken seriously and ingredients are as organic, free-range and delicious as can be. You might start with grilled Cornish mackerel, Bucksum Farm beetroot and horseradish salsa then move onto rabbit leg bourguignon with smoked pancetta and creamy mash, saving room for coconut panna cotta and crispy malt loaf. Wine drinkers have the choice of 31 by the glass; service is informed and friendly. Arrive early on a warm day to take your pick of the teak tables on the sun-trapping front terrace. *Path into Ashridge Forest opposite, with thousands of acres of beautiful ancient beech woods. Dogs welcome in the bar.*

Meals	Lunch, bar meals & dinner £11.75-£26.25.
Closed	Rarely.
Treats	Biscuits on bar, water bowls outside & large map by front door. Lovely circular walk on iFootpath.

David & Becky Salisbury
The Alford Arms,
Frithsden,
Hemel Hempstead, HP1 3DD

Tel	+44 (0)1442 864480
Email	info@alfordarmsfrithsden.co.uk
Web	www.alfordarmsfrithsden.co.uk

The Blue Ball Inn

252 years old this year and reigning champions of the annual Boxing Day Barrel Race, the Blue Ball with its bright whitewashed walls, bay window and flowing flower baskets is postcard-perfect. Ideally placed, with Granchester Meadows for a front garden and views across the river to the spires of Cambridge's colleges, the pub is thriving under the care of Toby and Angela. Inside all is spotless, scrubbed and poised to welcome hungry locals, walkers, twitchers and tourists. Tuck into shepherd's pie topped with cheese crusted leeks, or a bowl of hearty soup with a sandwich. At the back is a heated pavilion, shrine to the local cricket team, where you can while away a happy afternoon with a pint of Aspall's Harry Sparrow cider. Stroll across the Meadows to spend the day in Cambridge. Bliss. *Fenced back garden 'dog proof'; river 200 yards for dogs to get wet in (as ours does). Garden hose for dogs who've rolled in cow pats on the meadow. Watercolour montage of all our 'regular' dogs!*

Meals	Starters from £4. Mains from £9.
Closed	Rarely.
Treats	A dogs welcome sign at the front of pub, dog biscuits behind bar & bowls at front door & in back garden.

Tel	+44 (0)1223 846004
Email	info@blueballgrantchester.co.uk
Web	www.blueballgrantchester.co.uk

Toby & Angela Joseph
The Blue Ball Inn,
Broadway,
Grantchester, CB3 9NQ

The Fitzherbert Arms

In the old village of Swynnerton on Lord Stafford's estate is the once-forlorn Fitzherbert, all spruced up. If you've visited before you're in for a surprise: bar, lounge and snug now entwine with an open-plan feel, warmed by three delicious fires. A friendly vivacious team makes the place tick as they ferry platefuls of flavoursome food to elegant tables: seafood platters, steak and stout pies, crumbles, brownies and port-poached pears. They do a great line in comfort food, have a good list of local suppliers, and Staffordshire ales star at the pumps. There are 30 ports (more than any other pub in the country!), 16 wines by the glass and a real cider, too: something to be proud of. The 1818 building once held a forge and the Anvil Room is enticing: leather wingback chairs, a forge-like fire, hops above a soft-lit wall. *Autumn & winter pub walk available; enclosed garden; dogs welcome in the main bar area & snug.*

Meals	Bar snacks from £3. Starters from £5.75. Mains from £12.95.
Closed	Rarely.
Treats	Biscuit, water bowls & Doggie Beer.

Leanne Wallis
The Fitzherbert Arms,
Swynnerton,
Stone, ST15 0RA

Tel	+44 (0)1782 796782
Email	info@fitzherbertarms.co.uk
Web	www.fitzherbertarms.co.uk

The Three Greyhounds Inn

The bright, many-bottled bar winks and glows as you enter, while host Michael has a welcome for all. Fat purple cushions soften wooden benches around a huge dual-facing fireplace; reach for the 'Brandy Bible' and settle in. The clever layout makes the space cosy and intimate, with snugs around every corner – four with firesides – and nooks and crannies aplenty. Michael is proud of the atmosphere, and rightly so. Families nibble and natter with relish, while walkers and couples take their time over delicious smoked haddock and leek tart or pan-fried lamb's kidneys. During annual Cheshire Game Week you can tuck into dishes such as pheasant breast with sautéed white pudding and red leg partridge croquette.... Deep in the Cheshire countryside, this well-restored pub is conveniently close to the M6. *Enclosed extensive gardens to play in & great walks around Shakerley Mere nature reserve next to the pub.*

Meals	Lunch & dinner from £10.50.
	Bar meals from £5.95.
Closed	Rarely.
Treats	Biscuits & dogs' dinner menu, Doggie Beer & water bowls.

Tel	+44 (0)1565 723455
Email	info@thethreegreyhoundsinn.co.uk
Web	www.thethreegreyhoundsinn.co.uk

Michael Kettle
The Three Greyhounds Inn,
Holmes Chapel Road, Allostock,
Knutsford, WA16 9JY

The Bull's Head

You feel the warmth as soon as you walk through the door. Candles glow on the tables of this pretty village pub, fires crackle, and the staff couldn't be nicer. Under a low-beamed ceiling, seven hand pumps dispense the finest local ales from Bull's Head Bitter, White Bull and Cheshire Cat as well as the inimitable Mobberley Wobbly – ale is king! Add in a Highland extravaganza of over 100 whiskies and other tempting brews and you have the makings of a celebration. Chef Andy cooks 'pub classics from the heart' with full English flavours; the steak and ale pie is a fully encased masterpiece in itself, and the Irish whisky sticky toffee pudding too indulgent for words. With outside tables for sunny days, this is as good as it gets for a village pub. *A garden & the Whisky Snug for dogs. Beautiful Mobberley walk. Dog show every August: Saturday of the Bank holiday weekend or National Dog Day.*

Meals	Bar meals £2.85-£12. Lunch £3.95-£19.95. Sunday lunch £13.95.
Closed	Rarely.
Treats	Biscuits on bar, water bowls & Doggie Beer. A good walk between The Bull's Head & The Church Inn.

Barry Lawlor
The Bull's Head,
Mill Lane,
Mobberley, WA16 7HX

Tel	+44 (0)1565 873395
Email	info@thebullsheadpub.co.uk
Web	www.thebullsheadpub.co.uk

The Church Inn

Tim Bird and Mary McLaughlin's mini-pub empire continues to thrive and grow with the addition of the 18th-century Church Inn. Sister pub to the Bull's Head, also in Mobberley, it has been fully restored and refurbished, retaining the small intimate dining rooms with their wood and tiled floors, exposed brick and beams, soft lamplight, and glowing candles. On a wild winter's day it's hard to leave, with four craft ales on tap and decent wines to quaff and some great food: homemade venison burger, lamb hot pot or market fish of the day, then a sticky date bread and butter pud. Or try lighter lunch/afternoon dishes like Asian spiced fish cake or a flat iron steak sandwich with chips. Summer terraces give views of the church or across rolling fields. A village gem. *Secure terrace & garden. Own pub walk, lots more nearby; you can walk to sister pub in village, the Bull's Head.*

Meals	Lunch & dinner £15-£24.95.
	Sunday lunch £14.95.
Closed	Rarely.
Treats	Bowls, biscuits & Doggie Beer too. A great pub walk; extensive gardens & terrace to play in.

Tel	+44 (0)1565 873178
Email	info@churchinnmobberley.co.uk
Web	www.churchinnmobberley.co.uk

Simon Umpleby
The Church Inn,
Church Lane, Mobberley,
Knutsford, WA16 7RD

The Holford Arms, page 93

Index by town

Index by town

Pub index by town

Karl Maguire and Martha in Wales

The wild places

Canopy & Stars has a collection of over 300 inspiring, pet-friendly outdoor places to stay. From spectacular treehouses to remote riverside cabins, each one is an adventure for you and your dog.

canopyandstars.co.uk